The

OLD REBEL

The Lochlainn Seabrook Collection

Everything You Were Taught About the Civil War is Wrong, Ask a Southerner! - Correcting the Errors of Yankee "History"
Honest Jeff and Dishonest Abe: A Southern Children's Guide to the Civil War
A Rebel Born: A Defense of Nathan Bedford Forrest - Confederate General, American Legend (winner of the 2011 Jefferson Davis Historical Gold Medal)
Nathan Bedford Forrest: Southern Hero, American Patriot - Honoring a Confederate Icon and the Old South
The Quotable Nathan Bedford Forrest: Selections From the Writings and Speeches of the Confederacy's Most Brilliant Cavalryman
Give 'Em Hell Boys! The Complete Military Correspondence of Nathan Bedford Forrest
Forrest! 99 Reasons to Love Nathan Bedford Forrest
Saddle, Sword, and Gun: A Biography of Nathan Bedford Forrest For Teens
The Quotable Jefferson Davis: Selections From the Writings and Speeches of the Confederacy's First President
The Quotable Alexander H. Stephens: Selections From the Writings and Speeches of the Confederacy's First Vice President
The Alexander H. Stephens Reader: Excerpts From the Works of a Confederate Founding Father
The Quotable Robert E. Lee: Selections From the Writings and Speeches of the South's Most Beloved Civil War General
The Old Rebel: Robert E. Lee As He Was Seen By His Contemporaries
The Articles of Confederation Explained: A Clause-by-Clause Study of America's First Constitution
The Constitution of the Confederate States of America Explained: A Clause-by-Clause Study of the South's Magna Carta
The Quotable Stonewall Jackson: Selections From the Writings and Speeches of the South's Most Famous General
Abraham Lincoln: The Southern View - Demythologizing America's Sixteenth President
The Unquotable Abraham Lincoln: The President's Quotes They Don't Want You To Know!
Lincolnology: The Real Abraham Lincoln Revealed in His Own Words - A Study of Lincoln's Suppressed, Misinterpreted, and Forgotten Writings and Speeches
The Great Impersonator! 99 Reasons to Dislike Abraham Lincoln
The Quotable Edward A. Pollard: Selections From the Writings of the Confederacy's Greatest Defender
Encyclopedia of the Battle of Franklin - A Comprehensive Guide to the Conflict that Changed the Civil War
Carnton Plantation Ghost Stories: True Tales of the Unexplained from Tennessee's Most Haunted Civil War House!
The McGavocks of Carnton Plantation: A Southern History - Celebrating One of Dixie's Most Noble Confederate Families and Their Tennessee Home
Jesus and the Law of Attraction: The Bible-Based Guide to Creating Perfect Health, Wealth, and Happiness Following Christ's Simple Formula
The Bible and the Law of Attraction: 99 Teachings of Jesus, the Apostles, and the Prophets
The Way of Holiness: The Story of Religion and Myth From the Cave Bear Cult to Christianity
Christmas Before Christianity: How the Birthday of the "Sun" Became the Birthday of the "Son"
Britannia Rules: Goddess-Worship in Ancient Anglo-Celtic Society - An Academic Look at the United Kingdom's Matricentric Spiritual Past
The Book of Kelle: An Introduction to Goddess-Worship and the Great Celtic Mother-Goddess Kelle, Original Blessed Lady of Ireland
The Goddess Dictionary of Words and Phrases: Introducing a New Core Vocabulary for the Women's Spirituality Movement
UFOs and Aliens: The Complete Guidebook
Aphrodite's Trade: The Hidden History of Prostitution Unveiled
The Caudills: An Etymological, Ethnological, and Genealogical Study - Exploring the Name and National Origins of a European-American Family
The Blakeneys: An Etymological, Ethnological, and Genealogical Study - Uncovering the Mysterious Origins of the Blakeney Family and Name

THE OLD REBEL

Robert E. Lee

As He Was Seen By His Contemporaries

Collected and Edited, with an Introduction and Notes, by

LOCHLAINN SEABROOK

JEFFERSON DAVIS HISTORICAL GOLD MEDAL WINNER

FIRST CIVIL WAR SESQUICENTENNIAL EDITION

Foreword by Scott Bowden

SEA RAVEN PRESS, NASHVILLE, TENNESSEE, USA

THE OLD REBEL

Published by
Sea Raven Press, PO Box 1484, Spring Hill, Tennessee 37174-1484 USA
www.searavenpress.com • searavenpress@nii.net

First Sea Raven Press Civil War Sesquicentennial Edition: January 2012
Second Sea Raven Press printing: January 2014
ISBN: 978-0-9838185-4-0
Library of Congress Catalog Number: 2011941057

The Old Rebel: Robert E. Lee As He Was Seen By His Contemporaries / collected and edited, with an introduction and notes, by Lochlainn Seabrook. Foreword by Scott Bowden. Includes bibliographical references.

Front and back cover design, book design and layout, by Lochlainn Seabrook
Typography: Sea Raven Press Book Design
Front cover image: Library of Congress/Graphic art © Lochlainn Seabrook
All images © Lochlainn Seabrook

The views on the American "Civil War" documented in this book *are* those of the publisher.

The paper used in this book is acid-free and lignin-free. It has been certified by the Sustainable Forestry Initiative and the Forest Stewardship Council and meets all ANSI standards for archival quality paper.

PRINTED & MANUFACTURED IN OCCUPIED TENNESSEE, FORMER CONFEDERATE STATES OF AMERICA

Dedication

To my cousin, the Old Rebel

Epigraph

The grand old bard that never dies,
Receive him in our English tongue:
I send thee, but with weeping eyes,
The story that he sung.

Thy Troy is fallen, thy dear land
Is marred beneath the spoiler's heel:
I cannot trust my trembling hand
To write the things I feel.

Ah, realm of tombs! but let her bear
This blazon to the last of times:
No nation rose so white and fair,
Or fell so pure of crimes.

The widow's moan, the orphan's wail
Come round thee, yet in truth be strong:
Eternal right, though all else fail,
Can never be made wrong.

An angel's heart, an angel's mouth,
Not Homer's, could alone for me
Hymn well the great Confederate South,
Virginia first, and Lee!

PHILIP STANHOPE WORSLEY, 1866
Corpus Christi College, Oxford, England

CONTENTS

Notes to the Reader - 8
Foreword, by Scott Bowden - 9
Introduction, by Lochlainn Seabrook - 10

SECTION ONE: ANTEBELLUM PERIOD
1 Birth & Genealogy: 1807 - 17
2 Childhood: 1807-1825 - 21
3 West Point Years: 1825-1829 - 27
4 U.S. Army Years: 1829-1861 - 29
5 Marriage: 1831-1870 - 35
6 Fatherhood: 1832-1870 - 39

SECTION TWO: BELLUM PERIOD, LINCOLN'S WAR
7 C.S. Army Years: 1861-1865 - 47
8 Traveller: 1861-1870 - 99

SECTION THREE: POSTBELLUM PERIOD
9 Washington College Years: 1865-1870 - 107
10 Death: 1870 - 143
11 Legacy: 1807-1870 - 155

Appendix A - General Lee's Military Staff - 233
Appendix B - General Lee's Civil War Engagements - 235
Appendix C - Lees Who Were Born at Stratford Hall - 236
Appendix D - Robert E. Lee's Paternal Family Tree - 237
Appendix E - Lee Family Real Estate - 243
Notes - 245
Bibliography - 253
Meet the Author - 256

Notes to the Reader

Robert E. Lee had many nicknames, most flattering, a few not. Among them were: "Marse Robert," "Marse Bob," the "King of Spades," the "Great Virginian," "Granny Lee," the "Great Tycoon," "Marble Man," the "Incomparable Strategist," "Bobby Lee," "Captain of America," "Uncle Robert," and the "Grand Idol of the South." Out of my infinite respect for Lee, however, I entitled this book after the nickname he gave to himself: "The Old Rebel."

In an effort to retain the true character and meaning of the words of those I have quoted from, they have been printed here exactly as they appear in the original manuscripts, including typographical and grammatical peculiarities inherent to 19th-Century American writing and speaking (in some cases I have broken up long paragraphs). Quotes are marked with a traditional Victorian "hand" pointer. My chapter introductions are in normal font, my explanatory comments appear in italics above the writers' quotes, and my clarifications are in brackets within their quotes.

In any study of the "Civil War" it is vitally important to keep in mind that the two major political parties were then the opposite of what they are today. The Democrats of the mid 19th Century were conservatives, akin to the Republican Party of today, while the Republicans of the mid 19th Century were liberals, akin to the Democratic Party of today. Thus the Confederacy's Democratic president, Jefferson Davis, was a conservative (with libertarian leanings); the Union's Republican president, Abraham Lincoln, was a liberal (with socialistic leanings).

For those interested in the truth about the War for Southern Independence, see my books (partial list):

Everything You Were Taught About the Civil War is Wrong, Ask a Southerner! - Correcting the Errors of Yankee "History"

The Quotable Robert E. Lee: Selections From the Writings & Speeches of the South's Most Beloved Civil War General

The Quotable Jefferson Davis: Selections From the Writings & Speeches of the Confederacy's First President

A Rebel Born: A Defense of Nathan Bedford Forrest - Confederate General, American Legend

Nathan Bedford Forrest: Southern Hero, American Patriot - Honoring a Confederate Icon & the Old South

The Quotable Nathan Bedford Forrest: Selections From the Writings & Speeches of the Confederacy's Most Brilliant Cavalryman

Give 'Em Hell Boys! The Complete Military Correspondence of Nathan Bedford Forrest

The Alexander H. Stephens Reader: Excerpts From the Works of a Confederate Founding Father

The Quotable Stonewall Jackson: Selections From the Writings & Speeches of the South's Most Famous General

Abraham Lincoln: The Southern View - Demythologizing America's Sixteenth President

Lincolnology: The Real Abraham Lincoln Revealed in His Own Words - A Study of Lincoln's Suppressed, Misinterpreted, & Forgotten Speeches & Writings

The Unquotable Abraham Lincoln: The President's Quotes They Don't Want You to Know!

The Great Impersonator! 99 Reasons to Dislike Abraham Lincoln

FOREWORD

He was much more than a fearless soldier. He was more than a consummate gentleman, loyal compatriot-in-arms, faithful husband, loving father and Southern legend. From the time he ascended to command of the principal army of the Confederate States of America, until he was forced to cease the fight for Southern independence, Robert Edward Lee stood astride the North American continent like a colossus. On his shoulders bore the weight of a nation and his peoples' hope of a new republic forged in the rich traditions of their revolutionary forefathers.

His aura—so powerful that it filled a room as well as extended across dozens of battlefields—was perhaps best described by Erasmus D. Keyes, who was a comrade in the antebellum army and an adversary in the great war. "No man," admitted Keyes, "could stand in his presence and not recognize his capacity and acknowledge his moral force."

It is fitting that one of the Lee family's noble descendants, award-winning author Lochlainn Seabrook, brings together in one volume the excellent observations made by Lee's contemporaries. In no other single source can anyone more easily gain a complete compilation of observations about Lee, which leads to an understanding of how and why Lee became one of the most beloved army commanders in history. Seabrook's *The Old Rebel* is essential for anyone who treasures the facts about the great American, Robert E. Lee.

Scott Bowden, author

☛ *Last Chance For Victory: Robert E. Lee and the Gettysburg Campaign*

☛ *Robert E. Lee at War*

Historian Scott Bowden is a nine-time award-winning author of twenty-five works. He is a graduate of Texas Christian University, a member of the Sons of Confederate Veterans, and a recipient of the Douglas Southall Freeman American History Award and the SCV's Commander-in-Chief's Award. He lives in Arlington, Texas.

LEEATWAR.COM

INTRODUCTION

Why in the 21st Century should we care about "the Old Rebel" Robert E. Lee, a Victorian who was old fashioned even during his own time, and who died nearly 150 years ago? Why write a book about how his peers saw him, when the world he lived in disappeared long ago, making his life and death seemingly meaningless to those of us living in the modern age?

The answer is that a study of the life of General Lee is now more relevant than ever, for due to our depersonalized, cyber-oriented, mass society we are slowly but surely losing our connection with the natural world, with other people, and with God.

Lee's amazing life, his beliefs, thoughts, and statements, his actions and deeds, all serve as a moral compass; not only to guide us back to the path of righteousness, but to help keep us on track in the future. For Lee was something more than a mere mortal. Yes, he was a man. But he was no ordinary man. He was an individual of extraordinary attributes that set him, not above, but apart from much of the rest of humanity. That he refused to see himself as special is simply another manifestation of his uniqueness.

While bizarrely the North continues to venerate men like the megalomaniacal dictator and big government liberal Abraham Lincoln and the psychopathic murderer John Brown—even blasphemously comparing both to the crucified Jesus—we in the South hold up General Lee as the most Christ-like figure of the 19th Century. His flaws were few, his virtues many.

Here was a man of great wealth who remained modest; a man of great fame who preferred the company of little children; a man who held positions of great authority, but never abused his power; a general of great nobility who slept on the cold ground with his soldiers; a world renown celebrity who preferred the solitude of Nature and the companionship of his horse.

No one followed the spiritual teachings (rather than the

manmade religion) of Jesus more closely than Robert E. Lee. When the beloved Confederate chieftain was given a gift from his many admirers, whether it be a suit of new clothes or a roast turkey, he would always pass it on to someone more in need. When an individual requested a favor of him he would grant it if he was able, no questions asked. When he was offered fortunes, mansions, property, business opportunities, and titles, he turned them all down. He wanted to earn his own way; be his own man.

When liberal Lincoln's War came, conservative Lee remained faithful to both the Constitution and his home state, and, as painful as it was for him, seceded with her from the Union. When Northerners called him a "traitor," he ignored them; when they printed scurrilous lies and absurd slanders about him in the newspapers, he took the high road and refused to respond.

When his armies won battles, he bestowed the honor on his fellow officers; when his armies lost, he shouldered the full responsibility himself. Throughout his life he pushed for the abolition of slavery, and freed his wife's family's slaves even before Lincoln issued his fake, illegal, racist, and self-serving "military measure,"[1] the so-called Emancipation Proclamation.[2]

After the War, though Lee was cruelly and illegally indicted for "treason" against the U.S. government and was promised a humiliating trial and a long imprisonment, he publicly forgave the North and prayed for those who wished to do him harm.

He would not allow other Southerners to denigrate their old enemies in his presence, and he treated former Yankee soldiers with the same respect he treated former Confederate soldiers—even giving food, clothing, and money to indigent Union men. And when a New York corporation offered him the position, salary, and lifestyle of a tycoon, he turned it all down, saying he preferred living humbly with his family in the mountains of Virginia.

Literally everyone, no matter what their occupation or station in life, can gain from studying the life of a man such as this. Those in positions of authority can learn from Lee how to wield their power without abusing it: parents, for example, can learn how to properly socialize their children, teachers can learn how to properly impart knowledge to their students, employers can learn how to properly oversee their workers, and military officers can learn how to properly train and encourage their soldiers.

Those who are in subordinate positions can learn as well, however. Children, students, employees, and servicemen and women, for instance, can all learn the true meaning of duty, obedience, and respect, not only for God, their elders, and those above them, but most importantly, for themselves.

Let us consider the words of William A. Anderson, who said the following during an address he gave at Washington and Lee University for General Lee's 100th birthday celebration, January 19, 1907:

> His life and the lessons of his example served while he was here, and will serve for all time, to inculcate in the minds of the ingenuous youth of the country who, if we are true to his memory and his teachings, shall in increasing numbers gather here as the years and the centuries go by, not only the lessons of devotion to civic duty, of duty to man,—but the higher lessons of piety, and religion, of duty to God; for of all the Godly and Christian men who have been connected with this venerable institution as academy, college and university, none were more Godly, none more devout, none more sincere, consistent and humble followers of the meek and lowly Jesus, than the modest Christian gentleman who lies buried over yonder by the chapel for the worship of the living God, which he caused to be erected there. Well may we cherish his memory. Well may we again and again recall the lessons of his life and repeat those lessons to our children and our children's children.[3]

What more can be said of an individual such as this? Plenty!

Hear now what his contemporaries thought of him, and through their eyes let us be inspired to emulate one of history's most admirable and fascinating figures: the one and only Robert E. Lee.

Lochlainn Seabrook
Franklin, Williamson County, Tennessee, USA
January 2012, Civil War Sesquicentennial

The OLD REBEL

SECTION ONE

Antebellum Period

General Robert E. Lee as he appeared in April 1865, shortly after the fall of the Southern Confederacy.

BIRTH & GENEALOGY

1807

General Robert E. Lee as he looked after Lincoln's War, still wearing his colonel's uniform. The author descends from Lee's fourth great-grandparents, Richard Eltonhead and Ann Sutton of Lancashire, England.

Robert Edward Lee was born on January 19, 1807, into a Victorian family of wealth, fame, and power. A descendant of European royalty, numerous sheriffs, lawyers, military officers, judges, and state governors came from his family. Two of his first cousins, Francis Lightfoot Lee and Richard Henry Lee, signed the Declaration of Independence,[4] and his father, Henry "Light Horse Harry" Lee, was a celebrated Revolutionary War hero.

☛ "Robert Edward Lee came of a long line of illustrious ancestors whose names were conspicuous both in England and America. Indeed, it may be justly claimed that he was the product of the highest type of our Anglo-Saxon manhood.

"While we may insist that he was in himself a very king of men, and needs no royal lineage to add luster to his fame, yet it is gratifying to his admirers to know that his ancestry can be traced back to that noble

Chief—Robert the Bruce [King of Scotland].

"The Lee family, which has given so many great men to America, is of ancient and honorable descent. As early as the year 1333 we are informed by an old manuscript that Johes de Lee, a soldier, received lands from one Hugo de Hinton. The son of this Johes de Lee was Robertus de la Lee and he married Margarita, daughter and heiress of Thomas Astley, of Nordley, about the year 1400. Later still, we find the name Thomas Lee, of Cotton, in King's Nordley, in the Parish of Alvely, who was the son of Johannes Lee. Later still, in the reign of Charles I,

Stratford Hall, Stratford, Westmoreland County, Virginia, Robert E. Lee's birth place. Built in the 1720s, Stratford Hall has been preserved and is today a popular tourist destination.

of England, the Lee family were located in the county of Shropshire, and were of the Cavalier stock. One of these, Richard Lee [the General's third great-grandfather], a gentleman of good position and many accomplishments, determined to emigrate to the New World, concerning which such marvelous tales were being told. Bishop Meade of Virginia says of him, 'He was a man of good stature, comely visage, enterprising genius, a sound head, a vigorous spirit, and generous nature. When he got to Virginia, which at that time was not much cultivated, he

A chart showing some of the famous Lee family members who were born at or lived at Stratford Hall. General Robert E. Lee is on the far left.

was so pleased with the country that he made large settlements there with the servants he carried over.'"[5] — Reverend John W. Jones, chaplain, Army of Northern Virginia, C.S.A.

☛ "The Lees of Virginia, 'a family which has, perhaps, given more statesmen and warriors to their new home than any other of our old colonial progenitors,' came of an ancient and distinguished stock in England, and neither country can boast a nobler scion than the subject of these memoirs.

"General Lee had never the time or inclination to study genealogy, and always said he knew nothing beyond his first American ancestor, Colonel Richard Lee, who migrated to Virginia in the reign [1625-1649] of Charles I. He believed, however, from his inherited traditions and the Coat of Arms borne by his progenitors in this country, that his family came originally from Shropshire, England; and when the world rang with his name and fame, and he paid the usual penalty of greatness by being besieged with reiterated queries respecting his pedigree, this was all he would say."[6] — General Fitzhugh Lee, C.S.A.

(General Lee's nephew)

☛ "The long line of Lees may be traced back to Launcelot Lee, of Loudon, in France, who followed William the Conqueror to England. When Harold, the English king, had fallen on the bloody field of Hastings, Launcelot Lee was given by William an estate in Essex. From that time the name of Lee has ever been an honorable one in the history of England."[7] — Mary Lynn Williamson

A brief history of Stratford Hall, the place of Lee's birth:
☛ "The original Stratford House is supposed. . . to have been built by Richard Lee [the General's third great-grandfather], the first of the family in the New World. Whoever may have been its founder, it was destroyed in the time of Thomas Lee [1690-1750], an eminent representative of the name, early in the eighteenth century. Thomas Lee was a member of the King's Council, a gentleman of great popularity; and, when it was known that his house had been burned, contributions were everywhere made to rebuild it. The Governor, the merchants of the colony, and even Queen Anne [Stuart, of England] in person, united in this subscription; the house speedily rose again, at a cost of about eighty thousand dollars [the equivalent of about $2.5 million today]; and this is the edifice still standing in Westmoreland [County, Virginia]."[8] — John Esten Cooke, novelist, historian, and officer under Jeb Stuart, C.S.A.

The Lee Family Coat of Arms.

☛ "It is not generally known, I believe, that Robert E. Lee was the blood relative of John Marshall, the great Chief Justice, and of Thomas Jefferson, the author of the Declaration of Independence, and twice President of the United States. Marshall's mother, Mary Keith; Jefferson's mother, Jane Randolph, and Lee's grandmother, Mary Bland, were all three granddaughters of Colonel William Randolph."[9] — Emory Speer

CHILDHOOD

1807-1825

The product of a dynastic family of influence and prestige, Lee was raised and socialized according to the standards of the Southern Victorian upper class. Instilled with a militaristic sense of duty from early on, even as a youth he was widely known for his kindness, empathy, selflessness, and impeccable manners and behavior.

On Lee's childhood:
☛ "Robert was always good."[10] — Henry "Light Horse Harry" Lee (the General's father)

Robert E. Lee's father, Henry "Light Horse Harry" Lee.

Lee's father Henry died when he was only eleven, leaving the boy not only fatherless, but in charge of caring for his handicapped mother, Ann Hill (Carter) Lee:
☛ "She was an invalid and needed tender care. As her other sons and her daughters were away from home, the duty of watching over her fell to Robert. He took the keys and 'kept house' for her when she was sick, and also saw to all her outside work. He would run home from school to ride out with her, so that she might enjoy the fresh air and sunshine. When out riding, if she complained of the cold or of draughts, he would stuff paper in the cracks in the old coach with his penknife. He

was ever thoughtful of her comfort.

"Although he took such care of his mother, Robert found time to enjoy many outdoor sports. He liked hunting and would sometimes follow the hounds on foot all day long. In this way he gained the great strength of body which was never known to fail in after life. At school he was a faithful, hard-working student. He did well in all his studies. At first he went to school to a Mr. Leary, and later to a school kept by Benjamin H. Hallowell, who said that he never failed in a lesson.

"It was a happy life he led in Alexandria, and his old home there, in which his mother had lived, was always a sacred place to him. In later years a friend once found him looking sadly over the fence of the garden where he had played as a child. 'I am looking,' he said, 'to see if the old snowball trees are still here. I should be sorry to miss them.'"[11] — Mary Lynn Williamson

A similar observation about Lee's childhood:

☛ "This good mother [Ann] was a great invalid; one of Lee's sisters was delicate, and many years absent in Philadelphia, under the care of physicians. The eldest son, Carter, was at Cambridge, Sydney Smith in the navy, and the other sister too young to be of much aid in household

A drawing of General Lee's birthplace, Stratford Hall.

A photograph of the side of Stratford Hall.

matters. So Robert was the housekeeper, carried the keys, attended to the marketing, managed all the out-door business, and took care of his mother's horses.

"At the hour when other school-boys went to play, he hurried home to order his mother's drive and would there be seen carrying her in his arms to the carriage, and arranging her cushions with the gentleness of an experienced nurse. One of his relatives, who was often the companion of these drives tells us of the exertions he would make on these occasions to entertain and amuse his mother, assuring her, with the gravity of an old man, that unless she was cheerful the drive would not benefit her. When she complained of cold [drafts] or 'draughts,' he would pull from his pocket a great jack-knife and newspapers, and make her laugh with his efforts to improvise curtains, and shut out the intrusive wind, which whistled through the crevices of the old family coach."[12] — Emily V. Mason

☛ "To my mother [Mary], who was a great invalid from rheumatism for more than ten years, [my father] . . . was the most faithful attendant and tender nurse. Every want of hers that he could supply he anticipated. His considerate forethought saved her from much pain and trouble. During the war he constantly wrote to her, even when on the march and amidst the most pressing duties. Every summer of their life in Lexington he arranged that she should spend several months at one of the many medicinal springs in the neighbouring mountains, as much that she might be surrounded by new scenes and faces, as for the benefit of the waters. Whenever he was in the room, the privilege of pushing her wheeled chair into the dining-room and out on the verandas or elsewhere about the house was yielded to him. He sat with her daily, entertaining her with accounts of what was doing in the college, and the news of the village, and would often read to her in the evening. For her his love and care never ceased, his gentleness and patience never ended.

"This tenderness for the sick and helpless was developed in him when he was a mere lad. His mother was an invalid, and he was her constant nurse. In her last illness he mixed every dose of medicine she took, and was with her night and day. If he left the room, she kept her

A marred photo showing a distant view of Stratford Hall.

eyes on the door till he returned. He never left her but for a short time."[13] — Captain Robert E. Lee, Jr., C.S.A.

☛ "Robert's mother . . . was an invalid for many years. And if she was one of the most devoted of mothers, he not less was a faithful son. He watched over her very tenderly. When she was able to go out she was fond of taking long drives. He usually accompanied her, and always took the greatest pains to make her comfortable. He would often take several newspapers and a knife with him and if she was disturbed by draughts he would make paper curtains and hang them up at the sides of the carriage. She would laugh at his efforts, and the love and the laughing did her more good than the curtains."[14] — Evelyn Harriet Walker

☛ "When only eleven years old, he lost his father, who, prior to his death, had been absent from home for several years, so Robert Lee was reared almost entirely under the watchful and loving care of his mother. It is said she taught him, from his earliest childhood, to 'practice self-denial, and self-control, as well as the strictest economy, in all financial concerns,' traits which he ever exhibited through life."[15] — Frederick Warren Alexander

General Lee at the Battle of Chancellorsville, May 2, 1863.

WEST POINT YEARS

1825-1829

In 1825 Lee began his studies at West Point Military Academy at the age of eighteen. Four years later, on July 4, 1829, he graduated second (some say first) in his class with honors, a sterling reputation, and no demerits.

☛ "Robert Lee entered my school in Alexandria, Va., in the winter of 1824-25, to study mathematics, preparatory to his going to West Point. He was a most exemplary student in every respect. He was never behind time at his studies, never failed in a single recitation, was perfectly observant of the rules and regulations of the institution; was gentlemanly, unobtrusive, and respectful in all his deportment to teachers and fellow-students. His specialty was finishing up. He imparted a neatness and finish to everything he undertook. One of the branches of mathematics he studied with me was conic sections,

Robert E. Lee at age twenty-two, as second lieutenant of the U.S. army's Topographical Engineers in 1829. This is the earliest known portrait of Lee: he had just graduated from West Point.

An early illustration of the United States Military Academy at West Point, New York.

in which some of the diagrams were very complicated. He drew the diagrams on a slate, and although he well knew that the one he was drawing would have to be removed to make room for the next, he drew each one with as much accuracy and finish, lettering and all, as if it were to be engraved and printed. The same traits he exhibited at my school he carried with him to West Point, where I have been told, he never received a mark of demerit, and graduated at the head of his class."[16] — Benjamin Hallowell (one of Lee's early school teachers in Alexandria, Virginia)

Upon hearing that her eighteen year old son Robert was leaving for West Point, the General's mother said:

☛ "How can I live without Robert? He has been both son and daughter to me."[17] — Evelyn Harriet Walker

☛ "Young Lee entered West Point in 1825, when he was eighteen years of age. There he was distinguished for the excellence of his scholarship and the purity of his life at a time when according to the statement made by the superintendent to [U.S.] President [John Quincy] Adams, drunkenness and dissipation were very prevalent among the cadets. He graduated in 1829, with the second highest honors of his class, and with the record of never having received a demerit for neglect of duty."[18] — Major General Randolph H. McKim, C.S.A.

U.S. ARMY YEARS

1829–1861

In this 1852 portrait of Lee he is a captain in the U.S. army, and is just beginning his position as superintendent of West Point Military Academy.

Lee is so associated with his four years in the Confederate army that it is often forgotten that he spent thirty-two years before that serving in the U.S. army.

After graduating from West Point in 1829, he was appointed second lieutenant of Topographical Engineers in the U.S. army, and quickly began moving up the ranks. In 1834 he began work as assistant to the chief engineer of the U.S. army.

In 1835 Lee was appointed assistant astronomer "on the commission for marking out the boundary line between Ohio and Michigan," and on September 21, 1836, he was promoted to the rank of first lieutenant in the U.S. army.

In June 1837 Lee was placed in charge of "improving" the Mississippi River at St. Louis, Missouri, and in July 1838 he was promoted to captain of the engineer corps. In 1842 Lee was stationed at Fort Hamilton in New York Harbor, where he was placed in charge of defenses. In 1844 he was appointed a member of the board of visitors at West Point, and in 1845 he became a member of the U.S. Board of Engineers.

The year 1846 brought the start of the Mexican-American War, in which Lee fought with distinction. He was brevetted major for gallantry at the Battle of Cerro Gordo, April 18, 1847, and at the assault on Chapultepec, September 13, 1847, he was wounded and received the brevet promotion of lieutenant-colonel.

In 1849 Lee began constructing fortifications at Baltimore, Maryland, and from 1852 to 1855 he served as superintendent of West Point. In 1855 he was appointed lieutenant colonel of the Second Cavalry, and his family moved to Arlington, Virginia.

In 1856 Lee was sent to Jefferson Barracks, Missouri, then on to western Texas to reduce Indian attacks and protect the U.S. border from Mexican bandits. In 1857 he was stationed with the Second Cavalry at San Antonio, Texas, and in 1859 he was selected by the U.S. secretary of war to suppress the infamous "John Brown Raid" at Harper's Ferry.

In 1860 Lee was assigned to the command of the department of Texas, and on March 16, 1861, he received his last promotion in the U.S. army: Colonel in the First Cavalry, a position he held for only a few weeks before Lincoln launched his illegal war on states' rights and the constitutionally formed Southern Confederacy.

☛ "[During the Mexican-American War, in] making a reconnaissance from Cerro Gordo, Captain Lee ventured so far from his column, that he found himself in the midst of the enemy. He concealed himself under a fallen tree, near a spring where the Mexicans obtained water. The Mexicans passed and repassed over the tree, and even sat upon it, without discovering him. He remained there until night enabled him to make his escape."[19] — Judith White McGuire

☛ "As Superintendent of the Military Academy at West Point [1852-1855] my father had to entertain a good deal, and I remember well how handsome and grand he looked in uniform, how genial and bright, how considerate of everybody's comfort of mind and body. He was always a great favourite with the ladies, especially the young ones. His fine presence, his gentle, courteous manners and kindly smile put them at once at ease with him."[20] — Captain Robert E. Lee, Jr., C.S.A.

☛ "After the fall of Mexico [February 2, 1848], when the American army was enjoying the ease and relaxation which it had bought by toil and blood, a brilliant assembly of officers sat over their wine, discussing the operations of the siege, and indulging hopes of a speedy return to the United States.

"One among them rose to propose the health of [Lee] the captain of engineers, who had found a way for the army within the city; and then it was remarked that Captain Lee was absent. Magruder was dispatched to bring him to the hall, and, departing on his mission, at last found the object of his search in a remote room of the palace, busy on a map.

"Magruder accosted his friend, and reproached him for his absence.

"The earnest worker looked up from his labors with a calm, mild gaze, which we all remember, and, pointing to his instruments, shook his head.

"'But,' said Magruder, in his impetuous way, 'this is mere drudgery! Make somebody else do it, and come with me.'

"'No,' was the reply—'no, I am but doing my duty.'"[21] — The *Norfolk Virginian*

☛ "[While my father was superintendent at West Point, I went to day-school there,] and had always a sympathetic helper in . . . [him]. Often he would come into the room where I studied at night, and, sitting down by me, would show me how to overcome a hard sentence in my Latin reader or a difficult sum in arithmetic, not by giving me the translation of the troublesome sentence or the answer to the sum, but by showing me, step by step, the way to the right solutions. He was very patient, very loving, very good to me, and I remember trying my best to please him in my studies. When I was able to bring home a good report from my teacher, he was greatly pleased, and showed it in his eye and voice, but he always insisted that I should get the 'maximum,' that he would never be perfectly satisfied with less."[22] — Captain Robert E. Lee, Jr., C.S.A.

In the mid 1850s, while Lee was in the U.S. army, he was stationed in the American southwest where he was ordered to suppress Indian raids (shown above) and protect the U.S. border from hostile Mexicans.

☛ ". . . I recall an incident just prior to the civil or sectional war. General, then Lieutenant-Colonel Lee, in command of the First Cavalry, U. S. A., had his headquarters at Fort Mason, Texas. I was then a first lieutenant, temporarily in command of Company A of that regiment. I left him at the post when I went on a short leave of absence to San Antonio, Texas. On my return I stopped for lunch at a place about half way to Mason, where a cool spring and some large live oaks made an ideal camp or resting place.

"A few minutes after I got there, an ambulance came from the opposite direction, and I was pleasantly surprised to see General Lee step from it. After a cordial greeting he told me he had the day before received an order to report to General [Winfield] Scott at Washington, and he feared it was to consult in regard to a plan of campaign against the South. He also said that Virginia, true to its past history, would not act upon impulse or be controlled by other States, but in a patriotic, dignified manner would only secede after exhausting every honorable means to avert secession, but that if his State seceded, he should resign, as he deemed it his duty to do so.

"As he talked on, time and again he oft repeated, with emotion that came from his heart, the hope that Virginia would not secede and that the Union might be preserved. His emotion, emphasized by the tears that moistened his eyes, impressed me the more deeply, as he was usually entirely self-contained.

"Virginia seceded in the manner he prophesied, he resigned, and offered his services as he said he would. I next saw him when I reported to him at Richmond. Every day I met him off duty at our lonely post, I was more impressed with the simple grandeur of his private character, and speaking of him, eulogy becomes cold truth. I am unable to write except painfully with a pen, and must therefore beg to be excused for writing with a pencil."[23] — General George B. Cosby, C.S.A.

☛ "I remember with pleasure and affection my intimate associations with Lieutenant Lee [in the 1830s, when we worked together on an engineering project to improve the Mississippi River], a man then in the vigor of youthful strength, with a noble and commanding presence, and an admirable, graceful, and athletic figure. He was one with whom nobody ever wished or ventured to take a liberty, though kind and generous to his subordinates, admired by all women, and respected by all men. He was the model of a soldier and the *beau ideal* of a Christian man."[24] — General Montgomery C. Meigs, U.S. army

☛ "In 1845 the Mexican War broke out and Lieutenant Lee was ordered to the field. He was wounded once, he won many honors, and became a Colonel. But he was deeply pained by the horrors and cruelties of war. Many things in his letters at this time reveal his genuine kindness of heart.

"In a letter to his son he wrote some sad things about a

battlefield. He told how he found some poor wounded Mexicans and had them carried to a house by the side of the road. He found a little Mexican drummer boy with his arm broken to pieces by a bullet. A wounded soldier had fallen on him and died. The little drummer-boy could not get away and was moaning with pain. A little barefooted Mexican girl asked Colonel Lee to help him. '*Mille gracias, Signor*' [that is, 'a thousand thank-yous, Mister'] in Spanish, for that is the language the Mexicans speak. It is not hard to guess what she meant."[25] — Evelyn Harriet Walker

A scene from the Mexican-American War (1846-1848), at which Lieutenant Colonel Robert E. Lee fought with great distinction, launching his reputation as a masterful soldier. The illustration above depicts the charge of U.S. Captain Charles A. May at the Battle of Resaca De La Palma on May 9, 1846. May served under military hero General Zachary Taylor, soon to become the twelfth president of the U.S.—due in great part to his valor during the Mexican War. Taylor is the father of Sarah Knox Taylor (the first wife of Confederate President Jefferson Davis) and Confederate General Richard Taylor, who took over command of the Army of Tennessee in the Western theater after the resignation of General John Bell Hood in early 1865. The author is cousins with both the Taylor family and with General Hood.

MARRIAGE

1831-1870

On June 30, 1831, at Arlington, Virginia, Lee married his third cousin and childhood friend, Mary Ann Randolph Custis, the great-granddaughter of Martha (Dandridge) Washington, the wife of U.S. President George Washington. Unlike the vast majority of men today (at least 60 percent), Lee married only once and remained faithfully by his wife's side for the full length of their thirty-nine year union. By all accounts the Lee marriage was one of intense mutual respect, love, and tenderness.

General Lee's wife, Mary Anne Randolph Custis, the step great-granddaughter of President George Washington. The author descends from Mary's second great-grandparents, Robert Bolling and Anne Mary Cocke of Prince George County, Virginia.

☛ "During the first four years of Lee's professional life [in the early 1830s] he was assigned to Fortress Monroe, and assisted in strengthening the defenses of Hampton Roads. His nearness to Washington and Arlington made it possible for him to follow up a friendship which had long been of interest to him, and which had, of late, become deeply romantic. It was his friendship for Miss Mary Custis, granddaughter of the wife of George Washington.

"The young people had known each other nearly all their lives. During the latter part of Robert Lee's cadetship [at West Point] he had used at least a part of his furlough in visiting Mary Custis at her home in Arlington. She was a girl of great charm and exceptionally well educated. She had been proud, many a time, when the handsome young cadet, arrayed in gray uniform with bullet-shaped buttons and gold lace, had put himself to a good deal of trouble to visit her. Between the two there was mutual attraction; and each seemed worthy of the other.

"Probably the 'course of true love' did not run with entire smoothness; there is a tradition that Mary's father, George Washington Parke Custis, disapproved. Doubtless he thought that no man, not even the admirable son of 'Light Horse Harry' Lee, was quite worthy of his daughter. But she did not agree with him; and Robert himself, although he may have felt, with Mary's father, that he was not worthy of this lovely girl, did not give up his courtship; and he at length won her promise to be his wife."[26] — Bradley Gilman

☛ "The honeymoon seems to have been spent at Arlington, and must have given Lee occasion to ponder, in his serious way, over the responsibilities resting upon the owner of many slaves [Note: Robert E. Lee and his immediate family did not personally own slaves; only those inherited from his wife's father].[27] Neither he nor his father-in-law believed in the institution which was just beginning to array its warm partisans and violent opponents. Indeed, Mr. Custis manumitted his negroes; and Lee, as executor, carried out the provisions of his will [in 1862], although the War for the Union was raging at the time. So long, however, as circumstances forced him to be a master, the young officer was determined to be a kind one.

The father of Lee's wife, George Washington Parke Custis. A Marylander by birth, George passed on both his home Arlington House and his slaves to his daughter Mary. In 1862, five years after his death in 1857, General Lee emancipated his father-in-law's servants according to stipulations in his will. This was months *before* Lincoln issued his fake "Final Emancipation Proclamation," which freed no slaves in either the North or the South.

There is even a story . . . that he took a consumptive [black] coachman of his mother's to Georgia, and there had him cared for.

"But Virginia country life had its pleasures as well as its responsibilities; and, if Lee had been made of less strenuous stuff, he would have hesitated to serve his country three years longer in building coast defences, and would have settled down at Arlington to take his ease. He had loved hunting ever since boyhood, when he used to follow the hounds for hours unfatigued; the sights and sounds of Nature were dear to him through life; he could have made himself as methodical a farmer as Washington; he thoroughly enjoyed social visiting from plantation to plantation. In a word, he had in him the making of an ideal country gentleman; but he had also something more. He loved his [military] profession, and felt that it was a noble one; and he resolved to cling to it for his country's sake, although he was too good a man to wish for war and the personal distinction he might acquire therein."[28] — William Peterfield Trent

Another image of General Lee's wife, Mary Anne Randolph Custis. Like her husband Robert, Mary descends from European royalty.

☛ "[Prior to Lincoln's War, while] Lieutenant Lee was living at Hampton Roads, he was married to Miss Mary Custis, a great granddaughter of Martha Washington. She inherited the magnificent estates of her father, George Washington Parke Custis, who . . . was an adopted son of George Washington. Her mansion at Arlington [Arlington House] became henceforth for many years the home of the Lees, although the young Lieutenant was destined to spend the best of his life at a distance from Arlington in the fulfillment of his military duties. He had known Mary Custis when she was a little girl and had met her again when he was grown a handsome young cadet and was spending a vacation in Alexandria. They were married [June 30, 1831] two years after he graduated from West Point."[29] — Evelyn Harriet Walker

☛ "[In 1831 Lee] was united in marriage to Mary Custis, the daughter and heiress of George Washington Parke Custis, and the granddaughter of the wife of General Washington. She had received a fine classical education, and was the heiress of both Arlington and 'the White House,' on the Pamunkey River, which was the scene of the marriage of Gen. Washington with the widow Custis. Hence her father did not favor the match with the young lieutenant, devoted to a military career."[30] — Major General Randolph H. McKim, C.S.A.

☛ "General Lee's domestic life was noble in its purity, admirable in its loving indulgences and devotion, and happy in all the family pleasures that rule in refined homes. When one reflects upon the military qualities which won him rank as a ruler of men, his quiet home life, rich in all the affections, stands in admirable though striking antithesis; and yet the contrast disappears when his whole consistent career is passed in review.

"As a son his attachment to his mother knew no bounds. His affection for his wife was, if possible, even stronger. In social and domestic intercourse he was not the cold and austere man he appeared in the crisis of battle. No man more enjoyed quiet humor. In the home circle he was genial, captivating, and as unaffected in his ways as a child. He entered heartily into all the domestic rounds of amusement, and contributed by many little inventions to the enjoyment of guests. His children were fond of pets, and he indulged all their innocent propensities."[31] — Brigadier General Armistead L. Long, C.S.A. (served under Lee)

☛ "His wife had become a confirmed invalid, and to her he gave devoted attention. He spent much of his leisure time in her company, cheering her spirits by his conversation while he wheeled her invalid chair about."[32] — Brigadier General Armistead L. Long, C.S.A.

FATHERHOOD

1832–1870

Between 1832 and 1846, Robert and Mary bore seven children: George Washington Custis Lee, Mary Custis Lee, William Henry Fitzhugh Lee, Anne Carter Lee, Eleanor Agnes Lee, Robert E. Lee, Jr., and Mildred Childe Lee. Only William and Robert, Jr. married and bore children.

General Lee, of course, was the epitome of the doting, loving, gentle father, and, as the following comments reflect, he was adored by his entire family in return.

Robert E. Lee and his second son William Henry Fitzhugh Lee in 1845.

☛ "[My father] was always bright and gay with us little folk, romping, playing, and joking with us. With the older children, he was just as companionable, and I have seen him join my elder brothers and their friends when they would try their powers at a high jump put up in our yard. The two younger children he petted a great deal, and our greatest treat was to get into his bed in the morning and lie close to him, listening while he talked to us in his bright, entertaining way. This custom we kept up until I was ten years old and over.

"Although he was so joyous and familiar with us, he was very firm on all proper occasions, never indulged us in anything that was not good for us, and exacted the most implicit obedience. I always knew that it was impossible to disobey my father. I felt it in me, I never thought why, but was perfectly sure when he gave an order that it had to be obeyed. My mother I could sometimes circumvent, and at times took liberties with her orders, construing them to suit myself; but exact obedience to every mandate of my father was a part of my life and being at that time.

Another image of General Lee's son William, this one as an adult. During Lincoln's War William became a well respected general in the Confederate army.

"He was very fond of having his hands tickled, and, what was still more curious, it pleased and delighted him to take off his slippers and place his feet in our laps in order to have them tickled. Often, as little things, after romping all day, the enforced sitting would be too much for us, and our drowsiness would soon show itself in continued nods. Then, to arouse us, he had a way of stirring us up with his foot—laughing heartily at and with us. He would often tell us the most delightful stories, and then there was no nodding. Sometimes, however, our interest in his wonderful tales became so engrossing that we would forget to do our duty—when he would declare, 'No tickling, no story!'

"When we were a little older, our elder sister told us one winter the ever-delightful *Lady of the Lake*. Of course, she told it in prose and arranged it to suit our mental capacity. Our father was generally in his corner by the fire, most probably with a foot in either the lap of myself or youngest sister—the tickling going on briskly—and would come in at different points of the tale and repeat line after line of the poem—much to our disapproval—but to his great enjoyment."[33] — Captain Robert E. Lee, Jr., C.S.A.

☛ "[In September 1868, my sister] Mildred was still weak and nervous [from her recent sickness], nor did she recover her normal strength for several months. She was always my father's pet as a little girl, and during this illness and convalescence he had been very tender with her, humouring as far as he could all of her fancies. Not long before that Christmas, she enumerated, just in fun, all the presents she wished—a long list. To her great surprise, when Christmas morning came she found each article at her place at the breakfast-table—not one omitted."[34] — Captain Robert E. Lee, Jr., C.S.A.

The Lees' antebellum home, Arlington House, at Arlington, Virginia, was inherited by Lee's wife Mary from her father George Washington Parke Custis. In May 1861, while Lee was off fighting in Lincoln's War, Union troops pilfered and ransacked the estate, and Mary and her children were humiliated and driven into the street, becoming homeless refugees. After ruining much of the interior and stealing priceless family heirlooms (many of them belonging to family relation President George Washington), Yankee soldiers were purposefully buried in the yards so that the Lees could never move back in. After years of legal wrangling and a lawsuit against the U.S. government, it was eventually given back to the family after the General's death in 1870. However, it was now unliveable and the Lees formally sold it to the U.S. government for the modern equivalent of about $4 million. Today Arlington House is the architectural centerpiece of Arlington National Cemetery.

☛ "My father was the most punctual man I ever knew. He was always ready for family prayers, for meals, and met every engagement, social or business, at the moment. He expected all of us to be the same, and taught us the use and necessity of forming such habits for the convenience of all concerned. I never knew him late for Sunday service at the Post Chapel. He used to appear some minutes before the rest of us, in uniform, jokingly rallying my mother for being late, and for forgetting something at the last moment. When he could wait no longer for her, he would say that he was off and would march along to church by himself, or with any of the children who were ready. There he sat very straight—well up the middle aisle—and, as I remember, always became very sleepy, and sometimes even took a little nap during the sermon."[35] — Captain Robert E. Lee, Jr., C.S.A.

☛ "Further on the road, as our horses were climbing a steep rocky ascent, we met some little children, with very dirty faces, playing on the roadside. [My father] . . . spoke to them in his gentle, playful way, alluding to their faces and the desirability of using a little water [to clean themselves up]. They stared at us with open-eyed astonishment, and then scampered off up the hill; a few minutes later, in rounding this hill, we passed a little cabin, when out they all ran with clean faces, fresh aprons, and their hair nicely brushed, one little girl exclaiming, 'We know you are General Lee! We have got your picture!'"[36] — Mildred Lee (fourth daughter and youngest child of General Lee)

General Lee's third and youngest son, Robert E. Lee, Jr. Robert, Jr. was a captain in the Confederate army and after the War became a successful farmer, author, husband, and father.

☛ "My father always encouraged me in every healthy outdoor exercise and sport. He taught me to ride, constantly giving me minute instructions, with the reasons for them. He gave me my first sled, and sometimes used to come out where we boys were coasting to look on. He gave me my first pair of skates, and placed me in the care of a trustworthy person, inquiring regularly how I progressed. It was the same with swimming, which he was very anxious I should learn in a proper manner."[37] — Captain Robert E. Lee, Jr., C.S.A.

General Lee's first son George Washington Custis Lee. Like his younger brother William, he rose to the rank of general during Lincoln's War. However, unlike William, George remained single throughout his life and bore no children.

On young men courting his daughters:
☛ "[Local] students . . . were constant visitors [to the General's home], especially in the evenings, when young men came to see the girls. If his daughters had guests, my father usually sat with my mother in the dining-room adjoining the drawing-room. When the clock struck ten he would rise and close the shutters carefully and slowly, and, if that hint was not taken, he would simply say 'Good night, young gentlemen.' The effect was immediate and lasting, and his wishes in that matter, finally becoming generally known, were always respected."[38] — Captain Robert E. Lee, Jr., C.S.A.

☛ "'Baxter' and 'Tom, the Nipper' were [my sister] Mildred's pets. All of us had a fondness for cats, inherited from my mother [Mary] and her father, Mr. [George W. P.] Custis. My father was very fond of them in his way and in their place, and was kind to them and considerate of their feelings. My mother told of his hearing one of the house-pets, possibly Baxter or the Nipper, crying and lamenting under his window one stormy night. The General got out of bed, opened the window, and called pussy to come in. The window was so high that the animal could not jump up to it. My father then stepped softly across the room, took one of my mother's crutches, and held it so far out of the window that he became wet from the falling rain; but he persuaded the cat to climb up along the crutch, and into the window, before he thought of dry clothing for himself."[39] — Captain Robert E. Lee, Jr., C.S.A.

This photo of Arlington House, taken on June 28, 1864, shows Union troops pompously posing at the front entrance. Victorian Yankees considered the home the ultimate prize, and often used these types of propaganda photographs to try and humiliate both the Lee family and the Confederacy. But there was nothing to be proud of: hundreds of heavily armed Union troops had easily overpowered Mrs. Lee and her daughters while her husband and sons were off fighting. Thrown out of their own home, Yankee soldiers laughed at them and made fun of the terrified group of women and children as they fled. While President Davis and the rest of the Confederacy rightly criticized this type of so-called "fighting," as can plainly be seen in the above photograph, Lincoln and his army were proud of it and, apparently, considered it "manly"!

SECTION TWO

Bellum Period
Lincoln's War

7 C.S. ARMY YEARS

1861-1865

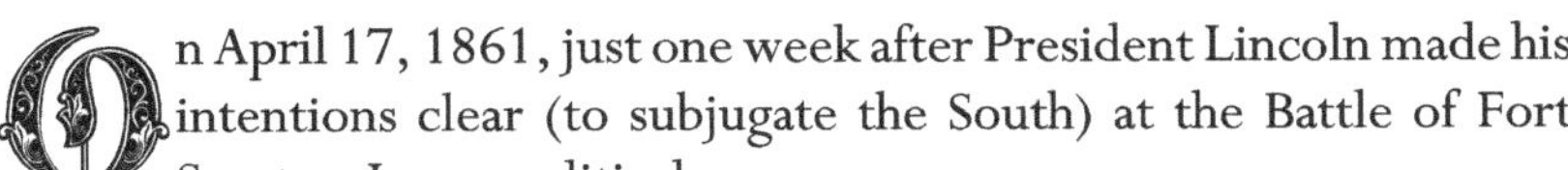

On April 17, 1861, just one week after President Lincoln made his intentions clear (to subjugate the South) at the Battle of Fort Sumter, Lee, a political conservative, made the painful and difficult decision to leave the Union with his home state Virginia—this after being offered the position of general-in-chief of U.S. armies by none other than Lincoln himself.

Lee as a Confederate general during Lincoln's War.

On April 20 Lee officially resigned from the U.S. army, and on April 23 he was promoted to major general and appointed commander-in-chief of Virginia's military and naval forces by Governor John Letcher.

As occurred in the U.S. army, Lee's climb up the C.S. army ladder was extraordinary. May 7 he was made commander of all forces from other States tendering their services to Virginia, on May 10 he was made commander of

Confederate States forces, and on May 14 he was appointed brigadier general.

By June 14 Lee was general of the Confederate States army, by August 3 he was commanding forces in the Army of the North-west, on November 5, 1861, he was assigned to the command of the department of Florida, South Carolina, and Georgia, and on March 13, 1862, he began his new position as "military advisor" to President Jefferson Davis at Richmond, Virginia.

On January 31, 1865, Lee was made general-in-chief of the Confederate States armies, and on February 6 he was made commander-in-chief of all Confederate States armies (unfortunately, too late to change the outcome of the War).

On April 9, 1865, Lee met with Yank General Ulysses S. Grant at Appomattox and negotiated the terms of the Confederacy's "surrender." Lincoln's War ended and Lee returned home a hero.

In April 1861, at the start of Lincoln's War, Lee was offered the command of the entire U.S. army. He, of course, declined, wishing to remain loyal to Virginia and the other seceding Southern states. Upon hearing of Lee's decision, U.S. General Winfield Scott went to him and said:

☛ "Lee, you have made the greatest mistake in your life; but I feared it would be so."[40] — Henry Stuart Foote

☛ "My husband has wept tears of blood over this terrible war; but he must, as a man and a Virginian, share the destiny of his state, which has solemnly pronounced for independence."[41] — Mrs. Robert E. Lee to General Winfield Scott (concerning her husband's agonizing decision, in 1861, to side with Virginia and the Confederate States against the United States)

James May, a Pennsylvania professor at the Theological Seminary, Episcopal Church, Alexandria, Virginia, wrote the following interesting letter to the General's cousin Cassius F. Lee on April 22, 1861, at the beginning of Lincoln's War. May, who sided with the South, was hoping that as a Christian, General Lee—then still a colonel—would be able to establish peace between the two countries before the conflict escalated any further:

☛ "My dear sir,—I am sure of your sympathy with me in the motive of

General Lee's railroad battery, with gun and crew, at Petersburg, Virginia, sometime between 1864 and 1865.

what I now write, even though you may think me presumptious and lacking in judgment. Two considerations prompt me; one, an Editorial in the *National Intelligencer*, of today, placed by yourself in Dr. Sparrow's hands and read by him to me a few minutes ago, the other a suggestion that Col. [Robert E.] Lee, now to be put in command of the Virginia troops, might, by God's blessing, bring peace to our distracted country. O, how my heart leaped at the thought! How many thousands, yea millions, would rise up to bless the man that should bring this to pass.

"I may be stepping out of my line in offering a word on the subject. But my heart is full, and I know you at least are willing to give me your attention. Who knows but that your cousin may be raised up by God for such a time as this? Could he bring about, at least, an armistice, preparatory to a National Assembly for a peaceful settlement of our troubles, how many hearts would he relieve and how large his share in the blessedness of peacemakers. I do not enter into the political considerations of the matter. That is not my province. It may suffice to say that, so far as became me, whether in the North or in the South, I always gave my opinion against the organization and the proposed measures of the [Lincoln] party now controlling the General Administration. I always held that organization to be not only needless, but mischievious.

"When it [the North] became so sectionally dominant, I hoped still that the more thoughtful members of it would shape its course. They seem to have been overborne. The unfortunate Proclamation of [War of] the President [Lincoln], and the measures which were its immediate antecedents, have utterly disappointed me and saddened me. But as I said, I do not enter into the political aspect of the great question now before us. I would regard it as a Christian should and especially a Christian minister.

"My feeble voice I lift for peace. I have often turned my thoughts to Col. Lee. The world knows his service in the Mexican War. Years ago I asked my brother-in-law, Major A. H. Bowman (now of West Point,) what army officers thought of him as a soldier? I remember well his emphatic answer. If those who were with him (Col. Lee) in Mexico, should answer, they would unanimously declare him to be, in all military qualifications, without a rival in the service. But my interest in him was quickened by hearing of his Christian character.

"During his absence in Mexico, I visited his family at Arlington, and heard from Mrs. Lee, allusions to his private letters. I received then my opinion of him as a Christian, and have had my eye on him ever since. May we not hope that God has put him in his present position to be an instrument of abating the storm which now threatens shipwreck to the whole country? It is sad that so few of our public men are Christians. Col. Lee is a grand exception.

"I know, in an official post, which is not that of head of the government, he would find it difficult to follow the private promptings of his own Christian mind, for a soldier's business is not to advise his superiors but to obey. But great respect would be shown to the judgment and Christian spirit of one so distinguished as he. Virginia gave us our original independence through her [George] Washington. She gave us our National Constitution through [Thomas] Jefferson, [James] Madison and others. Can she not now, while we are threatened with the immeasurable evils of civil war, give us through Col. Lee peace? In common with other States, she may justly complain of wrongs. But will civil war repair them?

"Christianity teaches not only the duty, but the wisdom of patience and forgiveness. Virginia, from her geographical position, from her glorious share in the past and from her great political weight, has it in her power (am I presumptious in saying it?) to come as a mediator, rather as an umpire and settle the question, not only for the happiness of the whole country, but for her own special property. Should Col. Lee be a leader in this matter and place his native State in this grand position (which I must think she could hold), he will have an honor never reached by Napoleon or Wellington. If Virginia may not call back the people of the continent to union, she yet may to peace. Standing apart from others, she would not, could not be invaded. She could be a healer or a peacemaker, and have all the blessedness of such an office.

"The wisdom of seniors has not been allowed its part in our great questions. Young, impetuous spirits seem to be leading the mind of the

Yankee General Gustavus A. De Russy (seated third from left) and his staff posing arrogantly on General Lee's front porch at Arlington House in May 1864.

country. Especially has not the Christian mind, the Church, been heard. Its voice must be for peace; Our sins may be too great to allow us to have again the blessedness of a united country, but may we not have peace? Is there not moral power in the Christian mind of the country to stay the hand of fraternal strife? How many wives, mothers, widows, sisters, how many quiet, peaceful citizens of all classes sigh for peace? How many families, now separated by wide geographical distances, would be divided in a way far more painful and dreadful by civil war?

"No quiet citizen, no Christian, can think of it without a fainting heart. During the civil wars of England, in the times of the Commonwealth, Lord Falkland was known in all Britain as one of the bravest men ever born in that land. After he had seen the indescribable wretchedness of the people of his native country in the strife of brothers, he would sit abstracted among his friends, and, sighing from the depth of his heart, exclaim, 'peace, peace.' I dare not say Col. Lee may bring us peace. The Lord can only do that. We may have so sinned that the wrath of God must lie upon us and make us suffer the awful judgment now threatening. How do all Christian sentiments, how do all the interests of the Christian Church, how do all our interests cry for peace.

"I do not say the Gospel forbids war absolutely. Its direct primary call is to peace: 'Blessed are the peacemakers, for they shall be called the children of God.' From my inmost soul, I pray that in this our day of trial, that blessedness may be enjoyed by Col. Lee. In thus writing, do I seem to be a meddler? I am not so in purpose and motive. Perhaps I mistake my calling. I think, as a Christian and a Christian minister, I cannot err in wishing and praying for peace. Our great national questions cannot be settled except in time of peace. O, may that peace come now, at the beginning, instead of the end of a fearful conflict. So praying, I am sure of your sympathy, and subscribe myself, most sincerely your friend, James May."[42] — James May

On April 23, 1861, Lee attended a massive convention at the Confederate Capitol where it was announced that he had been selected to be commander-in-chief of the Virginia forces. Southern journalist Edward A. Pollard describes the scene:

☛ "Every spectator admired the personal appearance of the man, his dignified figure, his air of self-poised strength, and features in which shone the steady animation of a consciousness of power, purpose, and position. He was in the full and hardy flush of ripe years and vigorous health. His figure was tall, its constituents well knit together; his head, well shaped and squarely built, gave indications of a powerful intellect; a face not yet interlined by age, still remarkable for its personal beauty, was lighted up by eyes black in the shade, but brown in the full light, clear, benignant, but with a deep recess of light, a curtained fire in them that blazed in moments of excitement; a countenance, the natural expression of which was gentle and benevolent, yet struck the beholder as masking an iron will.

"His manners were at once grave and kindly; without gayety or abandon, he was also without the affectation of dignity. Such was the man whose stately figure, in the Capitol at Richmond, brought to mind the old race of Virginians, and who was thereafter to win the reputation, not only as the first commander, but also as the first gentleman of the South, the most perfect and beautiful model of manhood in the war."[43] — Edward Alfred Pollard

☛ "One of the most impressive scenes recorded in the life of General Robert E. Lee was the last visit which he paid to the grave of his father [Henry 'Light Horse Harry' Lee]. This happened during the first year of the war, at the time when he was in charge of the defenses along that line of coast. 'He went alone to the tomb [at the time located on Cumberland Island, Georgia],'[44] says the officer who accompanied him to the island, 'and, after a few moments of silence, plucked a flower, and slowly retraced his steps, leaving the lonely grave to the guardianship of the crumbling stones, and the spirit of the restless waves that perpetually beat against the neighboring shore.'"[45] — Philip Alexander Bruce

☛ "While acting as Adjutant General of Virginia, and in the discharge of his duty to muster into the service new recruits, Colonel Baldwin one day found in one of the companies twenty-five or thirty youths under the prescribed age. He told them that he could not receive them, under the regulations, and the brave boys were very much disappointed, and clamored to see General Lee. Coming into the presence of the general, they begged him to allow them to enlist, and promised that they would prove themselves worthy to march by the side of their fathers and elder brothers.

"General Lee was very much affected by their appeal, but told them that he could not receive them, that they must go home and take care of their mothers and sisters, and that he would send for them when they were needed. After the young men had left, General Lee said to Colonel Baldwin: 'Those are beautiful boys, sir, and I very much disliked to refuse them; but it will not do to allow boys to enlist now. I fear we shall need them all before this war closes.'"[46] — Reverend John W. Jones, chaplain, Army of Northern Virginia, C.S.A.

☛ "Having for some time been reduced to very meagre fare, we were rejoiced to receive a present of a lot of chickens. One of the hens so distinguished herself as to be worthy of a place in history.

"Bryan, the steward of General Lee's mess, having discovered that she daily contributed an egg, spared her life. She proved to be a very discriminating hen, for she selected the general's tent to make her daily deposit. Instinct seemed to teach her that he was fond of fowls and domestic animals. Every day she would walk to and fro in front of his tent, and when all was quiet walk in, find a place under his bed, and deposit her egg; then walk out with a gratified cackle. Appreciating her partiality for him, he would leave his tent-door open for her to come in.

"General Lee's hen."

"This she kept up daily for weeks, Bryan always securing her contributions for the general's breakfast. She chose a roosting-place in the baggage-wagon, and on breaking up camp to meet Hooker at Chancellorsville, Bryan found room in the wagon for the hen. During the battle she seemed too much disturbed to lay, but as soon as the engagement was over she fell at once into her regular routine. She accompanied the army to Gettysburg.

"One night, when preparing for retreat, with the wagon loaded and everything ready, the question was raised, "Where is the hen?" By that time everybody knew her and took an interest in her; search was made in every direction, even General Lee joining in it. She was found at last perched on the wagon, where she had taken her place of her own accord. She accompanied the army in all its marches and countermarches for more than a year . . ."[47] — Brigadier General Armistead L. Long, C.S.A.

☛ "At this time [the Second Battle of Manassas, August 30, 1862] my company was detached from the Sixth Regiment and made a bodyguard to Gen. Lee. We kept close to his person both night and day.

"Part of the time Gen. Lee rode in an ambulance with both hands bandaged, his horse, 'Traveler,' having fallen over a log and crippled Lee's hands. This gave me a good opportunity of seeing the great soldier at close range.

"I remember one afternoon, when toward sunset the army having gone into camp for the night, Gen. Lee's headquarters being established in a little farmhouse near Chantilla, I think in Loudoun county, the General went out with one of his staff officers for a walk into an apple orchard. They were gone perhaps an hour. In the meantime a guard had been set around the cottage with instructions to let none pass without an order from Gen. Lee.

"When Gen. Lee returned with his aid by his side, he was halted by Frank Peak (a member of my company, now living in Alexandria, Va.). They both halted, and Peak said to them, 'My instructions are to let none pass without an order from Gen. Lee.' Gen. Lee turned to his aid and said, 'Stop, the sentinel has halted us.' The officer (I think it was Col. Marshall, who afterward lived in Baltimore, and died there not long ago) stepped forward and said, 'This is Gen. Lee himself, who gives all orders.' Peak saluted them, and they passed on.

"Before day the next morning the army was in motion toward Maryland, Gen. Lee still riding in the ambulance, very much, no doubt, to the chagrin of 'Traveler,' who was led by a soldier, just behind the ambulance."[48] — Luther W. Hopkins, C.S.A.

☛ "He had a great dislike to reviewing army communications; this was so thoroughly appreciated by me that I would never present a paper for his action unless it was of decided importance and of a nature to demand his judgment and decision. On one occasion, when an audience had not been asked of him for several days, it became necessary to have one. The few papers requiring his action were submitted.

"He was not in a very pleasant humour; something irritated him, and he manifested his ill humour by a little nervous twist or jerk of the neck and head peculiar to himself, accompanied by some harshness of manner. This was perceived by me, and I hastily concluded that my efforts to save him annoyance were not appreciated. In disposing of some cases of a vexatious character matters reached a climax; he became really worried, and, forgetting what was due to my superior, I petulantly threw the paper down at my side and gave evident signs of anger. Then in a perfectly calm and measured tone of voice, he said, 'Colonel Taylor, when I lose my temper don't you let it make you angry.'"[49] — Colonel Walter Herron Taylor, C.S.A. (one of Lee's aides)

☛ "General Lee accompanied the troops in person, and as they emerged from the fierce combat [at the Battle of Chancellorsville, April 30-May 6, 1863] they had waged in 'the depths of that tangled wilderness,' driving the superior forces of the enemy before them across the open ground, he rode into their midst. The scene is one that can never be effaced from the minds of those that witnessed it.

Fitzhugh Lee, a nephew of General Robert E. Lee, was a noted Confederate general in his own right. After Lincoln's War, Fitzhugh served as governor of Virginia and, under U.S. President Stephen Grover Cleveland, as consul-general at Havana, Cuba.

"The troops were pressing forward with all the ardor and enthusiasm of combat. The white smoke of musketry fringed the front of the line of battle, while the artillery on the hills in the rear of the infantry shook the earth with its thunder and filled the air with the wild shrieks of the shells that plunged into the masses of the retreating foe. To add greater horror and sublimity to the scene, the Chancellorsville house and the woods surrounding it were wrapped in flames. In the midst of this awful scene General Lee, mounted upon that horse which we all remember so well, rode to the front of his advancing battalions. His presence was the signal for one of those uncontrollable outbursts of enthusiasm which none can appreciate who have not witnessed them.

"The fierce soldiers, with their faces blackened with the smoke of battle, the wounded, crawling with feeble limbs from the fury of the devouring flames, all seemed possessed with a common impulse. One long, unbroken cheer, in which the feeble cry of those who lay helpless on the earth blended with the strong voices of those who still fought, rose high above the roar of battle and hailed the presence of the victorious chief. He sat in the full realization of all that soldiers dream of—triumph; and as I looked on him in the complete fruition of the success which his genius, courage, and confidence in his army had won, I thought that it must have been from some such scene that men in ancient days ascended to the dignity of the gods."[50] — Colonel Charles Marshall, C.S.A. (Lee's aid-de-camp)

☛ "General Lee, with coat buttoned to the throat, sabre-belt around his waist, and field-glass pending at his side, walked up and down in the shade of large trees near us, halting now and then to observe the enemy. He seemed full of hope, yet at times buried in deep thought."[51] — General John Bell Hood, C.S.A. (just prior to the Battle of Gettysburg, July 1-3, 1863)

☛ "As the years go by the students of history are more and more amazed at the boldness of Gen. Lee in placing his army of 75,000, some say 65,000, at Gettysburg, when he knew that between him and the capital of the Confederacy (which his army was intended to protect) was the capital of the United States protected by an army of not less than 200,000 soldiers, and I might add by the best equipped army in the world, for the United States Government had the markets of the world to draw supplies from.

"On the morning of the third day of the battle of Gettysburg [July 3, 1863] there had been a terrible artillery duel that made the earth tremble for miles around, and was heard far and wide.

"When the guns got too hot for safety the firing ceased, the noise died away and the soldiers lay down to rest.

"During this interval Gen. Lee called his generals together for counsel. The situation had grown serious. Lee's losses had been heavy in killed and wounded, and his stock of ammunition was growing low.

"After considerable discussion Lee mounted his gray horse [Traveller], rode off a few paces to a slight elevation, and lifting his field glass to his eyes looked intently at the long lines of blue that stretched along the slopes, in the hope of finding some weak point which he might attack. Then returning to his officers he said in a firm voice: 'We will attack the enemy's center, cut through, roll back their wings on either side and crush or rout their army.' Then he said: 'Gen. Pickett will lead the attack.'" — Luther W. Hopkins, C.S.A. (just prior to the doomed infantry assault known as "Pickett's Charge")

☛ "[General Lee] had the instincts of a soldier within him as strongly as any man. . . . No soldier could have looked on at Pickett's charge and not burned to be in it. To have a personal part in a close and desperate fight at that moment would, I believe, have been at heart a great pleasure to General Lee, and possibly he was looking for one." — General Edward Porter Alexander, C.S.A. (at the Battle of Gettysburg, July 1-3, 1863)

☛ "General Lee was perfectly sublime. He was engaged in rallying and encouraging the broken troops and was riding about, a little in front of the wood, quite alone—the whole of his staff being engaged in a similar manner farther to the rear. His face, which is always placid and cheerful, did not show signs of the slightest disappointment, care or annoyance, and he was addressing to every soldier he met a few words of encouragement; such as: 'All this will come right in the end; we'll talk it over afterward; but in the meantime all good men must rally.' . . . He spoke to all the wounded men that passed him, and the slightly wounded he exhorted to bind up their hurts and 'take a musket' in this emergency. Very few failed to answer his appeal, and I saw badly wounded men take off their hats and cheer him.

"[Confederate] General [Cadmus Marcellus] Wilcox now came up to him and in very depressed tones of annoyance and vexation, explained the state of his brigade. But General Lee immediately shook hands with him and said, in a cheerful manner: 'Never mind, General; all this has been my fault. It is I that have lost this fight, and you must help me out of it the best way you can.' In this manner did General Lee, wholly ignoring self and position, encourage and reanimate his somewhat dispirited troops, and magnanimously take upon his own shoulders the whole weight of the repulse. It was impossible to look at him, or to listen to him, without feeling the strongest admiration."[52] — Sir Arthur J. L. Fremantle, British officer (at the Battle of Gettysburg)

From a Yank:

☞ "I was at the battle of Gettysburg . . . and an incident occurred there which largely changed my views of the Southern people. I had been a most bitter anti-South man, and fought and cursed the Confederates desperately. I could see nothing good in any of them. The last day of the fight I was badly wounded. A ball shattered my left leg. I lay on the ground not far from Cemetery Ridge, and as General Lee ordered his retreat he and his officers rode near me.

"As they came along I recognized him, and, though faint from exposure and loss of blood, I raised up my hands, looked Lee in the face, and shouted as loud as I could, 'Hurrah for the Union!' The general heard me, looked, stopped his horse, dismounted, and came toward me. I confess that I at first thought he meant to kill me. But as he came up he looked down at me with such a sad expression upon his face that all fear left me, and I wondered what he was about. He extended his hand to me, and grasping mine firmly and looking right into my eyes, said, 'My son, I hope you will soon be well.'

"If I live a thousand years I shall never forget the expression on General Lee's face. There he was, defeated, retiring from a field that had cost him and his cause almost their last hope, and yet he stopped to say words like those to a wounded soldier of the opposition who had taunted him as he passed by! As soon as the general had left me I cried myself to sleep there upon the bloody ground."[53] — an unknown Union soldier

☞ "Our affections for you are stronger, if it is possible for them to be stronger, than our admiration for you."[54] — General James Longstreet, C.S.A. (to Lee, September 1863)

☞ "[Confederate General Jubal Anderson] Early was the only man who was ever known to swear in General Lee's presence. The General used to reprove him gently, yet at the same time to express his special affection for him by calling him 'my bad old man.'"[55] — Major Robert Stiles, C.S.A.

☛ "[During the Winter of 1863-1864] General Lee's . . . home was pitched in the midst of the camp. His small tent stood on a steep hillside, about two miles northeast of Orange Court House. Two or three additional tents furnished accommodations for his staff. Only the man himself was there to indicate the presence of one in authority. General

Yankee General Edward O. C. Ord with his wife and daughter, at the home of Confederate President Jefferson Davis in April 1865. Ord is leaning on the table at which General Robert E. Lee signed the papers of surrender over to Yankee General Ulysses S. Grant on April 9. Such photos were meant to heap further humiliation upon the South after the War.

Lee shared the sufferings and privations of his men. He allowed himself a small ration of meat only twice a week and sometimes declined even that. He lived on corn-bread or crackers or a bit of cabbage as each or all came with convenience. All luxuries sent him by friends went invariably to the sick and wounded in the hospitals. In reply to remonstrances he would always say, 'I am content to share the rations of my men.'"[56] — Henry Alexander White

☛ "One very cold morning a young soldier on the cars [train] to Petersburg was making fruitless efforts to put on his overcoat, with his arm in a sling. His teeth, as well as his sound arm, were brought into use to effect the object; but in the midst of his efforts an officer rose from his seat, advanced to him, and very carefully and tenderly assisted him, drawing the coat gently over his wounded arm, and buttoning it comfortably; then, with a few kind and pleasant words, returned to his seat.

"Now the officer in question was not clad in gorgeous uniform, with a brilliant wreath upon the collar, and a multitude of gilt lines upon the sleeves, resembling the famous labyrinth of Crete, but he was clad in 'a simple suit of gray,' distinguished from the garb of a civilian only by the three stars which every Confederate colonel is, by the regulations, entitled to wear. And yet he was no other than our chief general, Robert E. Lee, who is not braver than he is good and modest."[57] — an unnamed Southern newspaper, Winter 1864

Lee's soldiers not only used the Rebel Yell to terrorize their Yankee opponents in battle, but also to hunt rabbits (the banshee like scream startled the creatures just long enough for a kill). Thus, across the South it became a tradition that whenever a Rebel Yell was heard in the distance, someone would always say:

☛ "Well there goes Marse Robert, or an old hare."[58] — Henry Alexander White

☛ "While the Army was on the Rapidan, in the winter of 1863-4, it became necessary, as was often the case, to put the men on very short rations. Their duty was hard, not only on the outposts during the winter, but in the construction of roads, to facilitate communication between the different parts of the army.

"One day General Lee received a letter from a private soldier, whose name I do not now remember, informing him of the work that he had to do, and stating that his rations were not sufficient to enable him to undergo the fatigue. He said, however, that if it was absolutely necessary to put him upon such short allowance, he would make the best of it, but that he and his comrades wanted to know if General Lee was aware that his men were getting so little to eat, because if he was aware of it he was sure there must be some necessity for it.

"General Lee did not reply directly to the letter, but issued a general order in which he informed the soldiers of his efforts in their behalf, and that their privation was beyond his means of present relief, but assured them that he was making every effort to procure sufficient supplies. After that there was not a murmur in the army, and the hungry men went cheerfully to their hard work."[59] — Colonel Charles Marshall (Lee's aid-de-camp)

☛ "Not long after his West Virginia campaign General Lee was recommending a certain officer for promotion, when a friend urged him not to do so, alleging that this officer was accustomed to speak very disparagingly and disrespectfully of him. The quick reply was, 'The question is not what he thinks or is pleased to say about me, but what I think of him. I have a high opinion of this officer as a soldier, and shall most unquestionably recommend his promotion, and do all in my power to secure it.'"[60] — Reverend John W. Jones, chaplain, Army of Northern Virginia, C.S.A.

☛ "One day in July, 1863, after the battle of Gettysburg, when the Army of Northern Virginia lay on the north bank of the Potomac between Williamsport and Falling Waters, General Lee spoke pretty hotly to Lieutenant-colonel [Charles S.] Venable of his staff for making a report of an unsatisfactory condition of things at the Williamsport ford or ferry in too loud a tone of voice. Venable retired to his tent in no pleasant mood. Very soon, however, the general sent him an invitation to come and drink a glass of buttermilk with him. He of course accepted the invitation, but his angry feelings at what he esteemed an unmerited rebuke were only partially soothed by partaking of the friendly glass of the mild but sour beverage with his honored chieftain.

"On the next night the army recrossed the Potomac. About 3 A.M., after getting through the work of supervision of the crossing of the army-trains at one of the Williamsport fords, which had been assigned to Lieutenant-colonel [Briscoe G.] Baldwin and himself, Venable rode down, in a drizzling rain, to the vicinity of the pontoon bridge at Falling Waters. Having made his report, he threw himself on the ground near by, and soon fell asleep. When he awoke he found General Lee had taken the oil-cloth poncho from his own shoulders and thrown it over him. The hot-tempered aide-de-camp was thoroughly conquered."[61] — Brigadier General Armistead L. Long, C.S.A.

☛ "It is related that during the seven days' battle [June 26-July 2, 1862] General Lee was quietly sitting under a tree, the approaching shades of evening concealing even his stars, and none of his aides or couriers being present, when an impetuous surgeon galloped up and abruptly said: 'Old man, I have chosen that tree for my field-hospital, and I want you to get out of the way.'

"'I will cheerfully give place when the wounded come, doctor, but in the mean time there is a plenty of room for both of us,' was the meek rejoinder. The irate surgeon was about to make some harsh reply, when to his utter consternation a staff-officer rode up and addressed his 'old man' as General Lee. To his profuse apologies and explanations, the general quietly replied: 'It is no matter, doctor; there is plenty of room for both of us until your wounded are brought.'"[62] — Reverend John W. Jones, chaplain, Army of Northern Virginia, C.S.A.

☛ "[During the War, when] I again saw my father, he rode at the head of Longstreet's men on the field of Manassas, and we of [Stonewall] Jackson's corps, hard pressed for two days, welcomed him and the divisions which followed him with great cheers. Two rifle-guns from our battery had been detached and sent to join Longstreet's advance artillery, under [Confederate] General Stephen D. Lee, moving into action on our right. I was 'Number 1' at one of these guns.

"We advanced rapidly, from hill to hill, firing as fast as we could, trying to keep ahead of our gallant comrades, just arrived. As we were ordered to cease firing from the last position we took, and the breathless cannoneers were leaning on their guns, [my father] General Lee and staff

One of the thousands of anti-South, Yankee-centric cartoons that ran in newspapers across the North during Lincoln's War. This one, from a New York paper in 1864, concerns the Confederacy's numerous attempts at establishing peace with the U.S. (all were ignored or rejected by Lincoln) and the Northern antiwar movement (also heartily disliked by the warmongering Lincoln administration). General Lee and Confederate President Jefferson Davis stand in the middle trying to protect themselves from attack by Union Generals Philip H. Sheridan (far left), Ulysses S. Grant (second from left), William T. Sherman (far right), and David G. Farragut (second from right). The epitome of Yankee mythology and anti-Confederate Northern propaganda, Sheridan is pointing his sword at Lee, saying: "You commenced the war by taking up arms against the Government and you can have peace only on the condition of your laying them down again." Grant says to Lee: "I demand your unconditional surrender, and intend to fight on this line until that is accomplished." Lee replies: "Can't think of surrendering Gentlemen but allow me through the Chicago platform to propose an armistice and a suspension of hostilities." Davis agrees, saying: "That's it Lee, if we can get out of this tight place by an armistice, it will enable us to recruit up and get supplies to carry on the war four years longer." Farragut says: "'Armistice! and suspension of hostilities.' Tell that to the Marines, but sailors don't understand that hail from a sinking enemy." Lastly the always racist Sherman says to Davis: "We don't want your negroes or anything you have; but we do want and will have a just obedience to the laws of the United States."

galloped up, and from this point of vantage scanned the movements of the enemy and of our forces. The general reined in 'Traveller' close by my gun, not fifteen feet from me. I looked at them all some few minutes, and then went up and spoke to Captain Mason of the staff, who had not the slightest idea who I was. When he found me out he was greatly amused, and introduced me to several others whom I already knew.

"My appearance was even less prepossessing than when I had met my father at Cold Harbour, for I had been marching night and day for four days, with no opportunity to wash myself or my clothes; my face and hands were blackened with powder-sweat, and the few garments I had on were ragged and stained with the red soil of that section. When the General, after a moment or two, dropped his glass to his side, and turned to his staff, Captain Mason said:

"'General, here is some one who wants to speak to you.'

"The General, seeing a much-begrimed artillery-man, sponge-staff in hand, said: 'Well, my man, what can I do for you?'

"I replied: 'Why, General, don't you know me?' and he, of course, at once recognised me, and was very much amused at my appearance and most glad to see that I was safe and well."[63] — Captain Robert E. Lee, Jr., C.S.A.

☛ "Lee, while encamped at Culpeper, [Virginia,] was of course cordially received by the people of the town. One of these, a lady who had been somewhat scandalized by the friendly relations between some of her neighbors and the Yankees, took occasion to complain to the general that certain young ladies, then present, had been in the habit of visiting [Yankee] General [John] Sedgwick at his headquarters, which was pitched in the ample grounds of a citizen whose house he had declined to use.

"The young ladies were troubled, for the general [Lee] looked very grave. But they were soon relieved when he said, 'I know General Sedgwick very well. It is just like him to be so kindly and considerate, and to have his band there to entertain them. So, young ladies, if the music is good, go and hear it as often as you can, and enjoy yourselves. You will find that General Sedgwick will have none but agreeable gentlemen about him."[64] — General Henry J. Hunt, U.S.A.

On General Lee's propensity for "roughing it":
☛ "I, of course, selected a place where I thought he would be comfortable, although I firmly believe he concluded that I was thinking more of myself than of him. I took possession of a vacant house, and had his room prepared with a cheerful fire, and everything made as cosy as possible. It was entirely too pleasant for him, for he is never so uncomfortable as when comfortable."[65] — Colonel Walter Herron Taylor, C.S.A. (from the battlefield, November 1864)

☛ "We are told that on one occasion Lee received through the mail from an anonymous private soldier a very small slice of salt pork carefully packed between two oaken chips, with the statement in a letter that this was the daily ration of meat; the writer claimed to be unable to live on this allowance and, although a gentleman, had been compelled to steal. But the Commander himself fared no more sumptuously.

"It is stated that some officers once came to dine in General Lee's tent. The fare set before them was only a plate of boiled cabbage: in the centre of the dish rested a diminutive slice of bacon. With knife well poised above this morsel, General Lee invited each guest in turn to receive a portion. But the small size of the piece of bacon led them all to decline. The meat remained on the plate untouched; hunger was appeased with cabbage.

"On the following day, General Lee called again for the bit of swine-flesh, but his coloured servant, with many bows, gave the information that the bacon had been borrowed to grace the official board of the day before and had been already returned to the owner."[66] — Henry Alexander White

The caption of this 19th-Century drawing is: "The last of General Lee's headquarters, Petersburg - after the battle."

☛ "[Confederate] Gen. [Jeb] Stuart threw out his pickets across the fields, and just in front of us the enemy did likewise. The pickets were in full view of each other, and a long-range musket might have sent a bullet across the line at any time, but we did not molest each other. At night the lines came still closer together, and we could distinctly hear them relieving their pickets every two hours, and they doubtless could hear us doing the same.

"This state of things remained for several weeks. Not a shot was fired during all that time, and so well acquainted did the pickets of each army become, that it was not an uncommon thing to see them marching across the fields to meet each other and exchange greetings, and often the Confederates traded tobacco for coffee and sugar. I took quite an interest in this bartering and trading. This got to be so common that Gen. Stuart had to issue an order forbidding it.

"After a while conditions changed. Gen. Lee had sent Longstreet's corps to Tennessee to reinforce [General Braxton] Bragg, weakening his army to the extent of 20,000 men. Probably for this reason the enemy determined to make a demonstration, and began a movement toward our front. But so considerate were they that they did not open fire on us until we had gotten beyond range of their guns. This fraternal condition perhaps never existed before between two contending armies."[67] — Luther W. Hopkins, C.S.A. (near Brandy Station, Virginia, Summer 1863)

☛ "Two characteristics are stamped upon this army that follows Lee—the deep religious faith of many and the buoyant good temper of all. In the ranks march ministers of the Gospel and laymen who from youth have been devotees of the religious teachings handed down through pious ancestors from Knox, Cranmer, Wesley, and Bunyan. The labours of the chaplains during the winter on the Rapidan have been followed by a heightened religious devotion throughout the army.

"A veritable parallel to Cromwell's Ironsides is the Army of Northern Virginia in this Wilderness campaign, when it wards off weariness by keeping step to the vocal music of psalms and hymns. The piety of General Lee himself has reached as full a measure of religious devotion as that manifested by Havelock and Stonewall Jackson. Often is Lee found engaged in earnest prayer. With bowed head he is frequently beheld standing in the assemblies for prayer held by the soldiers. He constantly asks for the prayers of his friends, and always ascribes to Providence the successes of his army.

"The unfailing good humour of the men on the march is often their only panacea for thirst, hunger, and weariness. Privations furnish material for the spirit of innocent mirth. A lively fellow whistles an air, another chirps the fragment of a song, and all join in the chorus. Then a slip in the mud, a peculiar cry or quaint jest sets an entire regiment into a roar of laughter. After that follows the hum and the buzz of a bewildering medley of merriment and song that makes light the burden of the journey.

"This lightness of spirit is the most significant fact connected with Lee's army in the Wilderness. It indicates the superb morale of the Confederate troops. It is the sign of that cheerful endurance that carries them through the marching and starving and fighting of the fiercest campaign of the entire war. It follows them into battle. It marks them as they fight in the trenches. The men scarcely ever cease to talk and yell as they load and fire their muskets. We see the merriment and well-attempered buoyancy changed into the earnest enthusiasm of a

Another Yankee propaganda picture, this one showing Union General Irvin McDowell (fifth from right) and his staff standing in front of the Lee's stolen home, Arlington House, in 1862.

devoted soldiery when Lee gallops forward along Hill's column on the afternoon of May 4 [1864]. Affection for their great leader breaks out in the tumult of wild cheers and the rolling of the battle-yell as the soldiers catch sight of their hero in the plain slouch hat and the suit of grey."[68] — Henry Alexander White

☛ "The roar of the guns in the woods at that early hour in the morning was terrific. What was going on in front of us was being enacted up and down the river for at least three miles.

"Our forces then fell back into the open country, and the battle continued, at intervals, all day long.

"The Yankees were supported by infantry, while we had nothing but cavalry and artillery.

"Our enemies could have driven us back farther if they had tried to, but they seemed to be afraid of getting into trouble. I do not know what our commander, Gen. [Jeb] Stuart, knew, but I did not suppose that Gen. Lee was within 30 miles of us. Toward sunset I saw him come riding across the fields on his gray horse, 'Traveler,' accompanied by his staff. He seemed as calm and unconcerned as if he were inspecting the land with the view of a purchase.

"Whether it was the presence of Gen. Lee himself, or the fear that he had his army with him, I know not, but simultaneously with the appearance of Gen. Lee the enemy began to move back and recross the river. We did not press them, but gave them their own time."[69] — Luther W. Hopkins, C.S.A. (just prior to the Battle of Gettysburg, June 1863)

☛ "During the hottest portion of this engagement, when the Federals were pouring through the broken Confederate lines and disaster seemed imminent, General Lee rode forward and took his position at the head of General [John Brown] Gordon's column, then preparing to charge. Perceiving that it was his intention to lead the charge, Gordon spurred hastily to his side, seized the reins of his horse and excitedly cried, "'General Lee, this is no place for you. Do go to the rear. These are Virginians and Georgians, sir—men who have never failed—and they will not fail now.—Will you, boys? Is it necessary for General Lee to lead this charge?'

Confederate General Thomas J. Jackson (second from right) at the Battle of Manassas I, July 21, 1861. It was here that Jackson earned the nickname "Stonewall." Tragically he was cut down by friendly fire in May 1863. General Lee called him "my right arm" and said he would have gladly died in Jackson's place.

"'No! no! General Lee to the rear! General Lee to the rear!' cried the men. 'We will drive them back if General Lee will only go to the rear.'

"As Lee retired Gordon put himself at the head of his division and cried out in his ringing voice, 'Forward! charge! and remember your promise to General Lee!'"[70] — Brigadier General Armistead L. Long, C.S.A.

An example of Lee's great fatherly interest in the love lives of his soldiers:
☛ "It was in the winter of 1863-4, when we were camped near Orange Court House, that, meeting the General after I had come back from a short visit to Richmond, he asked after my father, and then said, 'Did you see Miss ______?' and I replied, 'No, sir; I did not.'

"Then again, 'Did you see Miss ______?' and when I still replied "'No,' he added, with a smile, 'How exceedingly busy you must have been.'"[71] — Lieutenant George W. Peterkin, C.S.A.

☛ "I think this was early in November [1863]. We felt winter approaching, and I remember when we reached the Rappahannock, although there was a bridge a mile below, the cavalry forded the stream, the men getting wet above their knees, as the water came well up to the sides of the horses. Gen. Lee, noticing that the men were wet from fording the river, said to our brigade commander, Gen. [Lunsford Lindsay] Lomax, in a kind and fatherly tone, 'My! general, you should have used the bridge below.' I suppose Gen. Lomax thought that as we were soldiers we ought not to mind a little wetting, even if the cold November winds were blowing."[72] — Luther W. Hopkins, C.S.A.

☛ 'As to [Union General Ulysses S.] Grant's grit and determination, all his predecessors together did not possess as much of these manly qualities, and we used to hear fine tales, too, of his imperturbability; for instance, that soon after he crossed the Rapidan in 1864, when some one dashed up to his headquarters and announced with great excitement the capture of his pontoons, every one else seemed to be shattered; but Grant deliberately removed his cigar from his mouth, blew a very fine smoke wreath or ring, and said quietly, 'If I beat General Lee I sha'n't want any pontoons; and if General Lee beats me I can take all the men I intend to take back across the river on a log.'"[73] — Major Robert Stiles, C.S.A.

☛ "[In the summer of 1864, General Lee] rode over from Petersburg, [Virginia,] and reached us quite late in the afternoon—too late to return to his headquarters that night. After some conversation about the line and troops[,] he mentioned the necessity of finding quarters for himself and those with him for the night. Apologizing for my inability to make him comfortable and to have him stay with me . . . I suggested that he should go to Chaffin's Bluff, where he would find houses occupied, I thought, by Major [Richard] Dick Taylor . . . and Colonel Jack Maury and others connected with the heavy and stationary artillery.

"He replied in his quiet, punctuating way of talking, as if weighing each word, 'Well, Colonel Carter, if I turn those gentlemen out of their rooms, where will they sleep?'—'On the ground,' I replied at once, 'like the rest of the army;' and I added, what I knew to be literally true, 'They will be delighted to give up their rooms to you.'—'None of your blarney, Colonel Carter—none of your blarney, sir,' he replied with a smile. Though not sure of it, I think he went there, but I am sure if he went the rooms were given up with delight."[74]
— Colonel Thomas H. Carter, C.S.A.

☛ "Already is the sun beaming upon the awful game of death; the forest wears the smile of the springtide; the birds in the tree-tops are singing while the tempest of wrath breaks below. The thunder of [Confederate Captain William T.] Poague's guns shakes the very earth. Lee rides forward to meet the head of Field's division. 'What boys are these ?' he asks. 'Texas boys,' is the quick reply from the brigade that once followed [John Bell] Hood but is now led by [Confederate General John] Gregg. The light of battle is shining in his deep, luminous eyes as he calls out, 'My Texas boys, you must charge.' The Confederates go fairly wild when they see before them the grey-bearded man with the grey slouch hat. The voices of the eight hundred Texans are hoarse with joy, and their blood catches fire as they hear Lee himself give the order to charge. Ragged caps fly into the air as the veterans rend the sky with their wild yell.

"Then the line of battle is formed, they advance beyond the batteries against [Union General Winfield Scott] Hancock. Immediately behind the line rides Lee to direct the charge in person. 'Charge, boys,' is Lee's deep, thrilling call as he advances into the thickest of the fight. Suddenly the men divine his desperate purpose and they begin to shout, 'Go back, General Lee—Marse Robert go back.' Then the artillerymen whom Lee has passed respond with the answering call, 'Come back, come back, General Lee.' Lee rides onward, waving his old grey hat, but the very heavens are rent with the cry, 'Lee to the rear! Lee to the

In this outlandish anti-South Northern cartoon, fantasy-prone Yanks imagine this ghastly scene after Lincoln's War. Titled "Freedom's Immortal Triumph! Finale of the Jeff Davis Die-nasty," President Davis (on the left) is pictured hanging from a "Sour Apple Tree" symbolically dressed in women's clothing. Beneath him the Devil waits to claim Davis' corpse in an open grave. To the right are the "Confederate Mourners" awaiting their own hangings (from left to right): Robert E. Lee, John C. Breckinridge, Judah P. Benjamin, William L. Yancey, Robert A. Toombs, Louis T. Wigfall, and Lincoln's assassin, John Wilkes Booth. Note that General Lee has been placed first in line! In the background are the notorious Southern prisons Andersonville and Libby, while Confederate artillery, shattered skulls, and copperhead snakes (a symbol of Northern Confederate sympathizers) litter the foreground. Above it all, in the upper far left, is Lady Liberty with the U.S. flag and a slave family looking beseechingly at a blindfolded Lady Justice (symbolizing, of course, "blind justice") in the center. To the far upper right is the sentimentalized image of the murdered Abraham Lincoln, being escorted into Heaven by a band of angels. The tragic irony of this simple-minded cartoon is that it was the conservative South that was fighting *for* personal freedom and self-determination (as promised in the Constitution). The North, led by the dictatorial big government liberal Lincoln, was fighting *against* liberty. General Lee, who was indicted for "treason" against the U.S. government after the War, is indeed lucky to have escaped the hangman's noose: brandished a "traitor" by postwar Yankees, he was grilled before a Reconstruction Committee made up of hostile and vengeful Northern politicians, who tried to trick him into saying something that would "prove his disloyalty to the Union" (they failed). Lee died in 1870, still a "prisoner on parole." So-called "Reconstruction" did not end until seven years later, in 1877, the final chapter of Lincoln's insane and illegal war against states' rights and the Constitution-loving Southern people.

rear!' A tall, lank, ragged Texas sergeant moves from the ranks, seizes the bridle-rein and turns Traveller's head to the rear. A look of disappointment crosses the face of General Lee, but he yields. A last earthly salute the entire line wave to their leader and forward they sweep to meet the advancing foe."[75] — Henry Alexander White (during the Battle of the Wilderness, May 5-7, 1864)

☛ "[On August 26, 1862, an] incident occurred which shows us the great Southern leader on his human and friendly side. A certain woman of wealth and social position, living near Salem, greatly desired to see the famous General Lee. Accordingly, she and her daughter, in a carriage drawn by a pair of superb horses, drove out to a point where Lee was likely to pass. She encountered, on the road . . . [a] squadron of Federal cavalry which had . . . [just] nearly captured General Lee; and they promptly took possession of her horses, leaving the disconsolate lady and her daughter sitting in their 'horseless carriage' in the middle of the highway.

"Soon afterward Lee arrived at that spot, inquired about their singular position, and, in his charming and courtly way, gave them all the sympathy he could. The mother afterward loved to tell this story of her interview with him, always ending with a laugh and the remark, 'I did indeed see him, as I had wished; but I don't feel quite reconciled, even to this day, at the price I had to pay—a pair of splendid horses—for that interview."[76] — Bradley Gilman

☛ "[It was the summer of 1864.] General Lee was visiting a battery on the lines below Richmond, and the soldiers, inspired by their affection for him, gathered near him in a group that attracted the enemy's fire. Turning toward them, he said, in his quiet manner, 'Men, you had better go farther to the rear; they are firing up here, and you are exposing yourselves to unnecessary danger.'

"The men drew back, but General Lee, as if unconscious of danger to himself, walked across the yard, picked up some small object from the ground, and placed it upon the limb of a tree above his head. It was afterward perceived that the object for which he had thus risked his life was an unfledged [baby] sparrow that had fallen from its nest. It was a marked instance of that love for the lower animals and deep feeling for the helpless which he always displayed."[77] — an unknown Confederate officer at the scene

☛ "I do not know how others [in Lee's army] felt about the bodies of the dead horses that lay scattered over the battlefields, but this sight distressed me almost as much as did the bodies of the soldiers. They [the horses] were so faithful and unfaltering. When the bugle sounded, any hour of the night, or any hour of the day, regardless of how short a time they had rested or how many miles they had marched, they were always ready to respond. They knew all the bugle calls. If it were saddle up, or the feed or the water call, they were as ready to answer one as the other. And they were so noble and so brave in battle. They seemed to love the sound of the guns. The cavalryman might lie low on the neck of his horse for shelter as the missiles of death hissed about him, but the horse never flinched, except when struck.

"The cavalryman often used his horse for a breastwork while he fired over his back, the horse standing like a Casabianca on the burning deck of his father's ship. Did you ever read *Black Beauty*? If you have not, read it. Lee had 75,000 'Black Beauties' in his army, every one of which, or nearly every one, is worthy of a monument. We build monuments for our dead soldiers, for those we know and for the unknown dead. What would you think of a monument some day, somewhere in Virginia, in honor of Lee's noble horses?"[78] — Luther W. Hopkins, C.S.A.

☛ "One day in Richmond a number of little girls were rolling hoops on the sidewalk, when word was passed from one to another that General Lee was riding toward them. They all gathered into a still group to gaze upon one of whom they had heard so much, when, to their surprise, he threw his rein to his attending courier, dismounted, and kissed every one of them, and then, mounting, rode away, with the sunny smile of childhood in his heart and plans of great battles in his mind."[79] — Reverend John W. Jones, chaplain, Army of Northern Virginia, C.S.A.

Luther W. Hopkins as he appeared in 1861, at the start of Lincoln's War. The young Hopkins served faithfully in General Lee's Northern Army of Virginia, and after the conflict wrote about his experiences in his wonderful book, *From Bull Run to Appomattox: A Boy's View*.

☛ "As one of the Army of Northern Virginia, I occasionally saw [my father] the commander-in-chief, on the march, or passed the headquarters close enough to recognise him and members of his staff, but a private soldier in Jackson's corps did not have much time, during that campaign, for visiting, and until the battle of Sharpsburg I had no opportunity of speaking to him. On that occasion our battery had been severely handled, losing many men and horses. Having three guns disabled, we were ordered to withdraw, and while moving back we passed General Lee and several of his staff, grouped on a little knoll near the road. Having no definite orders where to go, our captain, seeing the commanding general, halted us and rode over to get some instructions. Some others and myself went along to see and hear.

"General Lee was dismounted with some of his staff around him, a courier holding his horse. Captain [William T.] Poague, commanding our battery, the Rockbridge Artillery, saluted, reported our condition, and asked for instructions. The General, listening patiently, looked at us—his eyes passing over me without any sign of recognition—and then ordered Captain Poague to take the most serviceable horses and men, man the uninjured gun, send the disabled part of his command back to refit, and report to the front for duty. As Poague turned to go, I went up to speak to my father. When he found out who I was, he congratulated me on being well and unhurt. I then said:

"'General, are you going to send us in again?'

"'Yes, my son,' he replied, with a smile; 'you all must do what you can to help drive these people back.'"[80] — Captain Robert E. Lee, Jr., C.S.A.

☛ "On one of his daily visits to the lines at Petersburg, General Lee asked one of his officers who was riding with him if a work he had ordered to be performed was finished. The officer replied, hesitatingly, that it was. Lee then proposed to ride to the spot and inspect it.

"On arriving there he found that the work had made very little progress since his last visit to it, a week before. The officer in much confusion sought to excuse himself for his negligence, saying that he had ordered it to be completed at once, and had been told that it was finished, but had not himself been there. General Lee simply remarked, 'We must give our personal attention to the lines,' and rode quietly on. While doing so he began to compliment his companion on the fine charger he rode.

"'Yes, sir,' replied the general, 'he is a splendid animal, and I prize him the more highly because he belongs to my wife and is her favorite riding-horse.'

"'A magnificent horse indeed,'" was General Lee's reply, 'but I should not think him safe for Mrs. _____ to ride. He is entirely too spirited for a lady, and I would urge you by all means to take some of the mettle out of him before you suffer your wife to ride him again. And, by the way, general, I would suggest to you that the rough paths along these trenches would be admirable ground over which to tame him."[81] — Brigadier General Armistead L. Long, C.S.A.

☛ "It is related that one day during the war, as they were reconnoitering the countless [Yankee] host opposed to them, one of his subordinates exclaimed in bitter tones, 'I wish those people were all dead!' General Lee, with that inimitable grace of manner peculiar to him, promptly rejoined, 'How can you say so, General? Now I wish that they were all at home attending to their own business and leaving us to do the same.'"[82] — Reverend John W. Jones, chaplain, Army of Northern Virginia, C.S.A.

During the summer of 1863 several reviews of the Army of Northern Virginia were held before General Lee. One of these is described by his son, who witnessed the amazing event:

☛ "I remember being present when that of the Third Army Corps, [Confederate] General A. P. Hill commanding, took place. Some of us young cavalrymen, then stationed near the Rappahannock, rode over to Orange Court House to see this grand military pageant. From all parts of the army, officers and men who could get leave came to look on, and from all the surrounding country the people, old and young, ladies and children, came in every pattern of vehicle and on horseback, to see twenty thousand of that 'incomparable infantry ' of the Army of Northern Virginia pass in review before their great commander.

"The General was mounted on [his favorite horse] Traveller, looking very proud of his master, who had on sash and sword, which he very rarely wore, a pair of new cavalry gauntlets, and, I think, a new hat. At any rate, he looked unusually fine, and sat his horse like a perfect picture of grace and power.

"The infantry was drawn up in column by divisions, with their

General Lee (ninth from right) with some of his officers and military staff.

bright muskets all glittering in the sun, their battle-flags standing straight out before the breeze, and their bands playing, awaiting the inspection of the General, before they broke into column by companies and marched past him in review. When all was ready, General Hill and staff rode up to General Lee, and the two generals, with their respective staffs, galloped around front and rear of each of the three divisions standing motionless on the plain. As the cavalcade reached the head of each division, its commanding officer joined in and followed as far as the next division, so that there was a continual infusion of fresh groups into the original one all along the lines. Traveller started with a long lope, and never changed his stride. His rider sat erect and calm, not noticing anything but the gray lines of men whom he knew so well. The pace was very fast, as there were nine good miles to go, and the escort began to become less and less, dropping out one by one from different causes as Traveller raced along without a check.

"When the General drew up, after this nine-mile gallop, under the standard at the reviewing-stand, flushed with the exercise as well as with pride in his brave men, he raised his hat and saluted. Then arose a shout of applause and admiration from the entire assemblage, the memory of which to this day moistens the eye of every old soldier."[83] — Captain Robert E. Lee, Jr., C.S.A.

☛ "When the infantry was hurrying to the support of Fitz Lee's cavalry at Spottsylvania Court-house, as each division arrived it would form into line on the right of its predecessor. I happened to be near General Lee when a few bullets cut the limbs and struck the ground near him. Some general—I forget who—said, 'General, this is no place for you; do go away at once to a safe place.' He replied, with a half-complaining smile and manner, 'I wish I knew where my place is on the battlefield: wherever I go some one tells me it is not the place for me to be.' But he was always deeply touched by these indications of the devotion of his army and people to him."[84] — Colonel Thomas H. Carter, C.S.A.

☛ "On one occasion, when [his] headquarters were at Petersburg, [I] . . . happened to be there at meal-time, and was invited to dine with General Lee. It was a period in which rations were very short. A small bowl of soup graced the table, far too limited in quantity to go the rounds of the mess. General Lee accordingly divided it with . . . [me], and, as he looked around the table with a merry twinkle in his eye, quietly remarked, 'I am credibly informed that the young men of my staff never eat soup.'"[85] — General Wade Hampton, C.S.A.

☛ "The day after the battle of Cold Harbor [I, more commonly known as the Battle of Gaines' Mill, June 27, 1862], during the 'Seven Days' fighting around Richmond, was the first time I met my father after I had joined General [Stonewall] Jackson. The tremendous work Stonewall's men had performed, including the rapid march from the Valley of Virginia, the short rations, the bad water, and the great heat, had begun to tell upon us, and I was pretty well worn out. On this particular morning, my battery had not moved from its bivouac ground of the previous night, but was parked in an open field all ready, waiting orders. Most of the men were lying down, many sleeping, myself among the latter number. To get some shade and to be out of the way, I had crawled under a caisson, and was busy making up many lost hours of rest. Suddenly I was rudely awakened by a comrade, prodding me with a sponge-staff as I had failed to be aroused by his call, and was told to get up and come out, that some one wished to see me. Half awake, I staggered out, and found myself face to face with General Lee and his staff.

"Their fresh uniforms, bright equipments and well-groomed horses contrasted so forcibly with the war-worn appearance of our command that I was completely dazed. It took me a moment or two to realise what it all meant, but when I saw my father's loving eyes and smile it became clear to me that he had ridden by to see if I was safe and to ask how I was getting along. I remember well how curiously those with him gazed at me, and I am sure that it must have struck them as very odd that such a dirty, ragged, unkempt youth could have been the son of this grand looking victorious commander."[86] — Captain Robert E. Lee, Jr., C.S.A.

☞ "While in winter quarters at Petersburg a party of officers were one night busily engaged in discussing, at the same time, a mathematical problem and the contents of a stone jug which was garnished by two tin cups. In the midst of this General Lee came in to make some inquiry. He got the information he wanted, gave a solution of the problem, and went out, the officers expressing to each other the hope that the General had not noticed the jug and cups.

"The next day one of the officers, in the presence of the others, was relating to General Lee a very strange dream he had the night before.

Entitled "Three Heros," this 19th-Century drawing shows three famous Confederate generals (from left to right): Stonewall Jackson, Robert E. Lee, and Jeb Stuart. The author is cousins with all three.

The General listened with apparent interest to the narrative, and quietly rejoined, 'That is not at all remarkable. When young gentlemen discuss at midnight mathematical problems, the "unknown quantities" of which are a stone jug and two tin cups, they may expect to have strange dreams.'"[87] — Reverend John W. Jones, chaplain, Army of Northern Virginia, C.S.A.

☞ "On one occasion a demijohn [a large narrow-necked bottle encased in wicker] was observed to be carried into his [Lee's] tent, which excited in the minds of those who beheld it visions of good wine or brandy. (The general well knew that several of his staff enjoyed a glass of wine, or even something stronger.) About twelve o'clock he walked out of his tent, and with a twinkle in his eye remarked, 'Perhaps you gentlemen would like a glass of something ?' All assenting, he directed Bryan, the steward of the mess, to carry the demijohn to the mess-tent and arrange cups for the gentlemen. They followed him with pleasant anticipations of the unexpected treat. The general ordered the cork to be drawn and the cups filled. The disappointment of the expectants and Lee's enjoyment may be better imagined than described when the contents proved to be buttermilk [Lee's favorite beverage]."[88] — Brigadier General Armistead L. Long, C.S.A.

☞ "[During one of our many battles, it] was noticed that General Lee exposed himself unsparingly to fire. He sat for some time on his iron-gray [horse] close beside a section of Chamberlayne's battery, which on the brow of the hill was shelling the advancing enemy, and gazed intently through his glass at the movements of the approaching foe. Receiving a report from a staff officer, General Lee told him he had ridden up on the wrong side of the hill and unnecessarily exposed himself. When the officer remarked that he was ashamed to try to shelter himself when his commander was so exposed, General Lee remarked rather sharply, 'It is my duty to be here. I must see. Go back the way I told you, sir.'" —Colonel Thomas G. Jones, C.S.A.

☞ "After McClellan's change of base to Harrison's Landing on James River, the army lay inactive around Richmond. I had a short furlough on account of sickness, and saw my father; also my mother and sisters, who

Yankee General Samuel P. Heintzelman (fifth from the right) and his staff on the front steps of the Lee estate, Arlington House. The photographer, Matthew Brady, is in a top hat standing to Heintzelman's right.

were then living in Richmond. He was the same loving father to us all, as kind and thoughtful of my mother, who was an invalid, and of us, his children, as if our comfort and happiness were all he had to care for. His great [recent] victory [at the Battle of Gaines' Mill, June 27, 1862] did not elate him, so far as one could see."[89] — Captain Robert E. Lee, Jr., C.S.A.

☛ "After remaining in . . . camp a short time and receiving in Confederate paper money a portion of our pay, we [recently released Confederate prisoners] were marched into Richmond and to one of the depots. We did not know what disposition they [the Confederate authorities] intended making of us (perhaps we were going to a new camp), but there was a train that was just starting out for Gordonsville, so three of us got on the rear platform of the end car and thus beat our way to Gordonsville without being noticed. This was as far as the train could go in safety on account of the proximity of the enemy.

"When we got off we noticed Gen. Lee standing in the crowd, having just alighted from the train. I had often seen him, but had never got as close to him as I desired. Now, this was my chance. I went up within five feet of him, and took a good look. I never expect again to look upon such a splendid piece of humanity.

"He was dressed in a new Confederate uniform that fitted him perfectly, with long-legged boots, reaching above the knees. His collar was adorned on each side with three gold stars, surrounded by a gold wreath. His head was covered with a new soft black hat, encircled with a gold cord, from which dangled two gold acorns, one on each end. On his hands he wore yellow buckskin gauntlets, reaching one-third the way to his elbows. His full beard, closely clipped, was iron-gray, white predominating. I imagined that he was a little over six feet and would weigh 190 pounds. His eyes, I think, were brown, and as bright as stars. No picture could possibly do him justice. I suppose it would take cycles of time to produce another such as he—so perfect in form and feature."[90]
— Luther W. Hopkins, C.S.A.

On April 8, 1865, one day before the final surrender of the Confederacy, Rebel General William N. Pendleton approached Lee with the idea, expressed by several other officers as well, that the situation was hopeless and that it was now time to capitulate to Union forces. Here is the scene as Pendleton later described it:

☛ "General Lee was lying on the ground. No others heard the conversation between him and myself. He received my communication with the reply, 'Oh no, I trust it has not come to that;' and added, 'General, we have yet too many bold men to think of laying down our arms. The enemy do not fight with spirit, while our boys still do. Besides, if I were to say a word to the Federal commander he would regard it as such a confession of weakness as to make it the condition of demanding unconditional surrender—a proposal to which I will never listen. . . . I have never believed we could, against the gigantic combination for our subjugation, make good in the long run our independence unless foreign powers should, directly or indirectly, assist

A photo of General Lee's headquarters during the Battle of Gaines' Mill, June 27, 1862.

us. . . . But such considerations really made with me no difference. We had, I was satisfied, sacred principles to maintain and rights to defend, for which we were in duty bound to do our best, even if we perished in the endeavor.'

"Such were, as nearly as I can recall them, the exact words of General Lee on that most critical occasion. You see in them the soul of the man. What his conscience dictated and his judgment decided, there his heart was."[91] — General William N. Pendleton, chaplain, C.S.A.

☛ "In calling one day in Petersburg upon the accomplished lady of the gallant and lamented [Confederate] General Ambrose Powell Hill, his bright little girl met . . . [Lee] at the door and exclaimed, with that familiarity which the kind-hearted old hero had taught her: 'O General Lee, here is 'Bobby Lee' (holding up a puppy); 'do kiss him.'

"The general pretended to do so, and the little creature was delighted."[92] — Reverend John W. Jones, chaplain, Army of Northern Virginia, C.S.A.

☛ "Once General Lee had fallen asleep beneath a tree, on the roadside, over which 15,000 Confederates were defiling [marching]. On learning that their chief was tasting a repose of which he had so much need, there was the most absolute silence suddenly in their ranks, and the entire corps was able to pass without waking him."[93] — Edward Lee Childe (the General's nephew)

☛ "Lee waits behind his field-battery for the arrival of [Confederate General Richard Heron] Anderson's division of [Confederate General Ambrose Powell] Hill's corps. The fight is raging in his front; the guns of [Confederate General Richard Stoddert] Ewell are calling across from the turnpike that all is well on the left wing. An engineer is sent to find an opening for a flank attack against [Union General Winfield Scott] Hancock's left. At this moment of anxiety a courier—a mere lad—dashes up to General Lee with a message from Anderson. The courier's small pony is panting like a hunted deer. Lee reads the message and turns to look upon the tired pony. 'Young man,' he says, 'you should have some feeling for your horse; dismount and rest him.' Lee thereupon draws forth from the bag attached to his saddle a buttered biscuit, and half of this with his own hand he gives to the courier's pony."[94] — Henry Alexander White (during the Battle of the Wilderness, May 5-7, 1864)

☛ "I did not see my father at any time during the fighting [at the Battle of Fredericksburg, December 11-15, 1862]. Some days after it was all over, I saw him, as calm and composed as if nothing unusual had happened, and he never referred to his great victory, except to deplore the loss of his brave officers and soldiers or the sufferings of the sick and wounded. He repeatedly referred to the hardships so bravely endured by the inhabitants of Fredericksburg, who had been obliged to flee from the town, the women and children, the old and the feeble, whose sufferings cut him to the heart."[95] — Captain Robert E. Lee, Jr., C.S.A.

Though a compassionate man, the General did not like complaining or slacking, and was always encouraging his soldiers to show valor and strength, as the following story illustrates:

☛ "I happened to see a man lying flat on his face in a small ditch, and I remarked that I didn't think he seemed dead; this drew General Lee's attention to the man, who commenced groaning dismally. Finding appeals to his patriotism of no avail, General Lee had him ignominiously set on his legs by some neighboring gunners."[96] — Sir Arthur J. L. Fremantle, British officer

☛ "When we came back to our four guns and were leading them to the lines and the positions selected for them, just as we were turning down a little declivity we passed again within a few feet of General Lee, seated upon his horse on the crest of the hill, this time entirely alone, not even a courier with him. I was much impressed with the calmness and perfect poise of his bearing, though his center had just been pierced by forty thousand men and the fate of his army trembled in the balance. He was completely exposed to the Federal fire, which was very heavy. A half dozen of our men were wounded in making this short descent.

A war-torn Confederate Battle Flag, this one from the Thirteenth Mississippi Regiment.

"In this connection I have recently heard from a courier—who, with others, had ridden with the General to the point where we saw him—that, observing and remarking upon the peril to which they were subjected, he ordered all his couriers to protect themselves behind an old brick kiln some one hundred and fifty yards to the left, until their services were required, but refused to go there [behind the kiln] himself. This habit of exposing himself to fire, as they sometimes thought unnecessarily, was the only point in which his soldiers felt that Lee ever did wrong. The superb stories of the several occasions during this campaign when his men refused to advance until he retired, and with tears streaming down their faces led his horse to the rear, are too familiar to justify repetition . . ."[97] — Major Robert Stiles, C.S.A. (during the Battle of Spotsylvania, May 8-21, 1864)

☛ "I was on the march from home toward the army, and had reached a point not far from Charlottesville. There were about a dozen of us, all belonging to my regiment. About noon we saw advancing toward us a small body of cavalry. At first we took them for the enemy and approached them cautiously, they using the same precaution. When we discovered that we were fellow-Confeds we passed with a salute. One of them called to us and said, 'Boys, you may as well go home; Lee has surrendered his army.' We paid no attention to it, but moved on.

"A mile farther we met another squad and asked what was the news from the army. We got this reply: 'As we passed through Charlottesville we came near being mobbed for telling the news from the army. You had better go on and find out for yourselves.' Soon after this we met a colonel leading about 40 cavalrymen. By this time we began to feel that something was wrong. The colonel halted his men and frankly told us that it was a fact that Lee had surrendered his army. He stated that some of the cavalry had escaped and they were making their way toward their homes, and advised us to do the same.

"The colonel and his men moved on, and we halted for an hour in the road discussing the situation and trying to determine what to do. We were not prepared to act upon the evidence that we had had regarding the surrender, but were willing to admit that it might be true. One fellow from Company F, riding a gray horse, rose in his stirrups, and lifting his clinched hand high above his head, said, 'If Gen. Lee has had to surrender his army, there is not a just God in Heaven.'"[98] — Luther W. Hopkins, C.S.A. (mid April 1865)

☛ "Gen. Lee, seeing the peril in which his army was placed, ordered forward [John Brown] Gordon's division (which he was holding in reserve), placed himself at the head of it, and was about to lead them into battle in order to restore his broken lines. Shells were falling about Gen. Lee and his life was in peril. One of the officers rode up to him and said, 'Gen. Lee, this is no place for you; you must go to the rear.' His troops refused to go forward until Gen. Lee had retired from the front. One of the soldiers came forward, and taking the reins of Lee's horse, led him back. Then Gen. Gordon led his division forward, the enemy was driven back, the line was restored, and Gen. Lee's army was saved from destruction and another year added to the life of the Confederacy."[99] — Luther W. Hopkins, C.S.A. (Battle of the Wilderness May 5-7, 1864)

On Lee's teetotalism:

☛ "In the spring of 1861, while on an inspection tour to Norfolk, a friend there insisted that Lee should take two bottles of very fine old 'London Dock' brandy, remarking that he would be certain to need it, and would find it very difficult to obtain so good an article. The General declined the offer, saying that he was sure he would not need it. 'As proof that I will not,' he said, 'I may tell you that, just as I was starting to the Mexican War, a lady in Virginia prevailed on me to take a bottle

General Lee's headquarters during the Battle of Gettysburg in the Summer of 1863.

of fine old whiskey, which she thought I could not got on without. I carried that bottle all through the war without having had the slightest occasion to use it, and on my return home I sent it back to my good friend, that she might be convinced that I could get on without liquor.'"[100] — Reverend John W. Jones, chaplain, Army of Northern Virginia, C.S.A.

☛ "One of his brigadiers asked Lee one day, 'Why is it, general, that you do not wear the full [four-star] insignia of your rank, but content yourself with the [three] stars of a colonel?' 'Oh,' replied the modest chieftain, 'I do not care for display. And the truth is, that the rank of colonel is about as high as I ought ever to have gotten; or, perhaps, I might manage a good cavalry brigade if I had the right kind of subordinates.'"[101] — Reverend John W. Jones, chaplain, Army of Northern Virginia, C.S.A.

☛ "On one occasion some Confederate soldiers were gathered about a camp fire discussing the Darwinian theory of evolution, which had recently been brought to their attention. After a variety of opinions had been expressed about this famous speculation, one of the soldiers, who had remained silent, delivered his as follows:

"'Well, boys, the rest of us may have been developed from monkeys, but I tell you only God Almighty could make a man like Marse Robert.'"[102] — Franklin Lafayette Riley

Concerning Lee's religious influence on the Confederate army:
☛ "Military enthusiasm glowed around the brightening campfires, and to this was added a deep and growing religious sentiment. The Confederate chaplains were untiring in their labours. Each night found eager groups of men gathered in wooded glades, lending earnest attention to the appeals of these men of God. Among the men were often seen Lee and Jackson, with heads bowed reverently in prayer. In many brigades, increasing numbers accepted the Christian faith, and thus began that widespread interest in religion that rendered the Army of Northern Virginia more than the equal of Cromwell's Ironsides in piety and in fighting qualities."[103] — Henry Alexander White

☛ "[Throughout Lincoln's War] Lee's humility of spirit seemed to increase, if possible, day by day. His devout trust in God grew stronger and more childlike. His great heart was full of solicitude for the welfare of his men, and for the upbuilding of the strength of his army. Upon himself he laid the lowliest duties in order to relieve the sufferings of his soldiers. The man who always sat upon the most uncomfortable seat in his tent lest some one else might secure it, could also bring to the army for distribution the socks knit by his wife and daughters and other devoted women of Virginia."[104] — Henry Alexander White

☛ ". . . so dense was the fog and smoke of battle that [Union General Winfield Scott] Hancock's position was defined only by the sound of his muskets and the direction of the bullets. Lee spurred his horse toward the place of strife and found [Confederate General John Brown] Gordon arraying his men for the charge. Lee quietly took his position to lead the division. 'This is no place for General Lee,' said Gordon in stage-whisper. The soldiers heard the words and began to shout, 'General Lee to the rear.' 'These men are Georgians and Virginians; they have never failed you; they will not fail you now,' cried the impetuous Gordon to his commander. A ragged soldier stepped from the ranks and turned Traveller's head toward the rear. The cry of 'Lee to the rear' rang out again and again, and then it changed to the battle-slogan as the line advanced. Like a primitive bee-hunter, Gordon followed the course of the leaden messengers back to their origin. The din of battle swelled into a roar when Gordon met Hancock amid the dense growth of pines. The Federal left was thrust backward and Gordon set his flag above the eastern face of the salient."[105] — Henry Alexander White (describing an engagement during the Campaign in the Wilderness, May 1864)

Another view of Lee's Gettysburg headquarters.

☛ "On the morning of July 4, 1861, little Henry T_____ (a bright little boy of five, and an enthusiastic Confederate) went with his father to call on General Lee at his headquarters in Richmond, and to present him with a handsome copy of the Bible in four volumes.

"One of the staff met them at the door and reported that the general was too busy to see them; but, when the great chieftain heard the prattle of the little boy, he called to his aide to admit them.

"Receiving them with great cordiality, he accepted the gift of the

Bible with evident gratification, and was fondling [that is, gently caressing] the little boy on his knee, when the father inconsiderately asked Henry, 'What is General Lee going to do with General Scott?'

"The little fellow, who had caught some of the slang of the camp, and fully entered into the confident spirit which we all had in those early days of the war, instantly replied: 'He is going to whip him out of his breeches!'

"General Lee's voice and manner instantaneously changed, and, lifting Henry down, he stood him up between his knees, and, looking him full in the face, said, with great gravity: 'My dear little boy, you should not use such expressions; war is a serious matter, and General Scott is a great and good soldier. None of us can tell what the result of this contest will be.'"[106] — Reverend John W. Jones, chaplain, Army of Northern Virginia, C.S.A.

☛ "[General Lee] turned his head over his right shoulder, his cheeks became flushed and a sudden flash of the eye showed with what reluctance he retired before the fire directed upon him. No other course was left him, however, and he continued to ride slowly toward his inner line—a low earthwork in the suburbs of the city—where a small force was drawn up, ardent, hopeful, defiant, and saluting the shells now bursting above them with cheers and laughter. It was plain that the fighting spirit of the ragged troops remained unbroken; and the shout of welcome with which they received Lee indicated their unwavering confidence in him, despite the untoward condition of affairs."[107] — an eyewitness at the Siege of Petersburg (early April 1865)

☛ "[Not realizing the end was near, on April 2, 1865, Lee's troops were still] in excellent spirits, probably from the highly agreeable contrast of the budding April woods with the squalid trenches, and the long-unfelt joy of an unfettered march through the fields of spring. General Lee shared this hopeful feeling in a very remarkable degree. His expression was animated and buoyant, his seat in the saddle erect and commanding, and he seemed to look forward to assured success in the critical movement which he had undertaken."[108] — an unnamed soldier serving with Lee

This romanticized Yankee cartoon, entitled "The Last Offer of Reconciliation," shows a supposedly peace-loving Lincoln (left front center) extending his hand to a supposedly war-loving Jefferson Davis (as Lincoln intentionally started the "Civil War" while Davis did all he could to avoid it, the opposite is true). Some of Lincoln's cabinet members and military officers can be seen on the left, while to the right of Davis is (from left to right) John Wilkes Booth, Robert E. Lee, and the obligatory caricature of a "Southern slave in chains" (actually a rare sight in the South). Anti-South symbolism overwhelms the image, with peaceful background scenes and flowering fruits bordering Lincoln's side, contrasted with scenes of disaster and withering thorns bordering Davis' side. The subtitle, "In Remembrance of Pres. A. Lincoln: The Door is Open for All," is still more anti-Confederate Northern propaganda, all of it meant to whip up and maintain sectional hatred in the North for the South—which it has right into the present day. The truth is that Lincoln blocked black civil rights, delayed emancipation, and campaigned throughout his entire political career to have all American blacks deported to Africa, South America, and the Caribbean, hardly what any rational person would consider an "open door for all." Indeed, the man Yanks and New South scallywags continue to lovingly refer to as the "Great Emancipator," is the same man who used slaves (instead of free laborers) to finish constructing the White House, barred blacks from entering the Capitol Building, and, on July 17, 1858, told a Springfield, Illinois, audience: "What I would most desire would be the separation of the white and black races." Since knowledge of the real Abraham Lincoln destroys the Yankee myth that the "War was fought over slavery," it has been carefully suppressed for the last 150 years. But it is suppressed no longer.

An eyewitness account of Lee on the morning of April 9, 1865, the day the Confederacy "surrendered":

☛ "At three o'clock on the morning of that fatal day General Lee rode forward, still hoping that we might break through the countless hordes of the enemy who hemmed us in. Halting a short distance in rear of our van-guard, he sent me on to General [John Brown] Gordon to ask him if he could break through the enemy. I found General Gordon and

General Fitz Lee on their front line in the dim light of the morning arranging an attack. Gordon's reply to the message (I give the expressive phrase of the gallant Georgian) was this: 'Tell General Lee I have fought my corps to a frazzle, and I fear I can do nothing unless I am heavily supported by Longstreet's corps.'

"When I bore this message back to General Lee he said, 'Then there is nothing left me but to go and see [Yankee] General [Ulysses S.] Grant, and I would rather die a thousand deaths.'

"Convulsed with passionate grief, many were the wild words which we spoke as we stood around him. Said one, 'Oh, general, what will history say of the surrender of the army in the field?'

"He replied, 'Yes, I know they will say hard things of us: they will not understand how we were overwhelmed by numbers. But that is not the question, colonel: the question is, is it right to surrender this army? If it is right, then I will take all the responsibility.'"[109] — Lieutenant Colonel Charles S. Venable, C.S.A.

☛ "[On April 9, 1865, when] the flag of truce appeared on [Confederate General John Brown] Gordon's line, a feeling of surprise and curiosity to know what it meant pervaded the ranks. Soon it was told from man to man that the army was to be surrendered to the enemy. General Lee had been seen riding to the rear, dressed with more care than usual, and with his sword, which he rarely wore, buckled on.

"Later it was stated authoritatively that the service of the army was at an end. The emotions of the men are hard to describe. There was a feeling of relief that the long, unequal struggle was over, mingled with an agonized regret for the failure of the cause they had so nobly upheld. The troops were very silent, in their grief, and they moved about and spoke to each other with that hushed, subdued air which men wear when in the presence of death."[110] — James Dabney McCabe

On the afternoon of Lee's "surrender," April 9, 1865, Union General George G. Meade paid a visit to Lee's headquarters. Here, the following conversation took place, showing the overwhelming impression Lee's leadership had made on the Yanks during Lincoln's War:

☛ "Meade: 'Now that the war may be considered over, I hope you will not deem it improper for me to ask, for my personal information, the

One of the Lee's temporary homes. This one, which still stands, is located at 707 East Franklin St., Richmond, VA.

strength of your army during the operations about Richmond and Petersburg.'

"Lee: 'At no time did my force exceed 35,000 men; often it was less.'

"Meade: 'General, you amaze me! We always estimated your force at about 70,000 men.'"[111] — Brigadier General Armistead L. Long, C.S.A.

Here is another example of the banter that took place between Lee and Meade after the "surrender" of the Confederacy:

☛ "Lee: 'Meade, years are telling on you: your hair is getting quite gray.'

"Meade: 'Ah, General Lee, it is not the work of years: *you* are responsible for my gray hairs."[112] — General Francois A. de Chanal, a

French officer present at the scene

☛ "The disbanding of the Army of Northern Virginia [on April 9, 1865] marked the virtual downfall of the Southern Confederacy. The surrender of the remaining Confederate troops in the South and Southwest in the month of May, 1865, inevitably followed the capitulation of Lee at Appomattox. The soldiers of the Confederacy laid aside their arms, and turned from the bivouac to find desolate homes in a land laid waste. They uttered not a regret for the past nor a murmur concerning the present. They retained their former dauntless courage. They set themselves to work to restore their broken country.

"It was well that they were not broken in spirit, for the multiplied humiliations imposed upon the people of the South by the successful political party in the process called Reconstruction, were far more galling than the burdens laid upon them by a state of public warfare.

"When Lee returned from Appomattox he found Richmond partially in ashes. He sought privacy and rest in a rented house. He denounced the assassination of President Lincoln as a grievous crime, and deplored the intensified animosity toward the South on the part of the dominant political faction at Washington.

"On April 25, Lee wrote to Grant asking for the liberation from prison of all Confederate captives, at the same time remonstrating against the Federal practice of 'requiring oaths of paroled soldiers before permitting them to proceed on their journey. Officers and men on parole are bound in honour to conform to the obligations they have assumed. This obligation cannot be strengthened by any additional form or oath, nor is it customary to exact them.'"[113] — Henry Alexander White

The scene, on April 9, 1865, as depicted by an eyewitness, after Lee's "surrender" to Grant:

☛ "It is impossible to describe the anguish of the troops when it was known that the surrender of the army was inevitable. Of all their trials, this was the greatest and hardest to endure. There was no consciousness of shame; each heart could boast with honest pride that its duty had been done to the end, and that still unsullied remained its honor. When, after

This 19th-Century illustration shows General Lee riding back through his dispirited troops immediately after signing the papers of surrender to Grant at Appomattox.

his interview with Grant, General Lee again appeared, a shout of welcome instinctively ran through the army. But instantly recollecting the sad occasion that brought him before them, their shouts sank into silence, every hat was raised, and the bronzed faces of the thousands of grim warriors were bathed with tears.

"As he rode slowly along the lines hundreds of his devoted veterans pressed around the noble chief, trying to take his hand, touch his person, or even lay a hand upon his horse, thus exhibiting for him their great affection. The general then, with head bare and tears flowing freely down his manly cheeks, bade adieu to the army. In a few words he told the brave men who had been so true in arms to return to their homes and become worthy citizens.

"Thus closed the career of the noble Army of Northern Virginia."[114] — Brigadier General Armistead L. Long, C.S.A.

☛ "Among the Confederate soldiers themselves there had been scarcely a thought of surrender. When they saw their beloved leader riding back from the place of negotiation, their grief was wellnigh unspeakable. They halted his horse and gathered in clusters about him. Tears were running down every cheek as the grim, ragged veterans came up to wring his hand. Only sobs were heard or prayers uttered in broken words calling down the benedictions of heaven upon Lee. The tears in his own eyes formed his answer to the agony of his men. He could only say in a tone that trembled with sorrow, 'Men, we have fought through the war together. I have done the best I could for you. My heart is too full to say more.'"[115] — Henry Alexander White (on the day of Lee's "surrender" to Grant, April 9, 1865)

After Lee stacked arms at Appomattox on April 9, 1865:
☛ "The scene witnessed upon the return of General Lee was one certain to impress itself indelibly upon the memory; it can be vividly recalled now, after the lapse of many years, but no description can do it justice. The men crowded around him, eager to shake him by the hand; eyes that had been so often illumined with the fire of patriotism and true courage, that had so often glared with defiance in the heat and fury of battle, and so often kindled with enthusiasm and pride in the hour of success, moistened now; cheeks bronzed by exposure in many campaigns, and withal begrimed with powder and dust, now blanched from deep emotion and suffered the silent tear; tongues that had so often carried dismay to the hearts of the enemy in that indescribable cheer which accompanied 'the charge,' or that had so often made the air to resound with the paean of victory, refused utterance now; brave hearts failed that had never quailed in the presence of an enemy; but the firm and silent pressure of the hand told most eloquently of souls filled with admiration, love, and tender sympathy, for their beloved chief.

"He essayed to thank them, but too full a heart paralyzed his speech; he soon sought a short respite from these trying scenes and retired to his private quarters, that he might, in solitude and quiet, commune with his own brave heart and be still. Thus terminated the career of the Army of Northern Virginia—an army that was never vanquished; but that, in obedience to the orders of its trusted commander, who was himself yielding obedience to the dictates of a pure and lofty sense of duty to his men and those dependent on them, laid down its arms, and furled the standards never lowered in defeat."[116] — Colonel Walter Herron Taylor, C.S.A.

☛ "Whole lines of battle rushed up to their beloved old chief, and, choking with emotion, struggled with each other to wring him once more by the hand. Men who had fought throughout the war, and knew what the agony and humiliation of that moment must be to him, strove with a refinement of unselfishness and tenderness which he alone could fully appreciate, to lighten his burden and mitigate his pain. Not an eye that looked on that scene was dry."[117] — an unnamed eye-witness at the scene on April 9, 1865

☛ "Men who saw the defeated general when he came forth from the chamber [at Appomattox on April 9, 1865] where he had signed the articles of capitulation [to General Grant] say that he paused a moment as his eyes rested once more on the Virginia hills, smote his hands together as though in some excess of inward agony, then mounted his gray horse, Traveller, and rode calmly away." — Thomas Nelson Page

☛ "A day or two after the surrender, General Lee started for Richmond, riding Traveller, who had carried him so well all through the war. He was accompanied by some of his staff. On the way, he stopped at the house of his eldest brother, Charles Carter Lee, who lived on the Upper James in Powhatan County. He spent the evening in talking with his brother, but when bedtime came, though begged by his host to take the room and bed prepared for him, he insisted on going to his old tent, pitched by the roadside, and passed the night in the quarters that he was accustomed to.

"On April 15th he arrived in Richmond. The people there soon recognised him; men, women, and children crowded around him, cheering and waving hats and handkerchiefs. It was more like the welcome to a conqueror than to a defeated prisoner on parole. He raised his hat in response to their greetings, and rode quietly to his home on Franklin Street, where my mother and sisters were anxiously awaiting him. Thus he returned to that private family life for which he had always longed, and became what he always desired to be—a peaceful citizen in a peaceful land."[118] — Captain Robert E. Lee, Jr., C.S.A.

TRAVELLER

1861-1870

General Lee on his equally celebrated warhorse Traveller.

Traveller, whose name the Lees spelled in the traditional English manner (with two l's), was the General's constant companion for nine years: from the start of Lincoln's War until the General's death in 1870. The warhorse, nearly as famous as his owner, was such an integral part of Lee's life that I felt that he deserved his own chapter.

Traveller was born in 1857 in Greenbrier County, Virginia,

(now West Virginia), and was "adopted" by Lee in 1861 for use in the War due to his fitness and beauty. Both survived the conflict and were nearly inseparable for the rest of their lives.

During the General's funeral procession in October 1870, Traveller rode majestically behind the casket draped in black crepe. Not long afterward, in early 1871, Traveller stepped on a rusty nail, developed tetanus, and was euthanized. The noble steed was buried near Lee Chapel, the General's final resting place, so the two could be near one another in death.

General Lee on Traveller at the Battle of the Wilderness, May 5-7, 1864. His soldiers disliked seeing their beloved commander putting himself in harm's way at the front lines. They would jeopardize their own lives by grabbing Traveller's reigns and desperately yelling, "Lee to the rear!", as shown in this 19th-Century illustration.

☛ "One afternoon in July . . . the General rode down to the canal-boat landing to put on board a young lady who had been visiting his daughters and was returning home. He dismounted, tied Traveller to a post, and was standing on the boat making his adieux, when some one called out that Traveller was loose. Sure enough, the gallant gray was making his way up the road, increasing his speed as a number of boys and men tried to stop him.

"My father immediately stepped ashore, called to the crowd to stand still, and advancing a few steps gave a peculiar low whistle. At the first sound, Traveller stopped and pricked up his ears. The General whistled a second time, and the horse with a glad whinny turned and trotted quietly back to his master, who patted and coaxed him before tying him up again.

"To a bystander expressing surprise at the creature's docility the General observed that he did not see how any man could ride a horse for any length of time without a perfect understanding being established between them. My sister Mildred, who rode with him constantly this summer, tells me of his enjoyment of their long rides out into the beautiful, restful country. Nothing seemed to delight him so much."[119] — Captain Robert E. Lee, Jr., C.S.A.

General Lee on Traveller during the Confederate "surrender" at Appomattox, April 9, 1865.

☛ "Many times I have seen General Lee manifest affection for Traveller, and Traveller always seemed to appreciate it. I have seen General Lee stand and gaze at the faithful old animal, apparently recalling scenes of the war. Then he would stroke Traveller's nose and hand him a lump of sugar. Traveller was his pet. A comrade and I frequently walked the road leading toward the 'Peaks of Otter.' We often saw General Lee riding on the same road alone."[120] — Dr. Chalmers Deadrick

☛ "General Lee always [personally] took Traveller to the [farrier] shop to be shod, never trusting him to the care of a servant while undergoing this ordeal. As the faithful old war horse was spirited and nervous, the General always stood by his side while he was being shod, talking to him and enjoining patience on the part of the blacksmith. On these occasions the General would say: 'Have patience with Traveller; he was made nervous by the bursting of bombs around him during the war.'"[121] — Mr. Senseney (village blacksmith, Lexington, Virginia)

General Lee on Traveller at the Battle of Petersburg II, June 15-18, 1864.

☛ "[After the War my father] was very fond of horseback journeys, enjoyed the quiet and rest, the freedom of mind and body, the close sympathy of his old warhorse [Traveller], and the beauties of Nature which are to be seen at every turn in the mountains of Virginia. . . . He was a man of few words, very loath to talk about himself, nor do I believe any one ever knew what that great heart suffered. His idea of life was to do his duty, at whatever cost, and to try to help others do theirs."[122] — Captain Robert E. Lee, Jr., C.S.A.

☛ "The old iron-gray horse [Traveller] was the privileged character at General Lee's home. He was permitted to remain in the front yard where the grass was greenest and freshest, notwithstanding the flowers and shrubbery. General Lee was more demonstrative toward that old companion in battle than seemed to be in his nature in his intercourse with men. I have often seen him, as he would enter his front gate, leave the walk, approach the old horse, and caress him for a minute or two before entering his front door, as though they bore a common grief in their memory of the past."[123] — John B. Collyar

☛ "All [of the students at Washington College] felt an interest in

[General Lee's] old 'Traveller.' If there was ever any unbending it was towards this old horse. They were friends, and it was very pretty to see them together. Old Traveller was always at home in the front yard, and acted like a sentinel on guard. One could almost say that the toss of his head, whenever the General appeared, was both a military salute and an expression of love and admiration for his great master. Certain it is [that] there was love on both sides."[124] — J. W. Ewing

General Robert E. Lee (left) on Traveller, discussing strategy with General Stonewall Jackson near Chancellorsville, Virginia, in May 1863.

Confederate Generals Joseph E. Johnston (left) and Robert E. Lee (right).

SECTION THREE

Postbellum Period

WASHINGTON COLLEGE YEARS

1865-1870

General Lee as president of Washington College.

Soon after Lincoln's War came to an end, Lee began to cast about for a job to support his family. Instead, the job came to him in the form of an invitation from Washington College at Lexington, Virginia, to become its next president.

In a polite but firm two-page letter the General turned down the magnanimous offer, which the school board summarily disregarded. After some second thoughts, Lee wisely accepted the position, and was installed on October 2, 1865, leading to what was to become the most fulfilling and enjoyable period of his life.

The General served out his last five years at Washington College, helping to transform the antiquated and ravaged institution (during the War Yankee troops had destroyed parts of the campus and completely looted the library) into the magnificent and highly esteemed

Southern school that it is to this day.

After his death in 1870, General Lee's eldest son George became president and the college was renamed Washington and Lee University. And so it is still called.

☛ "General Robert E. Lee was to-day installed President of Washington College. There was no pomp or parade. The exercises of installation were the simplest possible, an exact compliance with the required formula of taking the oath by the new President, and nothing more. This was in accordance with the special request of General Lee. It was proposed to have the installation take place in the college chapel, to send invitations far and wide, to have a band of music to play enlivening airs, to have young girls robed in white and bearing chaplets of flowers, to sing songs of welcome, to have congratulatory speeches, to make it a holiday. That this programme was not carried out was a source of severe disappointment to many. But General Lee had expressed his wishes contrary to the choice and determination of the college Trustees and the multitude, and his wishes were complied with.

"The installation took place at 9 A.M., in a recitation-room of the college. In this room were seated the Faculty and the students, the ministers of the town churches, a magistrate, and the county clerk; the last officials being necessary to the ceremonial. General Lee was ushered into the room by the Board of Trustees. Upon his entrance and introduction all in the room rose, bowed, and then resumed their seats. Prayer by the Rev. Dr. White, pastor of the Presbyterian Church, directly followed. To me it was a noticeable fact, and perhaps worthy of record, that he prayed for the President of the United States [Andrew Johnson]. Altogether, it was a most fitting and impressive prayer.

"The prayer ended, Judge Brockenbrough, chairman of the Board of Trustees, stated the object of their coming together, to install General Lee as President of Washington College. He felt the serious dignity of the occasion, but it was a seriousness and dignity that should be mingled with heart-felt joy and gladness. Passing a brief eulogy upon General Lee, he congratulated the Board and College, and its present and future students, on having obtained one so loved, great, and worthy to preside over the college. General Lee remained standing, his arms quietly folded, calmly and steadfastly looking into the eyes of the speaker. Justice William White, at the instance of Judge Brockenbrough, now administered the oath of office to General Lee.

"For the benefit of those curious to know, I will give the oath, to which General Lee subscribed, entire. It is as follows:

"'I do swear that I will, to the best of my skill and judgment, faithfully and truly discharge the duties required of me by an Act entitled "An Act for incorporating the Rector and Trustees of Liberty Hall Academy," without favor, affection, or partiality: so help me God.'

"To this oath General Lee at once affixed his signature, with the accompanying usual jurat of the swearing magistrate appended. The document was handed to the county clerk for safe and perpetual custodianship, and at the same time the keys of the college were given up by the Rector into the keeping of the new President.

"A congratulatory shaking of hands followed, which wound up the day's brief but pleasing, impressive, and memorable ceremonial. President Lee and those of the Trustees present, with the Faculty, now passed into the room set apart for the use of the President—a good-sized room, newly and very tastefully furnished.

"General Lee was dressed in a plain but elegant suit of gray. His appearance indicated the enjoyment of good health—better, I should say, than when he surrendered at Appomattox Court-House, the first and only occasion, before the present, of my having seen him."[125] — An unnamed eyewitness at the ceremony (October 2, 1865)

☛ "[While a student at Washington College] I saw General Lee once on Traveller. He was passing just as I came out of the gate at the Episcopal church. I saw him but a moment; the picture is with me yet. Traveller moved as if proud of the burden he bore. To me the horse was beautiful and majestic. It was the only time that I was impressed with the greatness and beauty and power and glory of the man. He sat erect in the saddle. The gloved hand held the bridle, the other hung gracefully at his side. He was every inch a king. It was only a moment, but the impression will last a lifetime. It is one of the joyous moments of life on which my memory loves to dwell."[126] — W. H. Tayloe

☛ "The fact that General Lee was once its president, will have a lasting influence in favor of Washington and Lee University. I doubt whether, in the world's history, a college president ever exercised as powerful an influence for good over his students and faculty as did General Lee."[127] — Dr. Chalmers Deadrick

From a student at Washington College while General Lee was president:
☛ "On one occasion, I was told, that the General was noticed as deeply affected on coming out from prayers in the chapel. Some one ventured to ask, 'What is the matter, General?' To which he replied: 'I was thinking of my responsibility to Almighty God for these hundreds of young men.'"[128] — Reverend W. Strother Jones

☛ "[In 1868 the] commencement exercises of the [Washington] college began about June 1st and lasted a week. At this time, the town was crowded with visitors, and my father had his house full, generally of young girls, friends of my sisters who came to assist at the 'final ball,' the great social event connected with this college exercise. He seemed to enjoy their society as much as the young men did, though he could not devote so much time to them as the boys did, and I know that the girls enjoyed his society more than they did that of their college adorers. On the occasion of an entertainment at his house, in going amongst his guests saying to each group something bright and pleasant, he approached a young lady, a great belle, completely surrounded by her admirers—students, cadets, and some old 'Confeds.' He stopped and began to rally her on her conquests, saying:

"'You can do as you please to these other young gentlemen, but you must not treat any of my old soldiers badly.'"[129] — Captain Robert E. Lee, Jr., C.S.A.

☛ "In his intercourse with his faculty [at Washington College] he was courteous, kind, and often rather playful in manner. We all thought he deferred entirely too much to the expression of opinion on the part of the faculty, when we would have preferred that he should simply indicate his own views or desire. One characteristic of General Lee I noted then and have often recalled: I never saw him take an ungraceful posture. No matter how long or fatiguing a faculty meeting might be, he always preserved an attitude in which dignity, decorum, and grace were united.

"He was a very well built man, with rounded body and limbs, and seemed without the slightest affectation of effort to sit or stand or walk just as a gentleman should. He was never in a hurry, and all his gestures were easy and significant. He was always an agreeable companion. There was a good deal of bonhomie and pleasantry in his conversation. He was not exactly witty, nor was he very humorous, though he gave a light turn to table-talk and enjoyed exceedingly any pleasantry or fun, even. He often made a quaint or slightly caustic remark, but he took care that it should not be too trenchant. . . .

"General Lee did not talk politics, but he felt very deeply the condition of the country, and expressed to me several times in strong terms his disapproval of the course of the dominant party [the Northern Republicans, then the liberal party]."[130] — Colonel William Preston Johnston, C.S.A. (son of General Albert Sidney Johnston and aid-de-camp to President Jefferson Davis)

☛ "[As president of Washington College, General Lee] was not . . . of ardent temperament, or expansive, or particularly affable. He did not mingle much with us students. To us he was an Olympian, remote, seen in a haze of great deeds, in a great and tragic past. We knew him in the routine of collegiate duties as a just, firm, polite administrator, whose lightest word was law. Undoubtedly his presence was stimulative to professors and students.

"It was also restrictive. The boys were kept from many a bit of cantankerous disorder to which the student, reacting to dull drudgery, will sometimes turn. There was a feeling of awe inspired by the ex-commander of the C. S. army. The respect for him was profound. A word of disapproval quelled the most determined callithump [prank]."[131] — Dr. S. Z. Ammen

☛ "How very careful and thoughtful President Lee was of the students [at Washington College] can best be illustrated by telling how he treated me when my mother died. I was too far from home to attempt to return when I received a telegram announcing her death. I handed it to my roommate, asked him to take it to General Lee and tell him I would not attend any classes for two or three days. At the end of the month when my report came out there was not a single absent mark against me. This

The city of Washington, D.C., as it looked from the Lees' home Arlington House in the early 1800s.

can only be accounted for by General Lee's going to each professor to whom I recited and telling him. To me this is a remarkable illustration of his kindness to and care for the boys entrusted to him. If I had no other reason, I would love him for that yet."[132] — W. W. Estill

☛ "Lexington at this time was one of the most inaccessible points in Virginia. . . . On one occasion, a gentleman during his visit to Lexington called on General Lee and on bidding him good-bye asked him the best way to get back to Washington. 'It makes but little difference,' replied the General, 'for whichever route you select, you will wish you had taken the other.'"[133] — Captain Robert E. Lee, Jr., C.S.A.

☛ "In my short day at [Washington] college there was a tradition that four young men from New Hampshire were among the student body when some rather forward Southerners 'of the baser sort' attempted to ridicule them by publicly proclaiming them as 'Yankees' and 'out of their element' in a Southern college. This coming to the attention of General Lee greatly incensed him. He sent for all whose names he could ascertain and denounced their cowardice and gave them limited time to leave college."[134] — Reverend W. Strother Jones

☛ "When I was a student at Washington College, I would often see General Lee in conversation with the janitor of the grounds, and giving him instructions, evidently, as to his work about the lawn and grounds. It was remarkable to see him thus engaged, when he had so many other important duties to meet. I had the honor of being a dinner guest of his, on my return visit to Lexington, on one occasion; and I was impressed by the grace and ease with which he presided as a host. He made us all feel at home,—both the young and older men, who were his guests."[135] — Reverend Frank Bell Webb

☛ "My father's relations with the citizens of Petersburg [Virginia] were of the kindest description. The ladies were ever trying to make him more comfortable, sending him of their scanty fare more than they could well spare. He always tried to prevent them, and when he could do so without hurting their feelings he would turn over to the hospitals the dainties sent him . . ."[136] — Captain Robert E. Lee, Jr., C.S.A.

While the General was president of Washington College he was in charge of calling delinquent students to his office, an example of which follows:

☛ "I was a frolicsome chap at college, and, having been absent from class an unreasonable number of times, was finally summoned to the General's office. Abject terror took possession of me in the presence of such wise and quiet dignity; the reasons I had carefully prepared to give for my absence stood on their heads, or toppled over. In reply to General Lee's grave but perfectly polite question, I stammered out a story about a violent illness, and then, conscious that I was at that moment the picture of health, I hastened on with something about leaving my boots at the cobbler's, when General Lee interrupted me: "'Stop, Mr. M______,' he said; 'stop, sir! One good reason is enough.' But I could not be mistaken about the twinkle in the old hero's eyes!"[137] — a student from Washington College

☛ "General Lee was very approachable, easy to talk to and always appeared willing to hear. I have seen little girls go up to him on the street, take his hand, and walk and talk with him as with a parent."[138] — W. W. Estill

In 1869 Lee traveled to Baltimore, Maryland, to oversee the construction of a railroad:

☛ "A reception was given . . . in his honour. There his friends crowded to see him, and the greatest affection and deference were shown him. He had lived in Baltimore about twenty years before this time, and many of his old friends were still there; besides, Baltimore had sent to the Army of Northern Virginia a large body of her noble sons, who were only too glad to greet once more their former commander. That he was still 'a prisoner on parole,' disfranchised from all civil rights, made their love for him stronger and their welcome the more hearty.[139] On his return to Lexington, he was asked how he enjoyed his visit. With a sad smile, he said: 'Very much; but they would make too much fuss over the old rebel.'"[140] — Captain Robert E. Lee, Jr., C.S.A.

☛ "The greatest event in our lives has occurred—we have seen General Lee."[141] —Reverend Phillips of Abingdon, Virginia (after he and his wife had dinner with Lee)

During a visit with family and friends in the Spring of 1870, midway through so-called "Reconstruction":
☛ "One of his young cousins, in talking with him, wondered what fate was in store for 'us poor Virginians.' The General replied with an earnest, softened look: 'You can work for Virginia, to build her up again, to make her great again. You can teach your children to love and cherish her.'"[142] — Captain Robert E. Lee, Jr., C.S.A.

The General and his son Robert, Jr., were visiting friends near West Point, Virginia, in the Spring of 1870, when this recollection was recorded:
☛ "As was customary in this section of Virginia, the house was full of visitors, and I shared my father's room and bed. Though many a year had passed since we had been bedfellows, he told me that he remembered well the time when, as a little fellow, I had begged for this privilege. The next day he walked about the beautiful gardens, and was driven over the plantation and shown the landscapes and water views of the immediate neighbourhood. Mr. Graves, Dr. Tabb's overseer, who had the honour of being his coachman, fully appreciated it, and was delighted when my father praised his management. He had been a soldier under the General, and had stoutly carried his musket to Appomattox, where he surrendered it.

"When told of this by Dr. Tabb, my father took occasion to compliment him on his steadfast endurance and courage, but Graves simply and sincerely replied, 'Yes, General, I stuck to the army, but if you had in your entire command a greater coward than I was, you ought to have had him shot.' My father, who was greatly amused at his candour, spoke of it when he got back from his drive, saying 'that sort of a coward makes a good soldier.'"[143] — Captain Robert E. Lee, Jr., C.S.A.

☛ "[While president of Washington College General Lee] kept himself as well informed as possible on the financial condition of students; who and what their parents were;—in short all their home affairs. He made use of this information in his management of the students. On one occasion he happened to see a student from Nashville throw a stone against the upper part of the cupola of the chapel and knock a shingle off. He knew that the student's father was wealthy, and required the student to have the shingle replaced. This was done by a number of mechanics, who built scaffolding up to the necessary height. The expense was said to be thirty-odd dollars [about $500 in today's currency]."[144] — Professor M. W. Humphreys

☛ "During one of the public celebrations of 1870 I was the orator selected from the Washington Literary Society, and after my oration had been submitted to the committee I added a few closing sentences which were intensely Southern and which I knew would catch the popular applause. General Lee was surprised and shocked. How it was that I escaped a personal reprimand I do not now recall. I learned, however, of the General's indignation; that he had brought the subject up before the Faculty, and that I narrowly escaped expulsion."[145] — an unnamed student at Washington College

☛ "[While president of Washington College General Lee] knew the class standing of every student, and there were over four hundred of us. On inquiry of a father once as to his son's standing, General Lee replied: 'He is careful not to injure his health by too much study.'"[146] — Richard W. Rogers

On Lee's love of children:
☛ "Once in Petersburg, he called to see a child in whom he felt a special interest, and finding her sick, begged to be shown to her room.

When the mother, who was at a neighbor's for a moment, came home, she found him by the bedside of her sick child, ministering to her comfort and cheering her with his words."[147] — Reverend John W. Jones, chaplain, Army of Northern Virginia, C.S.A.

More on Lee's love of children:
☛ "On one occasion, having learned during a visit to a friend that two little boys in the family were sick with croup, he trudged back next day in the midst of a storm with a basket of pecans and a toy for his two little friends."[148] — Thomas Nelson Page

☛ "Another pretty story was of a little boy who, during a college commencement, slipped from his mother's lap, and going upon the platform where the general sat, seated himself at his feet, and snuggling against his knees, fell fast asleep, the general sitting motionless all the while, so as not to disturb the child."[149] — Thomas Nelson Page

☛ ". . . the sweetest and dearest memories of my college career, and of my life in fact, are associated with General Lee. I do not remember ever passing him upon the street or on the [Washington College] campus at Lexington but that he stopped and spoke to me often about some commonplace matter, but just enough to show me that he knew I was a student there and that I was one of his wards in the college, and enough to assure me that he felt an interest in me as he did in all the other boys. All that I know personally of General Lee is these little personal contacts."[150] — F. A. Berlin

President's House, Lee's campus home during his time at Washington College, Lexington, Virginia. While it was being built, the General and his family lived in the house to the right.

An example of the General's sympathetic nature was his great empathy for the

sick:

☞ "On one occasion, calling at Colonel [Robert] Preston's, he missed two little boys in the family circle, who were great favourites of his, and on asking for them he was told that they were confined to the nursery by croup. The next day, though the weather was of the worst description, he went trudging in great storm-boots back to their house, carrying in one hand a basket of pecan nuts and in the other a toy, which he left for his little sick friends."[151] — Captain Robert E. Lee, Jr., C.S.A.

☞ "During the fall of 1867 a student left the hill [Washington College], without leave, and spent the whole day off duty. When summoned before General Lee to give an excuse for his absence, he frankly admitted that he was fox hunting. Very quietly General Lee remarked: 'We did not come here to hunt foxes, Mr. ______.' Then followed some wholesome advice, which effectually settled the fox hunting matter for good. That boy never even wanted to go after foxes any more."[152] — Dr. Chalmers Deadrick

☞ "A few years after General Lee accepted the presidency of the then Washington College, I was sent to be entered in the preparatory department, along with an older brother who was to enter college. The morning after we reached Lexington we repaired to the office of General Lee, situated in the college building, for the purpose of matriculation and receiving instructions as to the duties devolving upon us as students.

"I entered the office with reverential awe, expecting to see the great warrior, whose fame then encircled the civilized globe, as I had pictured him in my own imagination. General Lee was alone, looking over a paper. He arose as we entered, and received us with a quiet, gentlemanly dignity that was so natural and easy and kind that the feeling of awe left me at the threshold of his door. General Lee had but one manner in his intercourse with men. It was the same to the peasant as to the prince, and the student was received with the easy courtliness that would have been bestowed on the greatest imperial dignitary of Europe.

"When we had registered my brother asked the General for a copy of his rules. General Lee said to him, 'Young gentleman, we have no printed rules. We have but one rule here, and it is that every student must be a gentleman.' I did not, until after years, fully realize the

Another view of General Robert E. Lee during his tenure as president of Washington College, 1865-1870, now Washington and Lee University.

comprehensiveness of his remark, and how completely it covered every essential rule that should govern the conduct and intercourse of men. I do not know that I could define the impression that General Lee left on my mind that morning, for I was so disappointed at not seeing the warrior that my imagination had pictured, that my mind was left in a confused state of inquiry as to whether he was the man whose fame had filled the world. He was so gentle, kind, and almost motherly, in his bearing, that I thought there must be some mistake about it. At first glance General Lee's countenance was stern, but the moment his eye met that of his entering guest it beamed with a kindness that at once established easy and friendly relations, but not familiar. The impression he made on me was, that he was never familiar with any man."[153] — John B. Collyar

☛ "I had a cousin, who at the time of my reaching Lexington was an assistant professor. He kindly allowed me to become an inmate of his home. As he was a resident of the town, an ex-Confederate officer, and well acquainted socially, I was soon by him introduced to all the homes where he visited. I well recollect my first visit to the home of General Lee. Just before we entered the house my cousin said, 'It is the custom here to introduce a stranger to the first member of the family we meet and after that you will allow that member to do as seems best.' I met Miss Mildred Lee [the General's youngest child, then in her early twenties] that night and was charmed with her manner and conversation. Subsequently I met all the family and was more than once invited to social gatherings at the house. I was never before so close to General Lee. I was struck with his looks and bearing. I thought then and still think that he was by far the handsomest man I ever saw. His splendid physique, grand carriage without 'airs,' universal politeness, and evident kind heart, impressed me greatly, and to this day I can see him as plainly as then."[154] — W. W. Estill

An illustration of the General's generosity and humility:
☛ "During his visit [to White Sulphur Springs—in what is now West Virginia], a circus came to 'Dry Creek,' a neighbouring settlement, and gave an exhibition. The manager rode over to the Springs, came to my father's cottage, and insisted on leaving several tickets, begging that

General Lee would permit him to send carriages for him and any friends he might like to take to his show. These offers my father courteously declined, but bought many tickets, which he presented to his little friends [that is, children] at the Springs."[155] — Captain Robert E. Lee, Jr., C.S.A.

☛ "Lord [Garnet J.] Wolseley, the commander of the English armies, was in Lexington, where he had come to pay his respects to our General [at Washington College]. Seeing that the General was engaged, we were about to leave when we were called back and asked to take seats in the adjoining room, where we could hear everything that was said. I remember the Englishman asked General Lee whom he thought the greatest military genius developed by the war, to which General Lee answered without hesitation, 'General Nathan Bedford Forrest, of Tennessee, whom I have never met. He accomplished more with fewer troops than any other officer on either side.'"[156] — J. W. Ewing

☛ "It is well known that General Lee was distinguished for mental and moral courage of the highest order. This was conspicuously displayed in more than one great crisis of his life. It is not so well known that he also had what we call 'nerve,' or physical courage, which never failed him. This was signally displayed in his personal scouting adventures in the Mexican war; and also to his staff when he passed from safe to very dangerous positions in the terrific battles of the Confederate war. One of these staff officers told me he could never discover by any word, gesture or change of countenance on the part of General Lee that he had any consciousness of personal danger. While president of the [Washington] college he had a somewhat singular adventure which signally displayed his 'nerve.'

"Colonel Ross had a fine farm near Lexington and the General used to ride out to this farm and talk 'farming' with his friend. The times were unsettled and Colonel Ross had a pack of rather vicious dogs to protect his property from petty thieves. These dogs were usually confined during the day, and turned out at night. One afternoon the Colonel seated in his hall heard these dogs barking in his front yard. Knowing that they had no business there, he hurried out and saw this scene: General Lee had ridden up on Traveller, dismounted, entered the gate, and was standing with his back to the gate, confronted by several dogs, the largest and fiercest of which stood on his hind feet with his front feet on the General's shoulders, and their noses not six inches apart.

"The General stood like a statue calmly looking into the dog's eyes. Colonel Ross called and beat off the dogs, and apologized for their attack. He told me that General Lee was entirely unruffled. He playfully chided him for not keeping his dogs tied up in the daytime. There was no change in his countenance; and, in the opinion of his host, his pulse had not quickened one beat a minute."[157] — Franklin Lafayette Riley

☛ "General Lee had only kindness and consideration for the boys of the school [Washington College] as well as others. Only once was I called before him for a lecture, having 'cut' recitations for one day. When asked why, I said 'To go hunting.' He said, 'Why you went hunting and yesterday was such a pretty day, and you would kill the birds that enjoy the day so much. I don't think I would do so again.' That was all of the lecture."[158] — John Blackmar

The barns and Yankee barracks at Arlington House as they appeared on June 29, 1864.

☛ "My father was much amused at an occurrence that took place during . . . [a trip to Baltimore in the Spring of 1869]. Late one afternoon a visitor was announced. As the General was very tired, [my] Uncle [Sydney] Smith Lee volunteered to relieve him. The visitor was found to be an Irishwoman, very stout and unprepossessing, who asked if she could see the General. The Admiral bowed, intimating that he was the desired person, when she said:

"'My boy was with you in the war, honey, and I must kiss you for his sake.' And with that she gave the Admiral an embrace and a kiss. Mr. Cassius Lee, to whom he told this [story], suggested that he should take [my brother] General Fitz Lee along to put forward in such emergencies."[159] — Captain Robert E. Lee, Jr., C.S.A.

☛ "I have often see General Lee on the campus [of Washington College] or on the street with a group of children clinging to both his hands."[160] — C. W. Hedger

☛ "As far as I know, Lee's chief recreation was horseback riding every afternoon; and many, many were the afternoons that we pedestrian students [at Washington College] would meet him, as he was out for his five or six miles ride; and we all invariably lifted our hats to him, which he responded to with a smile and salute. He almost always rode 'Traveller' in a sweeping walk, and sat as straight as an arrow in the saddle; and our boyish eyes always viewed him with the most intense admiration. His soldierly bearing and gentle spirit drew it from us."[161] — Reverend Frank Bell Webb

☛ "One of the proudest moments of my life, as a student [of Washington College], was during an examination in geometry when General Lee was present at the oral examination and listened with interest to the demonstration which I was fortunately able to give perfectly. His smile of approval was worth more than the class distinction that year."[162] — Reverend James R. Winchester

☛ "[At Washington College everyone] obeyed President Lee, not because they feared but because they loved him, and I don't think there was one of the about 800 boys who were there but would have died defending him if necessary. I was never called to his office, but I have heard the boys who were say his admonitions were as tender as a mother's and his warnings and instructions always fatherly and wise. In all the years that have passed I have thought of him and to this day the things I learned from listening to his conversation, watching his bearing and example I carry with me as a most important part of my education."[163] — W. W. Estill

☞ "[After the War every] afternoon, rain or shine, General Lee mounted 'Traveller' and had a ride. He always, as I recall him, wore a double-breasted gray coat, buttoned to the throat, with black buttons, top boots, a pair of spurs, gauntlet gloves, a large light-colored hat with a military cord around it. His poise was perfect, and I enjoyed looking at him every time he passed, and I suspect I stopped and looked at him hundreds of times."[164] — W. W. Estill

Despite the General's reputation as a strict disciplinarian, he had a soft side:
☞ "One winter [while Lee was serving as president of Washington College] a certain youth from the far South became fascinated by the ice and skating. He 'cut lectures' to indulge himself in what was to him a novel pastime. He was summoned before the president. 'You should not have broken the rules,' said the president, sternly. 'If you wished to go away, you should have asked permission.'

"'I understand, General,' was the lad's humble reply. Then his face brightened as he was about to leave the room; his eyes twinkled and he dared to say, 'The ice is fine, to-day, General.'

"'Yes?'

"'I'd like very much to be excused and go skating.'

"The wish was granted."[165] — Bradley Gilman

☞ "Upon the occasion of the delivery of an address at Washington College by a certain distinguished orator, General Lee came to me and said, 'I saw you taking notes during the address. It was in the main very fine; but if you propose publishing any report of it I would suggest that you leave out all of the bitter expressions against the North and the United States Government. They will do us no good under our present circumstances, and I think all such expressions undignified and unbecoming.'"[166] — Reverend John W. Jones, chaplain, Army of Northern Virginia, C.S.A.

Another example of the General's way with children:

☛ "There was a little [Southern] boy living with his mother, who had come from New York. His father had been killed in our [Confederate] army. The little fellow, now Colonel Grier Monroe, of New York City, was much teased at his playmates calling him 'Yankee' when he knew he was not one. One day he marched into my father's office in the college, stated his case, and asked for redress.

"'The next boy that calls you "Yankee" send him to me,' said the General, which, when reported, struck such terror into the hearts of his small comrades that the offense was never repeated."[167] — Captain Robert E. Lee, Jr., C.S.A.

☛ "As far as I could judge, with the exception of the General's family, my friend the late Professor J. J. White, of Washington and Lee University, was the closest person in Lexington to him. The two were accustomed to take long rides on horseback together. On one of these rides they were overtaken by darkness, and had to stop overnight at a farmhouse by the road. It so happened that there was only one vacant room in the house and one bed in that, which, to his horror, the professor found that he had to share with his old commander. It had to be done, but he said that he 'would as soon have thought of sleeping with the Archangel Gabriel as with General Lee.' He lay for the night on the very edge of the bed, and did not sleep a wink."[168] — Edward V. Valentine

☛ "He was a most regular attendant upon all of the services of his own church, his seat in the college-chapel was never vacant unless he was kept away by sickness, and if there was a union prayer-meeting or a service of general interest in any of the churches of Lexington, General Lee was sure to be among the most devout attendants.

"His pew in his own church was immediately in front of the chancel, his seat in the chapel was the second from the pulpit, and he seemed always to prefer a seat near the preacher's stand. He always devoutly knelt during prayer, and his attitude during the entire service

Yanks "on display" at the Lees' "captured" home, Arlington House.

was that of an interested listener or a reverential participant.

"He was not accustomed to indulge in carping criticisms of sermons, but was a most intelligent judge of what a sermon ought to be, and always expressed his preference for those sermons which presented most simply and earnestly the soul-saving truths of the Gospel. The writer heard him remark in reference to one of the Baccalaureate sermons preached at the college: 'It was a noble sermon—one of the very best I ever heard—and the beauty of it was that the preacher gave our young men the very marrow of the Gospel, and with a simple earnestness that must have reached their hearts and done them good.'"[169] — Reverend John W. Jones, chaplain, Army of Northern Virginia, C.S.A.

☛ "In the autumn of 1867, after an absence of two years from America, I entered Washington College, under the presidency of General Lee. It was my privilege, and I shall count it always a blessing, to be intimate with his charming family during my student life, and to see the General nearly every day at his home or in the class room. My reverence for the great soldier deepened into a personal attachment for the noble gentleman, the kind and gracious friend, so human and sympathetic with all his greatness. His very presence seemed to make purer the atmosphere around him, and there was in him a blended dignity and sweetness that made a man feel better for the seeing. The admiration and respect in which the students held him was universal, and during two years at college I never heard a jesting word spoken of General Lee. He took a personal interest in the students, and he was always open to approach in his home or his office. His influence with the wildest and most careless was wonderful, and yet no harsh word fell from his lips. A gentle reprimand to the most thoughtless was sufficient."[170] — Judge D. Gardiner Tyler

☛ "The last time I ever saw General Lee was on a summer's afternoon when I called to take leave of him at his house. A gentleman and two ladies were in the parlor at the time. During the conversation the General made a remark which was calculated to startle the company. 'I feel that I have an incurable disease coming on me,' he said—'old age. I would like to go to some quiet place in the country and rest.'"[171] — Edward V. Valentine

☛ "In the session of 1866-7 the students petitioned the [Washington College] faculty for a week's holiday at Christmas instead of the single day that had been adopted in imitation of the University of Virginia (as it then was). The petition was declined. A paper was started around for the signatures of students pledging themselves not to attend any lectures from Christmas to New Year's day. When sixty-nine students, including my roommate but not myself, had signed this paper, news of the movement came to General Lee's ears, and he merely said in the hearing of two or three students: 'Every man that signs that paper will be summarily dismissed. If all sign it, I shall lock up the college and put the keys in my pocket.' I told my roommate about this and he ran to college (a mile and a half) to scratch his name off . . ."[172] — Professor M. W. Humphreys

After the War, while the General was serving as president of Washington College, a steady stream of visitors came to his house, hoping to meet the world famous former Confederate chieftain. This account is about a Union soldier who paid Lee a visit:

☛ "One morning an Irishman who had gone through the war in the Federal ranks appeared at the door with a basket well filled with provisions, and insisted upon seeing General Lee. The servant protested and offered to carry a message, but Pat was not to be put off. The general, hearing the altercation, came from an adjoining room, and was greeted with profuse terms of admiration: 'Sure, sir, you are a great soldier, and it's I that know it. I've been fighting against you all these years, and many a hard knock we've had. But, general, I honor you for it; and now they tell me you are poor and in want, and I've brought this basket and beg you to take it from a soldier.' The general, touched by this spirit of sympathy, thanked him most kindly, and said, 'My man, I am not in need, but if you will carry your basket to the hospital you will find some poor fellow glad to be remembered by so generous a foe.'"[173] — Brigadier General Armistead L. Long, C.S.A.

In the Spring of 1870, with great fanfare from the local townspeople, Lee went to Charles City, Virginia, to visit his mother's childhood home, Shirley Plantation. Afterward one of the young women in attendance recorded this:
☛ "I can only remember the great dignity and kindness of General Lee's bearing, how lovely he was to all of us girls, that he gave us his photographs and wrote his name on them. He liked to have us tickle his hands, but when Cousin Agnes [the General's daughter] came to sit by him that seemed to be her privilege. We regarded him with the greatest veneration. We had heard of God, but here was General Lee!"[174] — An unnamed female from Virginia

An example of the General's sense of humor:
☛ "At a certain faculty meeting [at Washington College where Lee was serving as president] they were joking Mr. Harris, who so long and so ably filled the chair of Latin, about his walking up the aisle of the Presbyterian church with the stem of his pipe protruding from his pocket. Mr. Harris took out the offending stem and began cutting it shorter. My father, who had been enjoying the incident, said: "No, Mr. Harris, don't do that; next time leave it at home."[175] — Captain Robert E. Lee, Jr., C.S.A.

In and around the town of Lexington, postwar Lee was treated by the residents

with an almost godlike reverence, including those of African descent, who
☛ ". . . manifested for him on all occasions the most profound respect. When he approached, either walking or mounted on his famous horse Traveller, [the city's blacks] would stop, bow politely, and stand until he had passed. He never failed to acknowledge their salutes with kind and dignified courtesy."[176] — Brigadier General Armistead L. Long, C.S.A.

Washington College, Lexington, Virginia. General Lee spent the last five years of his life here serving as president, after which it was renamed in his honor: Washington and Lee University.

☛ "General Lee was not accustomed to talk of any thing that concerned himself, and did not often speak freely of his inner religious feelings. Yet he would, when occasion offered, speak most decidedly of his reliance for salvation upon the merits of his personal Redeemer, and none who heard him thus talk could doubt for a moment that his faith was built on the 'Rock of Ages.'

"He one day said to a friend, in speaking of the duty of laboring for the good of others: 'Ah! Mrs. P______, I find it so hard to keep one poor sinner's heart in the right way, that it seems presumptuous to try to help others.' And yet he did, quietly and unostentatiously, speak 'a word in season,' and exert influences potent for good in directing others in the path to heaven."[177] — Reverend John W. Jones, chaplain, Army of Northern Virginia, C.S.A.

☛ "[One day after the War, two] Confederate soldiers in very dilapidated clothing, worn and emaciated in body, came to see [my father at his home on Franklin Street in Richmond]. They said they had been selected from about sixty other fellows, too ragged to come themselves, to offer him a home in the mountains of Virginia. The home was a good house and farm, and near by was a defile [a narrow passage or gorge], in some rugged hills, from which they could defy the entire Federal Army. They made this offer of a home and their protection because there was a report that he was about to be indicted for treason. The General had to decline to go with them, but the tears came into his eyes at this hearty exhibition of loyalty."[178] — Captain Robert E. Lee, Jr., C.S.A.

☛ "[After the War] Mildred and her father [General Lee] were sitting one day in the back of the front hall when the door bell rang. Her father walked to the door and opened it. There stood in the door a long, tall, lean man, dressed in homespun and his shoes and lower part of his trousers covered with dust. He grabbed the General's extending hand and spoke about as follows: 'General Lee, I followed you four years and done the best I knowed how. Me and my wife live on a little farm away up on the Blue Ridge mountains. We heard the Yankees wasn't treating you right, and I come down to see 'bout it. If you will come up thar we will take care of you the best we know how as long as we live.'

"Before this was over the soldier held both of General Lee's hands and tears were dropping from the eyes of each. Pretty soon General Lee released one of his hands and reached out and took up a box containing a suit of clothes that had never been opened and spoke about as follows: 'My friend, I don't need a thing. My friends all over the country have been very kind and have sent me more clothes than I can possibly use, so I want to thank you for coming and give you this new suit.' The man snatched his hand from General Lee, crossed his arms, straightened himself up and said, 'General Lee, I can't take nothin' offen you.' After a few moments he relaxed, put one hand on the box and said, 'Yes, I will, General, I will carry them back home, put them away and when I die the boys will put them on me.'"[179] — W. W. Estill

An example of the General's sense of humor:

☛ "[On one occasion General Lee] received a letter from some Spirit Rappers [that is, psychics] asking his opinion on certain great military movements. He wrote in reply a most courteous letter in which he said that the question was one about which military critics would differ; that his own judgment about such matters was but poor at best, and that inasmuch as they had power to consult (through their mediums) Caesar, Alexander, Napoleon, Wellington, and all of the other great captains who have ever lived, he could not think of obtruding his opinion into such company."[180] — Reverend John W. Jones, chaplain, Army of Northern Virginia, C.S.A.

☛ "All the children knew and loved him, and felt no hesitation in approaching. A pleasant incident is related of Virginia Lee Letcher, his god-daughter, and her baby-sister, Fannie. Jennie had been followed by her persistent sister down the road, and all the coaxing and commanding of the six-year-old failed to make the younger turn home and leave her to continue her walk without company. Fannie had sat down by the roadside to pout, when General Lee came riding along. Jennie at once appealed to him: 'General Lee, won't you make this child go home to her mother?' The general immediately rode over to the refractory child, leaned over from his saddle, and drew her up into his lap. There she sat in royal contentment, and was thus grandly escorted home."[181] — Brigadier General Armistead L. Long, C.S.A.

☛ "There was one custom peculiar to the 'White' [the summer health retreat known as "White Sulphur Springs," where the Lees often stayed] and surviving long after the war. The long 'parlor' was the gathering place of the company after a meal. Here every one took part in a promenade up and down the great uncarpeted space, not usually in couples but in lines of three or four. Here introductions took place, here engagements were made, and this was the stranger's opportunity to be absorbed into the strenuous stream of life. It was only the old or the feeble who sat along the walls, unless a rare ostracism left the objectionable stranger stranded on the shore.

"Groups of young men, the newcomers, gathered about the doors to await fortunate opportunities, and were soon joined to some one of the constantly changing lines. It was a gay, informal scene, bewildering to the lookers-on. There was a graceful rhythm in the motion, as groups and couples threaded the winding maze, and there was harmony of sound in the mingling of tuneful Southern voices.

"The influence of General Lee was always present in these promenades. It was his time to dispense the kindly courtesies which made him the presiding genius of the place. He loved young people, especially young girls, for, to confess the truth, the young men were not thoroughly at ease with him; he seemed to test them with an Ithuriel spear, and they were inclined to shrink from the lofty standard he maintained. But he loved to see the girls surrounded by cavaliers and merry in the dance, and many a young Southerner owed his acquaintance with the belle of the season to General Lee's stately presentation. The keen, kindly eye was always alert lest some one should fail to share in the general happiness. This quiet influence, subtle and unacknowledged, permeated the throng and welded it into a gracious community regardful of mutual needs and pleasures."[182] — Christiana Bond

Another view of the Lees' home, Arlington House, now owned by the U.S. government.

☛ "Just once it was my lot to receive a severe rebuke from General Lee. While I was an undergraduate [at Washington College] my health seemed to become impaired, and he had a conversation with me about it, in which he expressed the opinion that I was working too hard. I replied: 'I am so impatient to make up for the time I lost in the army.' I got no further. [President] Lee flushed and exclaimed in an almost angry tone: 'Mr. Humphreys! However long you live and whatever you accomplish, you will find that the time you spent in the Confederate army was the most profitably spent portion of your life. Never again speak of having lost time in the army.' And I never again did."[183] — Professor M. W. Humphreys

☛ "On one occasion [during a faculty meeting at Washington College, where Lee was serving as president] a professor appealed to precedent, and added, "We must not respect persons." General Lee at once replied: "In dealing with young men I always respect persons, and care little for precedent."[184] — Professor Edward S. Joynes

☛ "[My father once] met a lady friend down in the town, who bitterly complained that she could get nothing to eat in Lexington suitable for Lent—no fish, no oysters, etc.

"'Mrs.,' the General replied, 'I would not trouble myself so much about special dishes; I suppose if we try to abstain from *special sins* that is all that will be expected of us.'"[185] — Captain Robert E. Lee, Jr., C.S.A.

☛ "[After the War General Lee] set to work to use his great influence to reconcile the people of the South to the hard consequences of their defeat, to inspire them with hope, to lead them to accept, freely and frankly, the government that had been established by the result of the war, and thus relieve them from the military rule [of Yankee Reconstruction]. . . . The advice and example of General Lee did more to incline the scale in favour of a frank and manly adoption of that course of conduct which tended to the restoration of peace and harmony than all the Federal garrisons in all the military districts."[186] — Colonel Charles Marshall, C.S.A.

A description of the Lee's new house in Lexington, which they moved into in the Spring of 1869:

☛ "My mother's room was on the first floor and opened out on the veranda, extending three sides of the house, where she could be rolled in her chair. This she enjoyed intensely, for she was very fond of the open air, and one could see her there every bright day, with Mrs. 'Ruffner,' a much petted cat, sitting on her shoulder or cradled in her lap. My father's favourite seat was in a deep window of the dining-room, from which his eyes could rest on rolling fields of grass and grain, bounded by the ever-changing mountains.

"After his early and simple dinner, he usually took a nap of a few minutes, sitting upright in his chair, his hand held and rubbed by one of his daughters. There was a new stable, warm and sunny, for [his warhorse] Traveller and his companion, 'Lucy Long,' a cow-house, wood-shed, garden, and yard, all planned, laid out, and built by my father. The increased room enabled him to invite a greater number to visit him, and this summer the house was full."[187] — Captain Robert E. Lee, Jr., C.S.A.

☛ "In 1867, in company with his daughter Mildred, he rode on horseback to the Peaks of Otter, fifty miles from Lexington. At a ferry on the route the boatman chanced to be an old soldier. When the usual charge was tendered the rough mountaineer's eyes filled with tears, and he shook his head while saying, 'I could not take pay from you, Master Robert: I have followed you in many a battle.'"[188] — Brigadier General Armistead L. Long, C.S.A.

☛ "As father and daughter rode on a sudden shower came down upon them, and they galloped up to a log hut by the roadside, and without ceremony sought shelter. The poor woman of the house did not view the intrusion with cordiality. Her floors were scrupulously clean and every footprint was an offence. On the wall were suspended rudely-colored portraits of Lee, Jackson, and Davis.

"When the storm abated the general stepped out to bring up the horses. In his momentary absence [his daughter] Miss Mildred gently intimated that the unceremonious caller was the original of one of the portraits. The woman was transfixed with astonishment, and, throwing up her hands, exclaimed, 'Lord bless my soul! That I should have lived to have General Lee in my house!' When the general returned her gratitude knew no bounds, and every attention was lavished upon the travellers."[189] — Brigadier General Armistead L. Long, C.S.A.

☛ "Though I have since sadly realized that I did not study while there [Washington College] as I should have done, and as the General was solicitous to have all who attended do, I count not as lost the time spent there, for at my impressionable age and with my intense feeling, simply to have met General Lee and to have watched so noble a hero daily performing such high duties, was almost equivalent to the beginning, at least, of acquiring a liberal education."[190] — Judge Robert Ewing

☛ "As memory turns back a long forgotten page, I can see myself with dozens of fellow [Washington College] students standing in front of the old Presbyterian church taking off our hats with heart-felt pleasure to General Lee as he rode by on his old war horse, that he loved and rode so well."[191] — John F. Ponder

☛ "On one occasion [Confederate] General [William N.] Pendleton at a vestry meeting complained to General Lee that the Episcopal students did not attend their church as they should. He said, 'even my son goes to the Presbyterian church; I suppose he is attracted by Dr. Pratt's eloquence.' 'I rather think,' replied General Lee, 'that the attraction is not so much Dr. Pratt's eloquence as it is Dr. Pratt's Grace,' referring to his attractive daughter of that name who was a favorite of the students."[192] — Richard W. Rogers

☛ "Some years ago we stood, in company with General Lee, watching a fire in the mountains, which blazed out with a baleful glare on the darkness of a winter's night. The scene was as picturesque as any Salvator ever painted, and the conversation naturally turned on its beauty.

"At last appealed to for an opinion, the general replied: 'It is beautiful, but I have been thinking of the poor animals which must perish in the flames.'

"There was no affectation in this. His tone was simple and

Mary Custis Lee, the General's first and eldest daughter, as she appeared in 1914, four years before her death.

earnest—his manner a complete negation of all art. With this wealth of tenderness, added to his grand and knightly attributes of character, it is no wonder that his people loved him with all their hearts, and cherish his memory with a passionate devotion." — The *Norfolk Virginian*, October 1870

☛ "It is not necessary for me to say anything about the devotion of the people of Virginia and of the entire South to General Lee and how they regarded him as on a pinnacle by himself as one of the truest, bravest, and noblest men, and yet in a certain way he was an effeminate man because he was so extremely kind, gentle, and considerate of everybody, and always had a spirit of deference for others. I remember often seeing him cross the street at the corner between his residence [in Lexington] and the Episcopal church. In winter that crossing was very bad in those days, and the only means of crossing, to keep out of the mud, was by a board plank about a foot wide. I have frequently seen General Lee crossing that plank and stepping off to the side when some one was coming in the opposite direction."[193] — F. A. Berlin

☛ "It is greatly to be regretted that an accurate and full account of this visit was not preserved, for the conversations during those two or three days were most interesting and would have filled a volume. It was the review of a lifetime by two old men. It is believed that General Lee never talked after the war with as little reserve as on this occasion. Only my father and two of his boys were present.

"I can remember his telling my father of meeting Mr. [William B.] Leary, their old teacher at the Alexandria Academy, during his late visit to the South, which recalled many incidents of their school life. They talked of the war, and he told of the delay of Jackson in getting on McClellan's flank, causing the fight at Mechanicsville, which fight he said was unexpected, but was necessary to prevent McClellan from entering Richmond, from the front of which most of the troops had been moved. He thought that if Jackson had been at Gettysburg they would have gained a victory, 'for' said he, 'Jackson would have held the heights which [Confederate General Richard Stoddert] Ewell took on the first day.' He said that Ewell was a fine officer, but would never take the responsibility of exceeding his orders, and having been ordered to Gettysburg, he would not go farther and hold the heights beyond the town. I asked him which of the Federal generals he considered the greatest, and he answered most emphatically 'McClellan by all odds.' He was asked why he did not come to Washington after second Manassas.

"'Because,' he replied, 'my men had nothing to eat,' and

pointing to Fort Wade, in the rear of our home, he said, 'I could not tell my men to take that fort when they had had nothing to eat for three days. I went to Maryland to feed my army.'

"This led to a statement of the mismanagement of the Confederate Commissary Department, of which he gave numerous instances, and mentioned his embarrassments in consequence. He was also very severe in his criticism of the newspapers, and said that patriotism did not seem to influence them in the least, that movements of the army were published which frustrated their plans, and, as an instance, he told of Longstreet's being sent to the Western Army and the efforts that were made to keep the movement secret, but to no purpose, the papers having heralded it at once to friend and foe alike. I also remember his saying that he advocated putting the negroes in the army, and the arguments he advanced in favour of it. My father remarked at table one day that he could not have starved in the Confederate service if he could have gotten bread and milk.

"'No,' replied the General, 'but frequently I could not get even that.'

"His love of children was most marked, and he never failed to show them patient consideration. On the occasion of this visit, his answers to all our boyish questions were given with as much detail and as readily as if we had been the most important men in the community.

"Several years before the war I remember that my sister, brother, and myself, all young children, drove over to Arlington Mills, and that while going there Colonel Lee rode up on a beautiful black horse. He impressed my childish fancy then as the handsomest and finest horseman I had ever seen—the beau-ideal of a soldier. Upon seeing us he at once stopped, spoke to each of us, and took my sister, then about ten years of age, upon his horse before him, and rode with us for two miles, telling her, I remember, of his boy Robby, who had a pony, and who should be her sweetheart. Often have I seen him on the road or street or elsewhere, and though I was 'only a boy,' he always stopped and had something pleasant to say to me."[194] — Cazenove Lee (son of the General's first cousin Cassius F. Lee, on a conversation between the two elderly men in the Summer of 1870)

☛ ["By late 1869 my father's] rides on Traveller in which he delighted so much were not so frequent now. He was not so strong as he had been through the spring and summer, and, indeed, during November he had a very severe attack of cold, from which he did not recover for several weeks. However, during the beautiful days of October he was often seen out in the afternoons on his old gray. His favourite route was the road leading to the Rockbridge Baths. A year previous to this time, he would sometimes go as far as the Baths and return in an afternoon, a trip of twenty miles. A part of this road led through a dense forest. One afternoon, as he told the story himself, he met a plain old soldier in the midst of these woods, who, recognising the General, reined in his horse and said:

"'General Lee, I am powerful glad to see you, and I feel like cheering you.'

"The General replied that this would not do, as they were all alone, only two of them, and there would be no object whatever in cheering. But the old soldier insisted that he must, and, waving his hat about his head, cried out:

"'Hurrah for General Lee!' and kept repeating it. As the General rode away he continued to hear the cheers until he was out of sight."[195] — Captain Robert E. Lee, Jr., C.S.A.

☛ "[During his travels in 1870 my father] was very unwilling to be made a hero anywhere, and most reluctant to show himself to the crowds assembled at every station along his route, pressing to catch sight of him.

"'Why should they care to see me?' he would say, when urged to appear on the platform of the train; 'I am only a poor old Confederate!'"[196] — Captain Robert E. Lee, Jr., C.S.A.

☛ "At Raleigh [North Carolina] and another place the people crowded to the depot and called 'Lee! Lee !' and cheered vociferously, but we were locked up and 'mum.' Everywhere along the road where meals were provided the landlords invited us in, and when we would not get out, sent coffee and lunches. Even soldiers on the train sent in fruit, and I think we were expected to die of eating. At Charlotte and Salisbury [South Carolina] there were other crowds and bands. . . . The train stopped fifteen minutes at Columbia [South Carolina]. Colonel

Lee bucked military protocol and wore his three-star colonel's uniform even after being made a full four-star general. The reason? Despite his promotion to the Confederacy's highest rank, the ever modest Lee felt he did not deserve it.

Alexander Haskell took charge of the crowd, which, in spite of the pouring rain, stood there till we left. General E. Porter Alexander was there, and was very hearty in his inquiries after all of us. His little girl was lifted into the car. Namesakes appeared on the way, of all sizes. Old ladies stretched their heads into the windows at way-stations, and then drew back and said 'He is mightily like his pictures.'

"We reached Augusta [Georgia] Wednesday night. The mayor and council met us, having heard a few minutes before that papa was on the train. We were whirled off to the hotel, and papa decided to spend Thursday there. They had a reception the whole of the morning. Crowds came. Wounded soldiers, servants, and working-men even. The sweetest little children—namesakes—dressed to their eyes, with bouquets of japonica—or tiny cards in their little fat hands—with their names."[197] — Agnes Lee (the General's daughter), from an April 3, 1870, letter to her mother Mary concerning her and her father's trip to Georgia

☛ "[After the War, wherever] he was seen [across the South], he was treated with the greatest love, admiration, and respect. It was with devotion, deep, sincere, and true, mixed with awe and sadness, that they beheld their old commander, on foot, in citizen's dress, grayer than three years ago, but still the same, passing along the ways where he had so often ridden on Traveller, with the noise of battle all around. What a change for him; what a difference to them! But their trust and faith in him was as unshaken as ever."[198] — Captain Robert E. Lee, Jr., C.S.A.

☛ "Inquiries are often made of me about General Lee as a disciplinarian [while he was president of Washington College]. Never was there a body of young men under finer control, and yet there was never any evidence of control. General Lee's slightest wish was law for the student body. We all honored and respected him, and obeyed, yet no word was ever said of discipline. At the end of each month, a list of names was published on the bulletin board with the request to call at General Lee's office. These were the boys who were not making good, either in class standing or in deportment. Each one was interviewed privately, no one on the outside ever knowing what passed.

"It was the rarest thing that a student needed a second interview. In a few instances, young men were quietly sent home, and no mention made of it in public. I once asked a student what General Lee said to him in his interview. He declared that he did not remember, but said that he talked to him like a father. He said: 'I was so frightened when I first went in that I forgot to say good morning.'"[199] — Richard W. Rogers

☛ "[As president of Washington College General Lee] held idleness to be not negative, but a positive vice. It often happened that the plea was made that an idle student was doing no harm and indirectly deriving benefit, etc. General Lee said, 'No, a young man is always doing something; if not good then harm to himself and others.' So that merely persistent idleness was with him always sufficient cause for dismissal."[200] — Professor Edward S. Joynes

☛ "I was so unfortunate while at [Washington] college as to have always an early class, and from time to time on winter mornings it was my habit 'to run late,' as the phrase went. This brought me in danger of meeting the president [General Lee] on his way from chapel, a contingency I was usually careful to guard against. One morning, however, I miscalculated, and as I turned a corner came face to face with him. His greeting was most civil, and touching my cap I hurried by. Next moment I heard my name spoken, and turning I removed my cap and faced him.

"'Yes, sir.'

"'Tell Miss _____' (mentioning the daughter of my uncle, General Pendleton, who kept house for him) 'that I say will she please have breakfast a little earlier for you.'

"'Yes, sir.' And I hurried on once more, resolved that should I ever be late again I would, at least, take care not to meet the general."[201] — Thomas Nelson Page

☛ "A new roadway of broken stone had just been laid through the [Washington] college grounds. Colonel James T. L. Preston, then professor in the Military Institute, came riding through on his way to town. As the stones were new and rough, the Colonel rode alongside on the grass. As he approached where the General was standing, he halted for a talk. General Lee, putting his arm affectionately around the horse's neck and patting him, said: 'Colonel, this is a beautiful horse; I am sorry he is so tenderfooted that he avoids our new road.' Afterwards Colonel Preston always rode on the stoneway."[202] — Professor Edward S. Joynes

Portrait of "the old Rebel," the nickname Lee used for himself.

10
DEATH
1870

General Lee departed from his physical body at around 9:00 AM on October 12, 1870, at the young age of sixty-three. His untimely death was the result of a number of varied factors. The most influential one, however, was Lincoln's War, which drained Lee's mental, physical, and emotional reservoirs and over stressed his immune system for four long years. Naturally, this unintended abuse left him open to a myriad of ailments.

Modern historians attribute the cause of death to "heart disease." But this is just science. It does not take into account the spiritual aspect, which is so important to us in the South. Here, we attribute the

An artist's rendering of General Lee's recumbent statue, Lee Chapel, Washington and Lee University, Lexington, Virginia.

General's premature demise to a "broken heart," shattered over the Confederacy's loss, and the humiliation at the South's so-called "surrender" to a larger but morally inferior army.

☛ "My husband [General Lee] came in. We had been waiting tea for him, and I remarked, 'You have kept us waiting a long time. Where have you been?" He did not reply, but stood up as if to say grace. Yet no word proceeded from his lips, and he sat down in his chair perfectly upright and with a sublime air of resignation on his countenance, and did not attempt a reply to our inquiries.

"That look was never to be forgotten, and I have no doubt he felt that his hour had come; for, though he submitted to the doctors, who were immediately summoned, and who had not even reached their homes from the same vestry-meeting, yet his whole demeanor during his illness showed one who had taken leave of earth. He never smiled, and rarely attempted to speak, except in his dreams, and then he wandered to those dreadful battlefields.

"Once, when [our daughter] Agnes urged him to take some medicine, which he always did with reluctance, he looked at her and said, 'It is no use.' But afterward he took it. When he became so much better the doctor said, 'You must soon get out and ride your favorite gray.' He shook his head most emphatically and looked upward.

"He slept a great deal, but knew us all, greeted us with a kindly pressure of the hand, and loved to have us around him. For the last forty-eight hours he seemed quite insensible of our presence. He breathed more heavily, and at last gently sank to rest with one deep-drawn sigh. And oh, what a glorious rest was in store for him!"[203]
— Mary (Custis) Lee, describing her husband's final moments

Just prior to Lee's death, his mind and body began to fail, more due to, as his family believed, emotional reasons than physical ones:
☛ "His health had always been so robust, and he was still so vigorous, that, at first, the physicians did not despair of him. But his family knew what the physicians were ignorant of. His heart, overwhelmed by the weight of his country's trials, had finished by breaking. Congestion of the brain was only a symptom of the moral malady that was slowly threatening him.

"Every messenger who came had been in the habit of bringing the most touching appeals from his old soldiers and their families, who were dying of starvation. These sufferings, which he could not relieve, were a torture to him. Year by year the hope of seeing times of perfect peace and prosperous tranquillity return became more remote. This anguish, for a long time hidden, even from his relatives, completed its work by destroying the buoyancy of that vigorous organization."[204] — Edward Lee Childe (Lee family relation)

☛ "The death of General Lee was not due to any sudden cause, but was the result of agencies dating as far back as 1863. In the trying campaign of that year he contracted a severe sore throat, that resulted in rheumatic inflammation of the sac inclosing the heart. There is no doubt that after this sickness his health was more or less impaired; and although he complained little, yet rapid exercise on foot or on horseback produced pain and difficulty of breathing. In October, 1869, he was again attacked by inflammation of the heart-sac, accompanied by muscular rheumatism of the back, right side, and arms. The action of the heart was weakened by this attack; the flush upon the face was deepened, the rheumatism increased, and he was troubled with weariness and depression.

"In March, 1870, General Lee, yielding to the solicitations of friends and medical advisers, made a six-weeks' visit to Georgia and Florida. He returned greatly benefited by the influence of the genial climate, the society of friends in those States, and the demonstrations of respect and affection of the people of the South; his physical condition, however, was not greatly improved. During this winter and spring he had said to his son, General Custis Lee, that his attack was mortal; and had virtually expressed the same belief to other trusted friends. And now, with that delicacy that pervaded all his actions, he seriously considered the question of resigning the presidency of Washington College, 'fearful that he might not be equal to his duties.' After listening, however, to the affectionate remonstrances of the faculty and board of trustees, who well knew the value of his wisdom in the supervision of the college and the power of his mere presence and example upon the students, he resumed his labours with the resolution to remain at his post and carry forward the great work he had so auspiciously begun.

"During the summer [of 1870] he spent some weeks at the Hot Springs of Virginia, using the [mineral] baths, and came home seemingly better in health and spirits. He entered upon the duties of the opening collegiate year in September with that quiet zeal and noiseless energy that marked all his actions, and an unusual elation was felt by those about him at the increased prospect that long years of usefulness and honour would yet be added to his glorious life.

"Wednesday, September 28, 1870, found General Lee at the post of duty. In the morning he was fully occupied with the correspondence and other tasks incident to his office of president of Washington College, and he declined offers of assistance from members of the faculty, of whose services he sometimes availed himself. After dinner, at four o'clock, he attended a vestry-meeting of Grace (Episcopal) church. The afternoon was chilly and wet, and a steady rain had set in, which did not cease until it resulted in a great flood, the most memorable and destructive in this region for a hundred years.

"The church was rather cold and damp, and General Lee, during the meeting, sat in a pew with his military cape cast loosely about him. In a conversation that occupied the brief space preceding the call to order, he took part, and told with marked cheerfulness of manner and kindliness of tone some pleasant anecdotes of Bishop Meade and Chief-Justice Marshall.

"The meeting was protracted until after seven o'clock by a discussion touching the rebuilding of the church edifice and the increase of the rector's salary. General Lee acted as chairman, and, after hearing all that was said, gave his own opinion, as was his wont, briefly and without argument. He closed the meeting with a characteristic act. The amount required for the minister's salary still lacked a sum much greater than General Lee's proportion of the subscription, in view of his frequent and generous contributions to the church and other charities, but just before the adjournment, when the treasurer announced the amount of the deficit still remaining, General Lee said in a low tone, 'I will give that sum.' He seemed tired toward the close of the meeting, and, as was afterward remarked, showed an unusual flush, but at the time no apprehensions were felt.

"General Lee returned to his house, and, finding his family waiting tea for him, took his place at the table, standing to say grace.

The effort was vain; the lips could not utter the prayer of the heart. Finding himself unable to speak, he took his seat quietly and without agitation. His face seemed to some of the anxious group about him to wear a look of sublime resignation, and to evince a full knowledge that the hour had come when all the cares and anxieties of his crowded life were at an end. His physicians, Doctors H. S. Barton and R. L. Madison, arrived promptly, applied the usual remedies, and placed him upon the couch from which he was to rise no more.

"To him henceforth the things of this world were as nothing, and he bowed with resignation to the command of the Master he had followed so long with reverence. The symptoms of his attack resembled concussion of the brain, without the attendant swoon. There was marked debility, a slightly impaired consciousness, and a tendency to doze; but no paralysis of motion or sensation, and no evidence of suffering or inflammation of the brain. His physicians treated the case as one of venous congestion, and with apparently favourable results.

"Yet, despite these propitious auguries drawn from his physical symptoms, in view of the great mental strain he had undergone, the gravest fears were felt that the attack was mortal. He took without objection the medicines and diet prescribed, and was strong enough to turn in bed without aid, and to sit up to take nourishment. During the earlier days of his illness, though inclined to doze, he was easily aroused, was quite conscious and observant, evidently understood whatever was said to him, and answered questions briefly but intelligently; he was, however, averse to much speaking, generally using monosyllables, as had always been his habit when sick.

"When first attacked, he said to those who were removing his clothes, pointing at the same time to his rheumatic shoulder, 'You hurt my arm.' Although he seemed to be gradually improving until October 10th, he apparently knew from the first that the appointed hour had come when he must enter those dark gates that, closing, open no more to earth. In the words of his physician, 'he neither expected nor desired to recover.' When [his son] General Custis Lee made some allusion to his recovery, he shook his head and pointed upward.

"On the Monday morning before his death, Doctor Madison, finding him looking better, tried to cheer him. 'How do you feel to-day, General?' General Lee replied slowly and distinctly: 'I feel better.' The

Lee Chapel, Washington and Lee University, Lexington, Virginia. The small but beautiful church is the site of the General's grave, along with those of his wife, children, and varied relations.

doctor then said: 'You must make haste and get well; [your loyal warhorse] Traveller has been standing so long in the stable that he needs exercise.' The General made no reply, but slowly shook his head and closed his eyes. Several times during his illness he put aside his medicine, saying, 'It is of no use,' but yielded patiently to the wishes of his physicians or children, as if the slackened chords of being still responded to the touch of duty or affection.

"On October 10th, during the afternoon, his pulse became feeble and rapid, and his breathing hurried, with other evidences of great exhaustion. About midnight he was seized with a shivering from extreme debility, and Doctor Barton felt obliged to announce the danger to the family. On October 11th, he was evidently sinking; his respiration was hurried, his pulse feeble and rapid. Though less observant, he still recognised whoever approached him, but refused to take anything unless prescribed by his physicians. It now became certain that the case was hopeless. His decline was rapid, yet gentle; and soon after nine o'clock, on the morning of October 12th, he closed his eyes, and his soul passed peacefully from earth.

"General Lee's physicians attributed his death in great measure to moral causes. The strain of his campaigns, the bitterness of defeat aggravated by the bad faith and insolence of the victor, sympathy with the subsequent sufferings of the Southern people, and the effort at calmness under these accumulated sorrows, seemed the sufficient and the real causes that slowly but steadily undermined his health and led to his death. Yet to those who saw his composure under the greater and lesser trials of life, and his justice and forbearance with the most unjust and uncharitable, it seemed scarcely credible that his serene soul was shaken by the evil that raged around him.

"General Lee's closing hours were consonant with his noble and disciplined life. Never was more beautifully displayed how a long and severe education of mind and character enables the soul to pass with equal step through this supreme ordeal; never did the habits and qualities of a lifetime, solemnly gathered into a few last sad hours, more grandly maintain themselves amid the gloom and shadow of approaching death. The reticence, the self-contained composure, the obedience to proper authority, the magnanimity, and the Christian meekness, that marked all his actions, still preserved their sway, in spite of the inroads of disease and the creeping lethargy that weighed down his faculties.

"As the old hero lay in the darkened room, or with the lamp and hearth-fire casting shadows upon his calm, noble front, all the massive grandeur of his form, and face, and brow remained; and death seemed to lose its terrors, and to borrow a grace and dignity in sublime keeping with the life that was ebbing away. The great mind sank to its last repose, almost with the equal poise of health. The few broken utterances that evinced at times a wandering intellect were spoken under the influence of the remedies administered; but as long as consciousness lasted there was evidence that all the high, controlling influences of his whole life still ruled; and even when stupor was laying its cold hand on the intellectual perceptions, the moral nature, with its complete orb of duties and affections, still asserted itself.

"A southern poet has celebrated in song those last significant words, 'Strike the tent': and a thousand voices were raised to give meaning to the uncertain sound, when the dying man said, with emphasis, 'Tell Hill he must come up!' These sentences serve to show most touchingly through what fields the imagination was passing; but generally his words, though few, were coherent; but for the most part, indeed, his silence was unbroken.

"This self-contained reticence had an awful grandeur, in solemn accord with a life that needed no defense. Deeds which required no justification must speak for him. His voiceless lips, like the shut gates of some majestic temple, were closed, not for concealment, but because that within was holy.

"Could the eye of the mourning watcher have pierced the gloom that gathered about the recesses of that great soul it would have perceived a presence there full of an ineffable glory. Leaning trustfully upon the all-sustaining Arm, the man whose stature, measured by mortal standards, seemed so great, passed from this world of shadows to the realities of the hereafter."[205] — Confederate General William Preston Johnston (1874)

☛ "I shall never forget the knock at the door of the lecture room and the notice handed in: 'General Lee died this morning. Academic exercises are suspended.' I read these words to the class and dismissed them. Already the church bells were beginning to toll."[206] — Professor C. A. Graves (at the announcement of Lee's death at Washington College, October 12, 1870)

☛ "On the 13th, Lee's body was borne to the college chapel, escorted by a guard composed of Confederate soldiers. Next to the hearse, 'Traveller,' the faithful gray that had borne him to so many battle-fields, was led. The Trustees and Faculty of the college, the students, and cadets of the Military Institute, and the citizens, followed in procession. Above the chapel floated the flag of Virginia draped in mourning. Through this and the succeeding day, the body, covered with flowers, lay in state, visited by thousands who came to look for the last time upon his noble features.

"On Friday, the 15th, the last rites were performed, amid the tolling of bells, the thundering of cannon, and the sound of martial music.

"The students of the college, officers and soldiers of the Confederate army, and about a thousand persons, assembled at the chapel. A military escort, with the officers of General Lee's staff, were in the front. The hearse followed, with 'Traveller' close behind it.

"Next came a committee of the Virginia Legislature, with citizens from all parts of the State. Passing the Military Institute, the cadets made the military salute as the body appeared, then joined the procession, and escorted it back to the chapel. The procession was more than a mile long. After the first salute, a gun was fired every three minutes.

"Moving still to the sound of martial music, the procession re-entered the grounds of Washington College and was halted in front of the chapel. The coffin was removed to the rostrum. Emblems of mourning met the eye in every direction. Feminine affection had hung garlands of flowers on the pillars and walls. Thousands were present, many surrounding the chapel.

"General Lee had requested that no funeral sermon should be preached over his body. The funeral service of the Episcopal Church was impressively read by his pastor, the [former Confederate general,] Rev. William N. Pendleton, D.D. The coffin was then carried by the pall-bearers to the library room in the basement of the chapel, where it was lowered into the vault prepared for its reception. The funeral services were concluded in the open air by prayer, and singing General Lee's favorite hymn:

> 'How firm a foundation, ye saints of the Lord,
> 'Is laid for your faith in His excellent word.'

"The sorrowful multitude then separated, and slowly returned to their own homes."[207] — Judith White McGuire

☛ "[At the General's funeral his] gray horse Traveller, who had carried him through so many battles, walked with the mourners to the grave. North and South mourned together for the dead hero. His enemies had long ago become his friends."[208] — Evelyn Harriet Walker

☛ "One morning, as I was coming from the old mess hall up the path by the chapel to the [Washington] college General Lee passed on his way toward home, bent and broken. He never passed that way again in life. The next day we knew that he was ill, and then he passed to that mysterious realm."[209] — W. H. Tayloe

☛ "In the late spring of 1870 I saw General Lee for the last time. He was on his way to the South under the advice of his physicians for the benefit of his health, which had begun to fail. I was painfully struck with the change in his appearance since I had left Lexington the year before, and I think he had little hope of recuperation. His face showed the deep lines, made more, I think, by grief for his people, than by disease, and he seemed weary and broken. In a few short months afterwards the South was weeping over his grave. The hero 'whose name is a blessing to speak' had become an eternal memory!"[210] — Judge D. Gardiner Tyler

☛ "General Lee died this morning at half past nine o'clock. He began to grow worse on Monday and continued to sink until he breathed his last this morning. He died as he lived, calmly and quietly, and in the full assurance of faith in the Lord Jesus Christ. The places of business are all closed, the bells are tolling, and the whole community thrown into the deepest grief."[211] — a Lexington, Virginia, newspaper

☛ "The death of General Lee was solemnly proclaimed to the residents of Lexington by the tolling of bells. With common accord all business was suspended. Tokens of mourning appeared on all buildings. The schools were closed and the college exercises ceased. The grief manifested by the people was profound. The little children whom he had cherished, and who had entertained for him a reverential love, wept over the absence of one whose death in the full measure of its bereavement they scarce understood. Women were affected to tears, and strong men turned aside to repress their emotion. It was a personal loss to them.

"In the Southern States his death was deplored as a calamity. Citizens, societies, and all associations of men met in some manner of assemblage and recorded their sense of the sad event. Resolutions of condolence and respect were adopted. Legislatures paused in their proceedings to add to the tokens of grief. All professions, all callings in mercantile life, were represented in the tributes. Rarely has sorrow been so universal, and seldom has genuine affection entered so deeply into the mourning over the death of a public benefactor."[212] — Brigadier General Armistead L. Long, C.S.A.

☞ "His death will awaken most profound and honest manifestations of grief throughout the entire South, and very many people in the North will forget political differences beside the open grave of the dead chieftain, and drop a tear of sorrow on his bier. And whatever may be the verdict as to his career in public life, the universal expression will be that in General Lee an able soldier, a sincere Christian, and an honest man, has been taken from earth."[213] — The New York *Sun*

☞ "The news from America that General Robert E. Lee is dead will be received with great sorrow by many in this county, as well as by his fellow-soldiers in America. It is but a few years since Robert E. Lee ranked among the great men of his time. He was the able soldier of the Southern Confederacy, the leader who twice threatened, by the capture of Washington, D.C., to turn the tide of success and cause a revolution which would have changed the destiny of the United States."[214] — *The Pall Mall Gazette* (England)

After Lincoln's illegal invaders passed through Richmond, Virginia, this is all that was left of the city's Exchange Bank on Main St. If the War was over slavery, as Yankee mythology alleges, why destroy Southern banks, and even universities, libraries, and hospitals? The answer is that the War was not over slavery, as both Presidents Davis and Lincoln attested.

This photo of General Lee was taken in April 1865, immediately following the Confederacy's "surrender" at Appomattox. He is standing at the back of his temporary house on Franklin, St., Richmond, Virginia. His beautiful home, Arlington House, had been stolen and plundered by Union troops at the start of Lincoln's War, but he wished them no ill will. Instead, he counseled his soldiers, family, and friends to pray for their former Yankee enemies and avoid derogatory speech. "We are all Americans," he urged, an important reminder that has been all but forgotten today by many in the North.

11 LEGACY

1807-1870

Richard Henry Lee I, born 1613 at Nordley Regis, Shropshire, England, is General Lee's third great-grandfather. A direct descendant of Launcelot De Le of Loudon, France, Richard emigrated from England to Virginia in the early 1640s, making him the progenitor of the Virginia Lees.

Robert E. Lee left behind a legacy that will stand the test of time, and which will continue to amaze, fascinate, and inspire generations long into the future. The following individuals are but a few examples of the thousands of Lee's contemporaries who recorded their thoughts, opinions, and views of the life and death of the great Confederate chieftain.

☛ "Whenever my father was asked if he was not 'intimate with General Lee,' his invariable reply was: 'No, sir, no man was great enough to be intimate with General Lee.'"[215] — Dr. Reid White

☛ "Posterity will rank General Lee above Wellington or Napoleon, before Saxe or Turenne, above Marlborough or Frederick, before Alexander or Caesar. Careful of the lives of his men, fertile in resource, a profound tactician, gifted with the swift intuition which enables a commander to discern the purpose of his enemy, and the power of rapid combination which enables him to oppose to it a prompt resistance;

modest, frugal, self-denying, void of arrogance or self-assertion, trusting nothing to chance; among men noble as the noblest, in the lofty dignity of the Christian gentleman; among patriots less self-seeking, and as pure as Washington; and among soldiers combining the religious simplicity of Havelock with the genius of Napoleon, the heroism of Bayard and Sidney, and the untiring, never-faltering duty of Wellington: in fact, Robert E. Lee, of Virginia, is the greatest general of this or any other age. He has made his own name, and the Confederacy he served, immortal."[216] — The Montreal *Telegraph* (Canada)

Anne Constable, born 1615, of London, England, wife of Richard Henry Lee I. The couple founded the first Lee family in Virginia in the mid 17th Century. Anne is General Lee's third great-grandmother.

☛ "Lee is the greatest military genius in America."[217] — General Winfield Scott, general-in-chief of the U.S. army under Lincoln

☛ "There never was a man more universally beloved and respected. He was conspicuous in [. . . my mind] for never having uttered a word among his most intimate associates that might not have been spoken in the presence of the most refined woman. It can always be said of him that he was never heard to speak disparagingly of any one, and when any one was heard so to speak in his presence he would always recall some trait of excellence in the absent one."[218] — James Eveleth, officer, U.S.A.

☛ "My father, always dignified and self-contained, rarely gave any evidence of being astonished or startled. His self-control was great and his emotions were not on the surface . . ."[219] — Captain Robert E. Lee, Jr., C.S.A.

☞ "Of all the men of my acquaintance, I remember General Lee as the most beloved and admired by both men and women. No one was ever jealous of him; all delighted to do him honor."[220] — Captain John Macomb, U.S.A.

☞ "Self-possessed and calm, Lee struggled to solve the huge military problem, and make the sum of smaller numbers equal to that of greater numbers. . . . His thoughts ever turned upon the soldiers of his army, the ragged gallant fellows around him—whose pinched cheeks told hunger was their portion, and whose shivering forms denoted the absence of proper clothing."[221] — General William Henry Fitzhugh Lee, C.S.A. (Lee's second son).

☞ "If Lee is not a general, I have none to send you."[222] — President Jefferson Davis, C.S.A. (responding to those Confederate officers who criticized him for replacing General Joseph E. Johnston with Lee after Johnston was injured at the Battle of Seven Pines in May 1862)

☞ "We had 120,000 men, Lee 60,000. Yet Lee handled his forces so skillfully that whenever he attacked he did it with a superior force, and in this way he overwhelmed our army and compelled its retreat, after suffering terrible losses not only in dead and wounded, but in prisoners."[223] — General Carl Schurz, U.S.A. (concerning the Battle of Chancellorsville, April 30-May 6, 1863)

☞ "I tell you that if I were on my death-bed to-morrow, and the President of the United States should tell me that a great battle was to be fought for the liberty or slavery of the country, and he asked my judgment as to the ability of a commander, I would say with my dying breath, 'Let it be Robert E. Lee.'"[224] — General Winfield Scott, U.S.A.

☞ "Everybody and everything—his family, his friends, his horse, and his dog—loves Robert E. Lee."[225] — two Victorian women overheard in conversation

☞ "All through the war Lee assumed the responsibility [for any battle losses], even when, at Gettysburg, his orders were not carried out, and the failure was manifestly due to others."[226] — Thomas Nelson Page (Virginia author, lawyer, and U.S. ambassador to Italy under President Woodrow Wilson)

☛ "[In the early 1840s Lee was] as fine-looking a man as one would wish to see, of perfect figure and strikingly handsome. Quiet and dignified in manner, of cheerful disposition, always pleasant and considerate, he seemed to me the perfect type of gentleman. . . . He was a peacemaker by nature."[227] — General Henry J. Hunt, U.S.A.

☛ "General Lee came to Washington College at a crisis, both for himself and for the college. As he had been impoverished by the war, his property confiscated, his ancestral home at Arlington made a national cemetery, it was necessary that he seek employment. Numerous positions were offered him at fine salaries, simply for the use of his name. But he turned from all of these. He wanted work, not charity.

Richard Henry Lee II, born in 1647 at Paradise, Gloucester County, Virginia, is the son of Richard Henry Lee I and Anne Constable. The Oxford-educated Richard II is General Lee's second great-grandfather.

"In Washington College, the man and the opportunity met. Her halls were empty, her faculty scattered, her treasury empty, her equipment deficient. At this crisis General Lee came. He opened and repaired the buildings, gathered a faculty of thoroughly equipped men, and then waited for students. And they came, from every part of the South, and even from the North. Under his wise administration, Washington College rose from the ashes of her poverty, and from a small denominational college grew into a splendid university, the inspiration being the lofty character of her president. While I was there a magnificent chapel was built, which afterwards became the 'Lee Memorial chapel.' His office was in the basement, near the mausoleum where he was buried."[228] — Richard W. Rogers

☛ ". . . In person General Lee was a notably handsome man. He was tall of stature and admirably proportioned; his features were regular and most amiable in appearance; and in his manners he was courteous and dignified. In social life he was much admired. As a slaveholder he was beloved by his slaves for his kindness and consideration toward them. [As noted earlier, the General and his immediate family did not personally own any slaves, and liberated those they had inherited from Mrs. Lee's side of the family in 1862—months before Lincoln issued his phoney Final Emancipation Proclamation.][229] General Lee was also noted for his piety. He was an Episcopalian, and was a regular attendant at church. Having a perfect command over his temper, he was never seen angry, and his most intimate friends never heard him utter an oath [that is, an expletive].

"Indeed, it is doubtful if there are many men of the present generation who unite so many virtues and so few vices in each of themselves as did General Lee. He came nearer the ideal of a soldier and Christian general than any man we can think of, for he was a greater soldier than Havelock, and equally as devout a Christian. In his death our country has lost a son of whom she might well be proud, and of whose services she might have stood in need had he lived a few years longer, for we are certain that, had occasion required it, General Lee would have given to the United States the benefit of all his great talents."[230] — The New York *Herald*

☛ "No one among men but his own brothers had better opportunity to know General Lee than I. We entered the [West Point] Military Academy together as classmates, and formed then a friendship never impaired. It was formed very soon after we met, from the fact that my father served under his in the celebrated Lee's Legion. We had the same intimate associates, who thought, as I did, that no other youth or man so united the qualities that win warm friendship and command high respect. For he was full of sympathy and kindness, genial and fond of gay conversation, and even of fun, that made him the most agreeable of companions, while his correctness of demeanor and language and attention to all duties, personal and official, and a dignity as much a part of himself as the elegance of his person, gave him a superiority that every one acknowledged in his heart. He was the only one of all the men I have known who could laugh at the faults and follies of his friends in such a manner as to make them ashamed without touching their affection for him, and to confirm their respect and sense of his superiority.

Letitia Corbin, born in the mid 1600s in Middlesex County, Virginia, is the wife of Richard Henry Lee II and the second great-grandmother of General Lee.

"I saw strong evidence of the sympathy of his nature the morning after the first engagement of our troops in the Valley of Mexico. I had lost a cherished young relative in that action, known to General Lee only as my relative. Meeting me, he suddenly saw in my face the effect of that loss, burst into tears, and expressed his deep sympathy as tenderly in words as his lovely wife would have done."[231] — General Joseph E. Johnston, C.S.A.

☛ "Lee was a man of great personal beauty and grace of body. . . . There were discerning minds that appreciated his genius, and saw in him the coming Captain of America. He belonged to a club which was then organized, together with General [George B.] McClellan, General Albert Sydney Johnston, General [Pierre G. T.] Beauregard, and a host of others, who recognized Lee as a master-spirit. He never swore an oath; he never drank; he was never violent; he never wrangled. He was averse to quarrelling, and not a single difficulty marked his career; but all acknowledged his justness and wonderful evenness of mind. Rare intelligence, combined with these qualities, served to make him a fit representative of his great prototype—General Washington."[232] —General William Preston, C.S.A.

☛ "An attempt has been made to throw a cloud upon the character of Robert E. Lee because he left the army of the United States to join in the struggle for the liberty of his State. Without entering into politics, I deem it my duty to say one word in reference to this charge.

"Virginian born, descended from a family illustrious in the colonial history of Virginia, more illustrious still in her struggle for Independence, and most illustrious in her recent effort to maintain the great principles declared in 1776, given by Virginia to the service of the United States, he represented her in the Military Academy at West Point. He was not educated by the Federal Government, but by Virginia; for she paid her full share for the support of that institution, and was entitled to demand in return the services of her sons.

"Entering the army of the United States, he represented Virginia there also, and nobly performed his duty for the Union of which Virginia was a member, whether we look to his peaceful services as an engineer, or to his more notable deeds upon foreign fields of battle. He came from Mexico crowned with honors, covered by brevets, and recognized, young as he was, as one of the ablest of his country's soldiers. And to prove that he was estimated then as such, not only by his associates, but by foreigners also, I may mention that when he was a captain of engineers, stationed in Baltimore, the Cuban Junta in New York selected him to be their leader in the revolutionary effort in that island.

"They were anxious to secure his services, and offered him every temptation that ambition could desire, and pecuniary emoluments far beyond any which he could hope otherwise to acquire. He thought the matter over, and, I remember, came to Washington to consult me as to what he should do. After a brief discussion of the complex character of the military problem which was presented, he turned from the consideration of that view of the question, by stating that the point on which he wished particularly to consult me was as to the propriety of entertaining the proposition which had been made to him. He had been educated in the service of the United States, and felt it wrong to accept place in the army of a foreign power, while he held his commission. Such was his extreme delicacy, such the nice sense of honor of the gallant gentleman we deplore [that is, whose passing we lament].

"But when Virginia—the State to which he owed his first and last allegiance—withdrew from the Union, and thus terminated his relations to it, the same nice sense of honor and duty, which had guided him on a former occasion, had a different application, and led him to share her fortune for good or for evil."[233] — President Jefferson Davis, C.S.A.

☛ "This officer was again indefatigable during these operations, in reconnaissances as daring as laborious, and of the utmost value. Nor was he less conspicuous in planting batteries and in conducting columns to their stations under the heavy fire of the enemy."[234] — General Winfield Scott, U.S.A. (on Lee's military service during the Mexican-American War, 1846-1848)

☛ "He examined everything thoroughly and conscientiously until master of every detail, ever too conscientious to act under imperfect knowledge of any subject submitted to him. And with all his stern sense of duty he attracted the love, admiration, and confidence of all. The little children always hailed his approach with glee, his sincerity, kindliness of nature, and cordial manners attracting their unreserved confidence."[235] — an unknown U.S. army officer who served under Lee in the 1850s

Thomas Lee, born in 1690 at Mount Pleasant, Westmoreland County, Virginia, is the son of Richard II and the great-granduncle of General Lee.

☛ "General Lee continued in excellent health and bore his many cares with his usual equanimity. He had aged somewhat in appearance since the beginning of the war, but had rather gained than lost in physical vigour, from the severe life he had led. His hair had grown gray, but his face had the ruddy hue of health, and his eyes were as clear and bright as ever. His dress was always a plain, gray uniform, with cavalry boots reaching to his knees, and a broad-brimmed gray felt hat. He seldom wore a weapon, and his only mark of rank was the stars on his collar. Though always abstemious in diet, he seemed able to bear any amount of fatigue, being capable of remaining in his saddle all day and at his desk half the night."[236] — General Armistead L. Long, C.S.A. (Autumn 1864)

☛ "Robert E. Lee was by far the ablest Confederate general which the war produced."[237] — General George Gordon Meade, U.S.A.

☛ "I shall never forget his sweet, winning smile, or his clear, honest eyes, which seemed to look into your heart. I have met many of the great men of my time, but Lee alone made me feel that I was in the presence of a man who was cast in a grander mold and made of a different and finer metal than all other men. I have met with but two men who realize my ideas of what a true hero should be—my friend Charles Gordon was one; General Lee was the other."[238] — British General Garnet J. Wolseley

☛ "General Lee was conspicuous for a lack of bitterness toward the United States authorities and the people of the North. He certainly had much which others would have taken as an occasion of bitterness if not absolute hatred. While he was suffering privation and hardship and meeting danger in opposing what he honestly believed to be the armed [Yankee] hosts of oppression and wrong, his home was seized (and held) by the [U.S.] Government, and his property destroyed [by Union troops].

"When at the close of the war he faithfully and scrupulously sought to carry out his parole, avoided the popular applause that his people were everywhere ready to give him, and sought a quiet retreat where he could labor for the good of the young men of the South, his motives were impugned, his actions were misrepresented, and certain of the Northern journals teemed with bitter slanders against him, while a United States grand jury (in violation of the terms of his parole, as General Grant himself maintained) found against him an indictment for 'treason and rebellion.' And yet amid all these provocations he uttered no word of bitterness, and always raised his voice for moderation and charity.

"Upon several occasions the writer has heard him rebuke others for bitter expressions, and the severest terms he was accustomed to employ were such as he used to his son [Robert, Jr.] to whom he said one day, as he was bravely working one of the guns of the Rockbridge Artillery, which was engaged in a fierce fight with the enemy, 'That's right, my son; drive those people back.' [During Lincoln's War, "those people" was the innocuous term Lee chose to use for Yankee soldiers, and for Northerners in general.]

"When told of [Stonewall] Jackson's wound and of his plan to cut [Union General Joseph] Hooker off from the United States ford and drive back his army on Chancellorsville, the eye of the great Captain sparkled, and his face flushed as he remembered that in the loss of his lieutenant he had been 'deprived of his right arm;' but his quiet reply was, 'General Jackson's plans shall be carried out—those people shall be driven today.'

"He used sometimes to speak of the enemy as 'General Meade's people,' 'General Grant's people,' or 'our friends across the river.'

Hannah Harrison Ludwell, born in 1701, is the wife of Thomas Lee and the great-grandaunt of General Lee.

"When in 1863 the head of the Army of Northern Virginia was turned northward, and it was understood that an invasion of Pennsylvania was contemplated, there resounded through the South a cry for retaliation there for the desolation inflicted by the Federal armies upon our own fair land. The newspapers recounted the outrages that we had endured, painted in vivid colors the devastation of large sections of the South, reprinted the orders of [brutal Yankee officers John] Pope, [Benjamin F.] Butler, and others of like spirit, and called upon the officers and men of the Army of Northern Virginia to remember these things when they reached the rich fields of Pennsylvania, arguing that the best way of bringing the war to a successful termination was to let the people of the North feel it as we had done.

"Prominent men urged these views on General Lee, and it would not have been surprising if he had so far yielded to the popular clamor as to have at least winked at depredations on the part of his soldiers. But he did not for a single moment forget that he led the army of a people who professed to be governed by the principles of Christian civilization, and that no outrages on the part of others could justify him in departing from these high principles.

"Accordingly, as soon as the head of his column crossed the Potomac he issued a beautiful address in which he called upon his men to abstain from pillage and depredations of every kind, and enjoined upon his officers to bring to speedy punishment all offenders against this order. If this had been intended for effect merely while the soldiers were to be allowed to plunder at will, nothing further would have been necessary."[239] — Reverend John W. Jones, chaplain, Army of Northern Virginia, C.S.A.

☛ "General Lee himself shared the lot of his soldiers. He constantly refused to establish his head-quarters in a house, even in the depth of winter; he slept under a tent, like the commonest of his men. This self-denial on the part of their chief produced its effect, and nobody was heard to complain."[240] — Edward Lee Childe

☛ "The opinion expressed by the General Assembly in regard to Gen. R. E. Lee [that is, that the General's appointment to commander-in-chief will "inspire increased confidence in the final success of our cause"] has my full concurrence. Virginia cannot have a higher regard for him, or greater confidence in his character and ability, than is entertained by me. When Gen. Lee took command of the Army of Northern Virginia, he was in command of all the armies of the Confederate States by my order of assignment. He continued in this general command, as well as in the immediate command of the Army of Northern Virginia, as long as I would resist his opinion that it was necessary for him to be relieved from one of these two duties.

"Ready as he has ever shown himself to be to perform any

Richard Henry Lee IV, born in 1732 at Stratford Hall, Westmoreland County, Virginia, is the son of Thomas Lee and Hannah Ludwell. One of the signatories to the Declaration of Independence, Richard IV is General Lee's first cousin.

service that I desired him to render to his country, he left it for me to choose between his withdrawal from the command of the army in the field, and relieving him of the general command of all the armies of the Confederate States. It was only when satisfied of this necessity that I came to the conclusion to relieve him from the general command, believing that the safety of the capital and the success of our cause depended, in a great measure, on then retaining him in the command in the field of the Army of Northern Virginia. On several subsequent occasions, the desire on my part to enlarge the sphere of Gen. Lee's usefulness, has led to renewed consideration of the subject, and he has always expressed his inability to assume command of other armies than those now confided to him, unless relieved of the immediate command in the field of that now opposed to [Union] Gen. Grant."[241] — President Jefferson Davis, C.S.A.

☛ "Capt. Lee, so constantly distinguished, also bore important orders from me, until he fainted from a wound and the loss of two nights' sleep at the batteries."[242] — General Winfield Scott, U.S.A. (of Lee's service in the Mexican-American War under Scott)

☛ "General Lee was Caesar without his ambition, Frederick without his tyranny, Napoleon without his selfishness, and Washington without his reward."[243] — Georgia Senator Benjamin Harvey Hill

☛ "Every man is to be judged, so far as human judgment may be passed upon him at all, by the tenor of the motives to which the main current of his days has responded. Judged by this standard, the career of Robert E. Lee must command the deliberate admiration even of those who most earnestly condemn the course upon which he decided in the most solemn and imperative crisis of his life.

"Of his genius as a military commander we do not speak. To that the unanimous voice of all the true and gallant men who fought our long battle out with him and his untiring army has borne abundant witness. The events which evoked it are still too near to us, too many melancholy memories still cluster about the names of those prodigious battle-fields of Virginia, to make it natural or possible for a Northern pen to dwell with complacency upon the strategic resources, the inexhaustible patience, the calm determination, of our most illustrious antagonist.

"But if the testimony of all honorable men who contended against the great Southern general agrees with the verdict of all competent foreign critics in awarding to him a place among the most eminent soldiers of history, the concord is not less absolute of all who knew the man in the private and personal aspects of his life, as to his gentleness, his love of justice, his truth, and his elevation of soul."[244] — The New York *World*

☛ "[General Lee] did not draw his sword to perpetuate human slavery, whatever may have been his opinions in regard to it; he did not seek to overthrow the Government of the United States. He drew it in defence of constitutional liberty. That cause is not dead, but will live forever. The result of the war established the authority of the United States; the Union will stand—let it stand forever. The flag floats over the whole country from the Atlantic to the Pacific; let it increase in lustre, and let the power of the Government grow; still the cause for which General Lee struck is not a lost cause.

"It is conceded that these States must continue united under a common government. We do not wish to sunder it, nor to disturb it. But the great principle that underlies the Government of the United States—the principle that the people have a right to choose their own form of government, and to have their liberties protected by the provisions of the Constitution— is an indestructible principle. You cannot destroy it. Like Milton's angels, it is immortal; you may wound, but you cannot kill it. . . . You may write General Lee's epitaph now. The principle for which he fought will survive him.

"His evening was in perfect harmony with his life. He had time to think, to recall the past, to prepare for the future. An offer, originating in Georgia, and I believe in this very city [Augusta], was made to him to place an immense sum of money at his disposal if he would consent to reside in the city of New York and represent Southern commerce. Millions would have flowed to him. But he declined. He said: 'No; I am grateful, but I have a self-imposed task which I must accomplish. I have led the young men of the South in battle; I have seen many of them fall under my standard. I shall devote my life now to training young men to do their duty in life.' And he did.

"It was beautiful to see him in that glorious valley where Lexington stands, the lofty mountains throwing their protecting shadows over its quiet home. General Lee's fame is not bounded by the limits of the South, nor by the continent. I rejoice that the South gave him birth; I rejoice that the South will hold his ashes. But his fame belongs to the human race. [George] Washington, too, was born in the South and sleeps in the South. But his great fame is not to be appropriated by this country; it is the inheritance of mankind. We place the name of Lee by that of Washington. They both belong to the world."[245] — Judge Hilliard

Francis Lightfoot Lee, born in 1734 at Stratford Hall, Westmoreland County, Virginia, is another son of Thomas Lee and Hannah Ludwell. Like his brother Richard, Francis signed the Declaration of Independence and is General Lee's first cousin.

☛ "Lee hated parade, display, and ceremony, hated above all things being made an object of public gaze and adulation. His idea of high position was high responsibility; a superior was simply one who had larger duties, and the mark of a gentleman was a keen sense of the feelings and susceptibilities of others."[246] — Gamaliel Bradford

☛ "In visiting the headquarters of the Confederate generals, but particularly those of General Lee, any one accustomed to see European armies in the field, cannot fail to be struck with the great absence of all the pomp and circumstance of war in and around their encampments.

"Lee's headquarters consisted of about seven or eight pole-tents, pitched, with their backs to a stake-fence, upon a piece of ground so rocky that it was unpleasant to ride over it, its only recommendation being a little stream of good water which flowed close by the general's tent.

"In front of the tents were some three or four army-wagons, drawn up without any regularity, and a number of horses turned loose about the field. The servants—who were, of course, slaves—and the mounted soldiers called couriers, who always accompany each general of division in the field, were unprovided with tents, and slept in or under the wagons. Wagons, tents, and some of the horses were marked 'U. S.,' showing that part of that huge debt in the North has gone to furnishing even the Confederate generals with camp-equipments.

"No guard or sentries were to be seen in the vicinity, no crowd of aides-de-camp loitering about, making themselves agreeable to visitors and endeavoring to save their generals from receiving those who had no particular business. A large farm-house stands close by, which in any other army would have been the general's residence *pro tem* [that is, temporarily]; but, as no liberties are allowed to be taken with personal property in Lee's army, he is particular in setting a good example himself.

"His staff are crowded together, two or three in a tent; none are allowed to carry more baggage than a small box each, and his own kit is but very little larger. Everyone who approaches him does so with marked respect, although there is none of that bowing and flourishing of forage-caps which occurs in the presence of European generals; and, while all honor him and place implicit faith in his courage and ability, those with whom he is most intimate feel for him the affection of sons to a father.

"Old General [Winfield] Scott was correct in saying that when Lee joined the Southern cause it was worth as much as the accession of 20,000 men to the 'rebels.' Since then every injury that it was possible to inflict[,] the Northerners have heaped upon him.

"Notwithstanding all these personal losses, however, when

speaking of the Yankees he neither evinced any bitterness of feeling nor gave utterance to a single violent expression, but alluded to many of his former friends and companions among them in the kindest terms. He spoke as a man proud of the victories won by his country and confident of ultimate success under the blessing of the Almighty, whom he glorified for past successes, and whose aid he invoked for all future operations."[247] — British General Garnet J. Wolseley

William Lee, born in 1739 at Stratford Hall, is a son of Thomas Lee and Hannah Ludwell, and is the first cousin of General Lee.

A description of Lee's estate, Arlington House, before it was captured, ransacked, and occupied by Yankee troops:

☛ "In resigning his commission and going over to the South, Lee sacrificed his private fortunes, in addition to all his hopes of future promotion in the United States Army. His beautiful home, Arlington, situated upon the heights opposite Washington, must be abandoned forever, and fall into the hands of the enemy. This old mansion was a model of peaceful loveliness and attraction. 'All around here,' says a writer, describing the place, 'Arlington Heights presents a lovely picture of rural beauty. The 'General Lee house,' as some term it, stands on a grassy lot, surrounded with a grove of stately trees and underwood, except in front, where is a verdant sloping ground for a few rods, when it descends into a valley, spreading away in beautiful and broad expanse to the lovely Potomac.

"This part of the splendid estate is apparently a highly-cultivated meadow, the grass waving in the gentle breeze, like the undulating bosom of Old Atlantic. To the south, north, and west, the grounds are beautifully diversified into hill and valley, and richly stored with oak, willow, and maple, though the oak is the principal wood. The view from the height is a charming picture. Washington, Georgetown, and the intermediate Potomac, are all before you in the foreground.

"In this old mansion crowning the grassy hill, the young officer had passed the happiest moments of his life. All around him were spots associated with his hours of purest enjoyment. Each object in the house—the old furniture and very table-sets—recalled the memory of [President George] Washington, and were dear to him. Here were many pieces of the 'Martha Washington china,' portions of the porcelain set presented to Mrs. Washington by Lafayette and others—in the centre of each piece the monogram 'M. W.' with golden rays diverging to the names of the old thirteen States. Here were also fifty pieces, remnants of the set of one thousand, procured from China by the Cincinnati Society, and presented to Washington—articles of elaborate decoration in blue and gold, 'with the coat-of-arms of the society, held by Fame, with a blue ribbon, from which is suspended the eagle of the order, with a green wreath about its neck, and on its breast a shield representing the inauguration of the order.

"Add to these the tea-table used by Washington and one of his bookcases; old portraits, antique furniture, and other memorials of the Lee family from Stratford—let the reader imagine the old mansion stored with these priceless relics, and he will understand with what anguish Lee must have contemplated what came duly to pass, the destruction, by rude hands, of objects so dear to him. That he must have foreseen the fate of his home is certain. To take sides with Virginia was to give up Arlington to its fate."[248] — John Esten Cooke

☛ "We honored General Lee beyond measure, and after nearly forty years, he is still the most imposing figure I ever saw."[249] — Thomas Nelson Page

☛ "At the opening of the war, with sublime self-sacrifice, General Lee had refused the headship of the Union Armies, and with full knowledge and foresight of the inevitable future, had elected to tread the fiery path to ruin with his native State rather than prove false to his ideals of patriotism and duty.

"His choice at its close reached even higher levels of heroic self-sacrifice, and I know of no more pathetic and sublime picture in American history than General Lee, on his warhorse Traveller, making his way alone across the Blue Ridge mountains, and riding quietly into the little village of Lexington to take up the burdens of a new profession and rebuild in a time of universal bankruptcy the fortunes of a disorganized and impoverished institution [Washington College]."[250] — Dr. Henry Louis Smith

☛ "His house was the abode of real 'old Virginia hospitality,' and many visitors to Lexington recall with sad pleasure the grace and dignity with which they were welcomed to that model home. Quiet and unobtrusive, a good listener and always ready to allow others to lead the conversation, General Lee was yet possessed of very fine conversational powers and showed the greatest tact in adapting himself to the tastes of his guests and making them feel at home. A plain farmer upon whose lands our troops were once camped told me that he had less difficulty in gaining access to General Lee, was treated by him with far more courtesy, and felt more at home in his tent than with certain quartermasters with whom he came in contact."[251] — Reverend John W. Jones, chaplain, Army of Northern Virginia, C.S.A.

Arthur Lee, born in 1740 at Stratford Hall, is a son of Thomas Lee and Hannah Ludwell, and is the first cousin of General Lee.

☛ "Robert E. Lee is worthy of all praise. As a man, he was peerless among men. As a soldier, he had no superior and no equal. As a humane and Christian soldier, he towers high in the political horizon."[252] — Reverdy Johnson

☛ ". . . a short time before his death, a large manufacturing company in New York offered him a salary of fifty thousand dollars if he would become their president. He answered that his duty to the college fully occupied his time, and he could not receive pay where he did not render service. When the college wished to raise his salary, he would not allow it; and when the Trustees deeded to Mrs. Lee a house and an annuity of three thousand dollars, in Mrs. Lee's name, he respectfully declined it. 'He declined all gratuities,' says the *Christian Observer*; 'and though a loving people, for whom he had toiled so heroically, would most joyously have settled on him a handsome property, he preferred to earn his daily bread by his personal exertion, and to set to his people an example of honest industry.'"[253] — Judith White McGuire

☛ "The much-talked of surrendering of Lee's sword [to me] and my handing it back, this and much more that has been said about it is the purest romance."[254] — General Ulysses S. Grant, U.S.A.

☛ "[After Lee was put in charge of heading the military operations of all the armies of the Confederacy on March 13, 1862] he revolutionized the plan of campaign hitherto followed. The South was already being shut in and throttled. Her sea-coast cities were being captured, her ports blockaded, and her country cut in two.

"His clear vision saw the imperative necessity of substituting an aggressive for a defensive policy, and he unleashed the eager [Stonewall] Jackson on the armies in the Valley of Virginia, keeping them fully occupied, and so alarming Washington [D.C.] as to hold [Union General Irwin] McDowell on the north side of the Rappahannock and withhold his 40,000 men from swelling [Union General George B.] McClellan's already powerful army on the Peninsula.

"Within a month after he was placed in actual command he perfected his plans and fell upon McClellan, and defeated the greatest army that had ever stood on American soil. The next three years proved beyond cavil that in the first campaign, as always, all that could have been done with his forces by any one was done by Lee. Within one year, indeed, he had laid the foundation of a fame as a great captain as enduring as Marlborough's or Wellington's.

"Three years from this time 'this colonel of cavalry' surrendered a muster-roll of 26,000 men, of which barely 8,000 muskets showed up, to an army of over 130,000 men, commanded by the most determined and able general that the North had found, and, defeated, sheathed his sword with what will undoubtedly become the reputation of the first captain and the noblest public character of his time.

Charles Lee, born in 1758 at Alexandria, Virginia, is the son of Henry Lee and Lucy Grymes and is the uncle of General Lee. A Princeton graduate, Charles served as one of the attorneys for the controversial American political figure Aaron Burr.

"In this period he had fought three of the greatest campaigns in all the history of war, and had destroyed the reputation of more generals than any captain had ever done in the same space of time. His last campaign alone, even ending as it did in defeat, would have sufficed to fix him forever as a star of the first magnitude in the constellation of great captains. Though he succumbed at last to the 'policy of attrition,' pursued by his patient and able antagonist, it was not until Grant had lost in the campaign over 124,000 men, better armed and equipped—two men for every one that Lee had had in his army from the beginning of the campaign."[255] — Thomas Nelson Page

☛ "[General Lee] was emphatically a man of prayer, was accustomed to have family prayers, and had his season of secret prayer which he allowed nothing to interrupt. He was a devout and constant Bible reader, and found time to read the old book even amid his most pressing duties. He became president of the Rockbridge County Bible Society, and in his letter of acceptance spoke of 'the inestimable knowledge of the priceless truths of the Bible.'"[256] — Reverend John W. Jones, chaplain, Army of Northern Virginia, C.S.A.

☛ "It is related that as his army was crossing the James [River], in 1864, and hurrying on to the defense of Petersburg, General Lee turned aside from the road, and, kneeling in the dust, devoutly joined a minister in earnest prayer that God would give him wisdom and grace in the new stage of the campaign upon which he was then entering."[257] — Reverend John W. Jones, chaplain, Army of Northern Virginia, C.S.A.

☛ "Soldiers looked with devotion upon a leader who dared to give battle against heavy odds, and who showed, also, the generous daring to shoulder the responsibility for every movement."[258] — Henry Alexander White (on Lee's bitter win against the superior forces of General McClellan at the Seven Days' Battle, Summer 1862)

☛ ". . . his lips were never soiled by a profane or obscene word, and that when the provocation was great for a display of angry feelings, it was his course to use the 'soft answer which turneth away wrath.'"[259] — an unnamed member of a local Christian church

☛ "[After the War] in his seclusion, while honored by the best of those who had bravely fought against him, General Lee was pursued by the malignity of those haters of the South who, having kept carefully concealed while the guns were firing, now that all personal danger was over, endeavored to make amends by assailing with their clamor the noblest of the defeated.

"It was a period of passion, and those who, under other conditions, might have acted with deliberation and reason, gave the loose to their feeling and surrendered themselves blindly to the direction of their wildest and most passionate leaders. Those against whose private life the purity of his life was an ever-burning protest reviled him most bitterly. The hostile press of the time was filled with railing against him; the halls of Congress rang with denunciation of him as a traitor—the foolish and futile yelping of the cowardly pack that ever gather about the wounded and spent lion. And with what noble dignity and self-command he treated it all! To the nobility of a gentleman he added the meekness of a Christian. When, with a view to setting an example to the South, he applied to be included in the terms of the general amnesty finally offered, his application was ignored, and to his death he remained 'a prisoner on parole.'

"He was dragged before high commissions and was cross-examined by hostile prosecutors panting to drive or inveigle him into some admission which would compromise him, but without avail, or even the ignoble satisfaction to his enemies that they had ruffled his unbroken calm."[260] — Thomas Nelson Page

This ode to Lee was written by a Yank:

☛ "[I recall visiting] the college Chapel at Lexington, gazing upon the recumbent statue of General Lee. While standing here, in the very presence of the dead, I am moved to say a few words in regard to the life that ended in his tomb, and the character of the man whose name is carved upon this stone.

"As I read history, and compare the men who have figured in the events that make history—in wars and revolutions—it seems to me that General Lee was not only a great soldier, but a great man, one of the greatest that our country has produced. After his death, the college which had hitherto borne the name of Washington, by whom it was endowed, was rechristened 'Washington and Lee University'—a combination which suggests a comparison of the two men whose names are here brought together. Can we trace any likeness between them?

Anne Lee born in 1770 at Chantilly, Westmoreland County, Virginia, is the first wife of Charles Lee. Anne is the daughter of Richard Henry Lee IV and Anne Gaskins, making her General Lee's second cousin.

"At first it seems that no characters, as well as no careers, could be more alien to each other than those of the two great leaders, one of whom the Founder of the Government which the other did his utmost to destroy.[261] But nature brings forth her children in strange couples, with resemblances in some cases as marked, and as yet unexpected, as are contrasts in others. Washington and Lee, though born in different centuries, were children of the same mother, Old Virginia and had her best blood in their veins. Descended from the stock of the English Cavaliers, both were born 'gentleman,' and never could be any thing else. Both were trained in the school of war, and as leader of armies it would not be a violent assumption to rank Lee as the equal of Washington. But it is not in the two soldiers, but in the two men, that the future historian will find point of resemblance.

"Washington was not a brilliant man; nor a 'man of genius,' such as now and then appears to dazzle mankind; but he had what was far better than genius—a combination of all the qualities that win human trust; in which intelligence is so balanced by judgment and exalted by character as to constitute a natural superiority; indicating one who is born to command, and to whom all men turn, when their hearts are 'failing them for fear,' as a leader. He was great not only in action, but in repose; great in his very calm—in the fortitude with which he bore himself through all changes of fortune, through dangers and disasters, neither elated by victory nor depressed by defeat—mental habitudes which many will recognize as re-appearing in the one who seems to have formed himself upon that great model.

"Washington was distinguished for his magnanimity. Was not Lee also? Men in public station are apt to be sensitive to whatever concerns their standing before the world; and so, while taking to themselves the credit of success, they are strongly tempted to throw upon others the blame of failure. Soldiers especially are jealous of their reputation; and if a commander loses a battle his first impulse is to cast the odium of defeat upon some unfortunate officer. Somebody blundered; this or that subordinate did not do his duty.

"Military annals are filled with these recriminations. If Napoleon met with a check in his mighty plans he had no scruple in laying it to the misconduct of some lieutenant; unless, as in Russia, he could throw it upon the elements, the wintry snows and the frozen rivers—anything to relieve himself from the imputation of the want of foresight or provision for unexpected dangers. At Waterloo it was not he that failed in his strategy, but Marshal Ney, that failed in the execution.

"In this respect General Lee was exactly his opposite. If he suffered a disaster he never sought to evade responsibility by placing it upon others. Even in the greatest reverse of his life, the defeat at Gettysburg, when he saw the famous charge of [Confederate General George E.] Pickett melt away under the terrible [Yankee] fire that swept the field, till the ranks were literally torn in pieces by shot and shell, he did not vent his despair in rage and reproaches, but rushing to the front, took the blame upon himself, saying, 'It is all my fault.' Perhaps no incident of his life showed more the nobility of his nature.

Richard Bland Lee, born in 1753 at Leesylvania, Prince William County, Virginia, is the son of Henry Lee and Lucy Grymes. Richard is the uncle of General Lee.

"When the war was over General Lee had left to him at Lexington, about the same number of years that Napoleon had at St. Helena; and if he had had the same desire to pose for posterity in the part of an illustrious exile, his mountain home would have furnished as picturesque a background as the rocky island in the South Atlantic, from which he could have dictated 'Conversations' that should furnish the materials of history. He need not have written or published a single line, if he had only been willing to let others do it for him. By their pens he had opportunity to tell of the great part he had acted in the war in a way to make the whole chain of events contribute to his fame.

"But he seemed to care little for fame, and, indeed, was unmoved when others claimed the credit of his victories. If it be, as Pascal says, 'the truest mark of a great mind to be born without envy,' few men in history have shown more of this greatness than he. And when, as was sometimes the case, old companions-in-arms reflected upon him to excuse their own mistakes, he had only to lift the veil from the secrets of history to confound them. But under all temptations he was dumb. Nothing that he did or said was more truly grand than the silence with which he bore the misrepresentations of friend or foe. This required a self-command such as Washington had not to exercise at the end of his military career: for he retired from the scene crowned with victory, with a whole nation at his feet ready to do him honor, while Lee had to bear the reproach of the final disaster—a reproach in which friends sometimes joined with foes. Yet to both he answered only with the same majestic calm, the outward sign of his magnificent self-control. Such magnanimity belongs to the very highest order of moral qualities, and shows a character rare in any country or any age.

"This impression of the man does not grow less with closer observation. With the larger number of 'great men' the greatness is magnified by distance and separation. As we come nearer they dwindle in statue, till, when we are in their very presence and look them squarely in the face, they are found to be but men like ourselves, and sometimes very ordinary men—with some special ability, perhaps which gives them success in the world, but who for all that are full of selfishness, which is the very essence of meanness, and puffed up with paltry conceit and vanity that stamps them as little rather than great.

"Far different was the impression made by General Lee upon those who saw him in the freedom of private intercourse. It might be expected that the soldiers who fought under him should speak with pride and admiration of their old commander; but how did he appear to his neighbors?

"Here in Lexington, everybody knew him, at least by sight. They saw his manner of life from day to day, in his going out and his coming in, and on all the impression was the same; the nearer he came to them the greater he seemed. Everyone has some anecdote to tell of him, and it is always of something that was noble and lovable. Those who knew him best loved him most and revered him most. This was not a greatness that was assumed, that was put on like a military cloak; it was in the man, and could not be put on or off; it was the greatness which comes from the very absence of pretension. And those who came closest to him, give us a still further insight into his nature by telling us that what struck them most was the extent of his sympathy.

"Soldiers are commonly supposed to be cold and hard—a temper of mind to which they are inured by their very profession. Those whose business is the shedding of blood are thought to delight in human suffering. It is hard to believe that a soldier can have a very tender heart. Yet few men were so sensitive to others' pain as General Lee. All came near him perceived that with his manly strength there was united an almost womanly sweetness. It was this gentleness which made him great, and which has enshrined him in the heart of his people forever.

"This sympathy for the suffering showed itself, not in any public act so much as in a private and delicate office which imposed upon him a very heavy burden—one that he might have declined, but the taking of which showed the man. He had an unlimited correspondence. Letters poured in upon him by the hundred and the thousand. They came from all parts of the South, not only from his old companions-in-arms, but from those he had never seen or heard of. Every mother that had lost a son in the war felt that she had a right to pour her sorrow into the ear of one who was not insensible to her grief. Families left in utter poverty appealed to him for aid.

"Most men would have shrunk from a labor so great as that of answering these letters. Not so General Lee. He read them, not only patiently, as a man performs a disagreeable duty, but with a tender interest, and so far as was possible, he returned the kindest answers. If he had little money to give, he could at least give sympathy, and to his old soldiers and their wives and children, it was more than money to know that they had a place in that great heart.

"While thus ministering to his stricken people, there is one public benefit which he rendered that ought never to be forgotten. Though the war was over, he still stood in public relations in which he could render an immeasurable service to the whole country. There are no crisis in a nation's life more perilous than those following civil war. The peace that comes after it, is peace only in name, if the passions of the war still live. After our great struggle, the South was full of inflammable materials. The fires were but smoldering in ashes and might break out at any minute, and rage with destructive fury. If the spirit of some had had full swing, the passions of the Civil War would have been not only perpetuated, but increased, and have gone down as an inheritance of bitterness, from generation to generation.

Theodoric Lee was born in 1766 in Westmoreland County, Virginia, and married the author's cousin Catherine Hite. Theodoric is General Lee's uncle.

"This stormy sea of passion, but one man could control. He had no official position, civil or military. But he was the representative of the 'Lost Cause.' He had led the Southern armies to battle, and he had the unbounded confidence of millions; and it was his attitude and his words that did more than any thing else to still the angry tempests that the war had left behind. It was the sight of the great chieftain, so calm, so ready to bear the burden with his people, that soothed their anger and their pride; and made the old soldiers of the Confederacy feel that they could accept what had been accepted by their leader; and that, as he had set the example, it was no unworthy sacrifice to become loyal supporters of the restored American Union. It is therefore not too much to say that it is owing in great measure to General Lee, that the Civil War has not left a lasting division between the North and the South, and that they form to day one United Country.[262]

"These are the grateful memories to be recalled now that he who was so mighty in war, and so gentle in peace, has passed beyond the reach of praise or blame. Do you tell me that he was an 'enemy,' and that by as much as we love our country we ought to hate its enemies? But there are no enemies among the dead. When the grave closes over those with whom we have been at strife, we can drop our hatreds, and judge of them without passion, and even kindly, as we wish those who come after us to judge of us. In a few years all the contemporaries of General Lee will be dead and gone; the great soldiers that fought with him and that fought against him, will alike have passed to the grave; and then perhaps there will be a nearer approach of feeling between friend and foe.

"'Ah, yes,' say some who admit his greatness as a soldier and leader, 'if it were not for his ambition, that stopped not at the ruin of his country.' . . . But was that ambition in him which was patriotism in us? How is it that we who were upborne for four years by a passion for our country, that stopped at no sacrifices, cannot understand that other men, of the same race and blood, could be inspired with the same passion for what they looked upon as their country, and fight for it with the same heroic devotion that we fought for ours? They as well as we, were fighting for an idea: we [Northerners] for union, and they for independence—a cause which was as sacred to them as ours to us. Is it that what was patriotism on one side was ambition on the other? No; it was not disappointed ambition that cut short that life, but a wound that struck far deeper.

"One who watched by him in those long night hours, tells me that he died of a broken heart. This is the most touching aspect of the warrior's death; that he did not fall on the field of battle, either in the hour of defeat or victory, but in silent grief for sufferings which he could not relieve. There is something infinitely pathetic in the way that he entered in the condition of the whole people, and gave his last strength to comfort those who were fallen and cast down. It was this constant strain of hand and brain and heart that finally snapped the strings of life so that the last view of him as he passes out of sight, is one of unspeakable sadness. The dignity is preserved, but it is the dignity of woe. It is the same tall and stately form, yet not wearing the robes of a conqueror, but bowed with sorrows not his own. In the mournful majesty, silent with a grief beyond words, this great figure passes into history. There we leave him to the judgment of another generation, that standing afar off, may see some things more clearly than we.

Edmund Jennings Lee I, born at Leesylvania in 1772, is the son of Henry Lee and Lucy Grymes. Edmund married Sarah Lee, a daughter of Richard Henry Lee IV and Anne Gaskins. Edmund is General Lee's uncle and his wife Sarah is the General's second cousin.

"When the historian of future ages comes to write the History of the Great Republic, he will give the first place to that War of the Revolution, by which our country gained its independence, and took its place among the nations of the earth; and the second to the late Civil War, which, begun for separation, ended in a closer and consolidated union. That was the last act in the great drama of our nation's life, in which history cannot forget the part was borne by him whose silent form lies within this sepulchre. As I took a last look at the sarcophagus, I observed that it bore no epitaph; no words of praise were carved upon the stone; only a name, with two dates:

Robert Edward Lee
Born January 19, 1807
Died October 12, 1870

"That is all; but it is enough: all the rest may be left to the calm, eternal judgment of history."[263] — Reverend Henry M. Field, Northern editor

☛ "All classes in the South beheld with pride the dignity of their cause nobly represented in the person and character of the commander of their most important army. While so many others in the Separatist ranks, as brave, as patriotic as Lee, but of a different temperament, allowed themselves to indulge in violent language against the North, he remained calm and moderate, in spite of all provocations. His reports are without emphasis, without exaggeration, his language always modest. The day after his most brilliant successes, he rendered an account of his victories with a tone of such moderation, that in reading them at this distance of time, it appears almost impossible he could have written them in the burning atmosphere of a war which displayed the most ardent passions of the human heart.

"This was a very remarkable side of his character. Perhaps this rare moderation and this elevated sense of justice are answerable for the general idea, widely spread, that Lee was cold and unimpressionable. On the contrary, nobody more than he had a heart susceptible of emotion, nor experienced a more profound indignation at seeing the South invaded. But he knew how to control himself, and was never drawn beyond what was compatible with the dignity of the supreme military commander of a people struggling for its independence.

"The South had come to regard Lee in his private and public character with an admiration that soon knew no bounds, and there was placed in him, as general, the most absolute confidence, a confidence never withdrawn, even in the hour of the greatest disasters.

"The army first set an example of blindly trusting to him; it saw him always at work, and in each of the terrible blows which he struck at the enemy, his brave soldiers had a further proof that their confidence was justified. The extreme care which he took on every occasion not to expose them without necessity, (especially at Fredericksburg, where an ambitious commander would not have hesitated to shed torrents of blood to complete his triumph,) singularly contributed to increase their affection.

"In spite of the reserved air which seldom left him, Lee received with kindness the humblest of his soldiers. Naturally very simple in his manners, and kind, endued with great sweetness and much patience, he made no difference in his fashion of receiving those of all ranks who came to him. He often used to say that the common soldiers, who fought without being enticed by the allurement of rank, pay, or glory, but only from a sense of duty and love of country, were the most deserving class in the army, and had a right to the utmost consideration and best treatment. This extreme simplicity of life and manners rendered him peculiarly dear to the troops."[264] — Edward Lee Childe

☛ "General Grant's behavior [during the surrender] at Appomattox was marked by a desire to spare the feelings of his great opponent. There was no theatrical display; his troops were not paraded with bands playing and banners flying, before whose lines the Confederates must march and stack arms. He did not demand Lee's sword, as is customary, but actually apologized to him for not having his own, saying it had been left behind in the wagon; promptly stopped salutes from being fired to mark the event, and the terms granted were liberal and generous. 'No man could have behaved better than General Grant did under the circumstances,' said Lee to a friend in Richmond. 'He did not touch my sword; the usual custom is for the sword to be received when tendered,

Samuel Phillips Lee, born in 1812 at Westmoreland County, Virginia, is the son of Francis Lightfoot Lee II and the author's cousin Elizabeth Blair—the daughter of noted American politician and journalist Francis Preston Blair, Sr. A rear admiral in the Union navy during Lincoln's War, Samuel fought against his famous third cousin, Confederate General Robert E. Lee, and is buried at Arlington National Cemetery.

and then handed back, but he did not touch mine.' Neither did the Union chief enter the Southern lines to show himself or to parade his victory, or go to Richmond or Petersburg to exult over a fallen people, but mounted his horse and with his staff started for Washington, D.C. [George] Washington, at Yorktown, was not as considerate and thoughtful of the feelings of [British Commander] Cornwallis or his men.

"Charges were now withdrawn from the guns, flags furled, and the [U.S.] Army of the Potomac and the [C.S.] Army of Northern Virginia turned their backs upon each other for the first time in four long, bloody years. The Southern soldiers, wrapped in faded, tattered uniforms, shoeless and weather-beaten, but proud as when they first rushed to battle, returned to desolate fields, homes in some cases in ashes, blight, blast, and want on every side.

"A few days afterward General Lee rode into Richmond, accompanied by his staff, and the cheering crowds which quickly gathered told in thunder tones that a paroled prisoner of war was still loved by his people. It was a demonstration in which men forgot their own sorrow and gave way to the glory and gratitude of the past. They adored him most, not in the glare of his brilliant victories, but in the hour of his deepest humiliation."[265] — General Fitzhugh Lee, C.S.A. (General Lee's nephew)

☛ "Not only his soldiers, but the people of the South loved him and still love him with a devotion which is very nearly akin to adoration. Thousands of his soldiers would have esteemed it a privilege to die for him. The world would understand this, if the world could have seen and known him as we saw and knew him.

"It would be difficult to conceive of a nobler presence or a more attractive personality than his! A form 'of noblest mold' crowned by a countenance perfect in its calm benignity, and manly beauty. Large lustrous dark brown eyes, kindly eyes—honest, earnest eyes— which you saw at once were the windows of a great soul. Eyes that gleamed with a high unfaltering purpose, and a dauntless courage, and could serenely look impending disaster and death in the face; and anon would beam with a loving sympathy and a tenderness which were almost divine. A bearing, simple, graceful, and natural, in which there was modesty without diffidence, and supreme dignity without self-assertion.

"It was this actual personal Lee whom his soldiers, and hundreds of thousands of the women and children of the Southern States knew and loved as no leader of men, certainly none of this continent, has ever been loved, before, or since his day."[266] — William A. Anderson

☛ "For quickness of perception, boldness in planning, and skill in directing Lee had no superior . . ."[267] — Colonel Walter Herron Taylor, C.S.A.

On Lee the man:
☛ ". . . here it is difficult to find suitable words in which to speak of him. In a private conversation a gentleman once said to an officer who had been intimately associated with him, 'Most men have their weak point. What was General Lee's?' After a thoughtful pause, the answer was, 'I really do not know.' This answer may be taken for that of the great majority of those who knew him personally or who have studied his character. He was singularly free from the faults which so often mar the character of great men. He was without envy, jealousy, or suspicion, self-seeking, or covetousness; there was nothing about him to diminish or chill the respect which all men felt for him. . . .

"I should . . . say that he was clothed with a natural dignity which could either repel or invite as occasion might require. He could pass with perfect ease from familiar, cheerful conversation to earnest conference, and from earnest conference to authoritative command. He had a pleasant humor, could see the ludicrous side of things, and could enjoy an anecdote or a joke. But even in his lightest moods he was still the cultivated gentleman, having that just degree of reserve that suited his high and responsible position.

"His character was perfectly simple; there were in it no folds or sinuosities. It was simple because guided by a single principle. It is common to say that this principle was duty. This is not the whole truth. Duty is faithfulness to obligation, and is measured by obligation. That which moulded General Lee's life was something more than duty. It was a fine soldierly instinct that made him feel that it was his business to devote his life and powers to the accomplishment of high impersonal ends. Duty is the highest conception of Roman stoicism; it was the ambition of the Christian soldier to serve. General Grant interpreted him correctly when he said, 'I knew there was no use to urge him to anything against his ideas of right.'"[268] — General Armistead L. Long, C.S.A.

Elizabeth Blair, a relative of the author, born in 1818 at Abingdon, Washington County, Virginia, is the wife of Samuel Phillips Lee. Like Samuel, Elizabeth descends from European royalty.

☛ "[While president of Washington College] General Lee's interest in the student body, in my judgment and experience, was the crowning feature of his administration. What could be more vital to the hundreds of students, composed of youths—some mere boys—young men, and battle-scarred veterans who had fought under him, than the parental interest he felt and showed to all alike? To the youth he was indeed a father, gently admonishing, if wayward, encouraging, if backward, and praising, if successful,— always mindful of our moral and physical welfare. To the mature he was both friend and counselor, exercising the same watchful care—encouraging, complimenting, and admonishing, if necessary. To all he was the same, a peerless model, influencing by wise precept and noble example."[269] — Hubbard G. Carlton

☛ "General Lee was my friend, and in that word is included all that I could say of any man. His moral qualities rose to the height of his genius. Self-denying; always intent upon the one idea of duty; self-controlled to an extent that many thought him cold, his feelings were really warm, and his heart melted freely at the sight of a wounded soldier, or the story of the sufferings of the widow and orphan."[270] — President Jefferson Davis, C.S.A.

☛ "The North had the men, money and the munitions of war, but the South had Lee and Stonewall Jackson. And in having them they felt that they were more than a match for the North."[271] — Luther W. Hopkins, C.S.A.

☛ "If ever there lived a man who might of right be proud, it was General Lee! Descended from a long line of illustrious ancestors—allied by marriage to the family of George Washington—of manly beauty, rarely equaled—with honors constantly clustering around his brow, until his fame was coextensive with two continents—it would surely have been excusable had he exhibited, if not a haughty spirit, at least a consciousness of his superiority and his fame.

"But modest humility, simplicity, and gentleness, were most conspicuous in his daily life.

"Scrupulously neat in his dress, he was always simply attired, and carefully avoided the gold-lace and feathers in which others delighted. During the war, he usually wore a suit of gray, without ornament, and with no insignia of rank save three stars on his collar, which every Confederate colonel was entitled to wear. But he always kept a handsomer (though equally simple) uniform, which he wore upon occasions of ceremony. [Confederate] General William Nelson Pendleton—chief of artillery of the Army of Northern Virginia—relates that on the morning of the surrender [April 9, 1865] he found him before daybreak dressed in his neatest style, and that to his inquiries he pleasantly replied: 'If I am to be General Grant's prisoner to-day, I intend to make my best appearance.'"[272] — Reverend John W. Jones, chaplain, Army of Northern Virginia, C.S.A.

☛ "The daring courage of Lee, so signally shown at [the battle at] Contreras [Mexico], was melted into tenderness when he saw in [fellow soldier] Joseph E. Johnston's face the grief caused by the death of a relative in the battle. To his old friend, through the gathering tears, Lee 'expressed his deep sympathy as tenderly in words as his lovely wife would have done.'"[273] — Henry Alexander White

On the soldiers in Lee's army:

☛ "It may seem strange to the present age that a country devastated as this portion of Virginia was at this time, with so many homes mourning the loss of their brave sons slain in battle, or maimed for life, with starvation almost staring them in the face, with the capital of their country besieged by great armies, with what we would call at this day deprivation and suffering incomparable, that the people could have any heart for festivities, such as dances and plays. But such was the fact. The soldiers during their furlough were received everywhere as heroes, and were banqueted and entertained as if peace and plenty reigned throughout the land. Many a parody like the following was made: 'There was a sound of revelry by night,' and 'Les Miserables' (Lee's miserables) had gathered there.

John Fitzgerald Lee, born in 1813 at Sully, Fairfax County, Virginia, is the son of Francis Lightfoot Lee II and Jane Fitzgerald. The West Point graduate is General Lee's third cousin.

"But it must be remembered that it was this spirit among the Southern people that made them endure their hardships and sustain the conflict as long as they did. It was the women standing loyally by their husbands, brothers and lovers that made the Southern soldiers ready to play or ready to fight, regardless of what they had in their haversacks or wore on their backs."[274] — Luther W. Hopkins, C.S.A.

☛ "[I speak now] . . . of his gentleness and moderation in all his views and utterances. Of these eminent virtues—eminent and striking, above all, in a defeated soldier with so much to embitter him—General Lee presented a very remarkable illustration. The result of the war seemed to have left his great soul calm, resigned, and untroubled by the least rancor. While others, not more devoted to the South, permitted passion and sectional animosity to master them, and dictate acts and expressions full of bitterness toward the North, General Lee refrained systematically from every thing of that description; and by simple force of greatness, one would have said, rose above all prejudices and hatreds of the hour, counselling, and giving in his own person to all who approached him the example of moderation and Christian charity. He aimed to keep alive the old Southern traditions of honor and virtue; but not that sectional hatred which could produce only evil."[275] — John Esten Cooke

☛ "I remember . . . that he always recognized us boys when he met us on his strolls through the town or the grounds of the [Washington] college and called us all by name. It seemed remarkable to me that he was able to remember our faces and names among as many as four hundred and ten students. I also recall that his custom was to write to the parent of each boy a letter, sometimes in his own handwriting, about once a year, concerning the young man's conduct, and that he wrote such a letter to my father commending me for good conduct, etc."[276] — Graham Robinson

☛ "Many children all through the land were named after Lee, and, instead of being annoyed by it, as some men of distinction have been, he seemed to regard it as a compliment, which he always acknowledged."[277] — Reverend John W. Jones, chaplain, Army of Northern Virginia, C.S.A.

☛ "On the subject of slavery, [General Lee] . . . assured me that he had always been in favour of the emancipation of the negroes, and that in Virginia the feeling had been strongly inclining in the same direction, till the ill-judged enthusiasm (amounting to rancour) of the abolitionists in the North [of whom the principle instigator was William Lloyd Garrison of Newburyport, Massachusetts] had turned the Southern tide of feeling in the other direction.

"In Virginia, about thirty years ago [about 1835], an ordinance for the emancipation of the slaves had been rejected by only a small majority, and every one fully expected at the next convention it would have been carried, but for the above cause. [General Lee] . . . went on to say that there was scarcely a Virginian now who was not glad that the subject had been definitely settled, though nearly all regretted that they had not been wise enough to do it themselves the first year of the war."[278] — Herbert C. Saunders, of London, England (1866)

☛ "[The year 1831] saw the beginning of the Abolitionist assault, under

[William Lloyd] Garrison's leadership, against the institution of slavery in the Southern States.[279] Mr. Custis [General Lee's father-in-law] himself was a believer in gradual emancipation, and left provision in his will that his servants should become freedmen a certain number of years [five] after his own demise [in 1857]. As executor, Robert E. Lee carried out that provision to the very letter, and, in 1862, sent these manumitted servants with passes through his own military lines into the Northern States.

"Throughout life he was the gentlest and most indulgent of masters to his African retainers. We are told that one of the earliest duties laid upon himself by the young commissioned officer was to take his mother's negro coachman, a consumptive, to the mild climate of Georgia, and there to provide tender nursing until the end came."[280] — Henry Alexander White

☛ "General Lee is, almost without exception, the handsomest man of his age I ever saw. He is fifty-six years old, tall, broad-shouldered, very well made, well set up—a thorough soldier in appearance; and his manners are most courteous and full of dignity. He is a perfect gentleman in every respect. I imagine no man has so few enemies, or is so universally esteemed.

"Throughout the South, all agree in pronouncing him to be as near perfection as a man can be. He has none of the small vices, such as smoking, drinking, chewing, or swearing, and his bitterest enemy never accused him of any of the greater ones. He generally wears a well-worn long grey jacket, a high black felt hat, and blue trousers tucked into his Wellington boots. I never saw him carry arms; and the only mark of his military rank are the three stars on his collar. He rides a handsome horse [Traveller], which is extremely well groomed. He himself is very neat in his dress and person, and in the most arduous marches he always looks smart and clean."[281] — Sir Arthur J. L. Fremantle, British officer

☛ "[While he was attending West Point, Lee] always kept his uniform neat and his brass buttons rubbed so bright that you could see your face in them. His shoes were always well blacked and his musket shining. He was a handsome young fellow, six feet tall and as straight as an arrow. He liked to look well, but did not care for gold lace and feathers. After he had become a General in the army, he often went without his General's uniform and sometimes wore simply his Colonel's stars. When asked why he did this, he replied that he did not care about making a show of himself. Besides, he added, perhaps he did not deserve to rank higher than a Colonel anyway."[282] — Evelyn Harriet Walker

☛ "In May, 1861, General Lee was fifty-four years old. All his faculties had arrived at their complete development. Of tall figure, he had still at that time a carriage somewhat stiff, owing to his military education; but gradually his appearance changed, and gave place to a grave and reflective air, the result of his heavy responsibility as commander-in-chief. The rude trials of the Civil War had not yet whitened his hair. His moustache was black, the rest of his beard close-shaved. His fine clear blue eyes, full of sweetness and benevolence, shone beneath his black eyebrows. One could not meet his look without loving him. His temperance was nearly absolute; he seldom drank anything but water, and was completely indifferent as to what he ate. Excess had never enfeebled his robust vigour. Grave, silent, shut up in himself, he impressed those who saw him for the first time with the idea that he was a man endued with little sensibility. His sincerity, his frankness at all times, his great and generous heart, full of honour and candid simplicity, could only become known during the war."[283] — Edward Lee Childe

Charles Carter Lee, born in 1798 at Stratford Hall, is the son of Henry "Light Horse Harry" Lee and Ann Hill Carter. Charles is the brother of General Lee.

☛ "My father never could bear to have his picture taken, and there are no likenesses of him that really give his sweet expression. Sitting for a picture was such a serious business with him that he never could 'look pleasant.'"[284] — Captain Robert E. Lee, Jr., C.S.A.

☛ "When Lee sheathed his sword [at Appomattox] the Confederate Government vanished like a morning cloud. Of its policy, he declared, he knew nothing and 'had no hand nor part in it.' He was only a soldier, obeying his country's laws, and striving with all his might to preserve the blessing of peace."[285] — Thomas Nelson Page

☛ "I regard him as the noblest specimen of manhood I ever came in contact with. I often mention with pride that I received my diploma from his hands [at Washington College] in June, 1870."[286] — A. H. Hamilton

☛ "General Lee rarely slept in a house—never outside of his lines—during the war, and when on the march some convenient fence-corner would be his most frequent place of bivouac. The writer has not unfrequently seen some [lower-ranked] colonel, or major-quartermaster, entertained in princely style at some hospitable mansion, while near by the commander-in-chief would bivouac in the open air.

"He never allowed his mess to draw from the commissary more than they were entitled to, and not unfrequently he would sit down to a dinner meagre in quality and scant in quantity.

"He was exceedingly abstemious in his own habits. He never used tobacco, and rarely took even a single glass of wine. Whiskey or brandy he did not drink, and he did all in his power to discourage their use by others."[287] — Reverend John W. Jones, chaplain, Army of Northern Virginia, C.S.A.

☛ "It was his constant feeling that he was living and working to an end that constituted the source of General Lee's magnanimity and put him far above any petty jealousy. He looked at everything as unrelated to himself, and only as it affected the cause he was serving. This is shown in his treatment of his subordinates. He had no favorites, no unworthy partialities.

"On one occasion he spoke highly of an officer and remarked that he ought to be promoted. Some surprise was expressed at this, and it was said that that particular officer had sometimes spoken disparagingly of him. 'I cannot help that,' said the general; 'he is a good soldier, and would be useful in a higher position.' As he judged of the work of others, so he judged of his own.

"A victory gave him pleasure only as it contributed to the end he had in view, an honorable peace and the happiness of his country. It was for this cause that even his greatest victories produced in him no exaltation of spirits: he saw the end yet far off. He even thought more of what might have been done than of what was actually accomplished. In the same way a reverse gave him pain, not as a private but as a public calamity. He was the ruling spirit of his army. His campaigns and battles were his own."[288] — General Armistead L. Long, C.S.A.

☛ "As to my dear General Robert E. Lee, what can I say? He was almost a second father to me. I do not know how to express my deep admiration for him. I was not there when he became connected with the university [Washington College]. To me he was the grandest of men. His unobtrusive demeanor; his dignity and gentleness; his firmness in and devotion to principle, elevated, graced and gave dignity to official and personal associations."[289] — Jo Lane Stern, telegrapher, C.S.A. (Washington College graduate)

☛ "After two years of official relationship which was cordial and pleasant from the beginning to the end, I left the college to pursue my professional studies with the conviction that in all the elements of true greatness General Lee was far in advance of any man I had ever known. I have known many great and good men since; but I have had no good reason to modify the judgment I then formed. If extensive knowledge, if far-seeing wisdom, if a wondrous self-control, if ability to manage great enterprises and to master minute details, if the spirit of meekness and of self-sacrifice, if simplicity in thought and speech, if courtesy and an exquisite sense of honor, if ability to estimate other men and to mold them to his will, are elements of greatness, then General Lee was, and is, my beau-ideal of the highest type of Christian gentleman. I may add that this is the estimate formed of him by all who were so fortunate as to know him intimately."[290] — Edward Clifford Gordon

☛ "As a man General Lee will be remembered in history as a man of the epoch. . . . We all know that he was great, noble, and self-poised. He

Edmund Jennings Lee II, born in 1797 at Alexandria, Virginia, is the son of Edmund Jennings Lee I and Sarah Lee. The Princeton-educated lawyer is the first cousin of General Lee.

was just and moderate, but was, perhaps, misunderstood by those who were not personally acquainted with him. He was supposed to be just, but cold. Far from it. He had a warm, affectionate heart.

"During the last year of that unfortunate struggle [Lincoln's War] it was my good fortune to spend a great deal of time with him. I was almost constantly by his side, and it was during the two months immediately preceding the fall of Richmond that I came to know and fully understand the true nobility of his character. In all those long vigils he was considerate and kind, gentle, firm, and self-poised.

"I can give no better idea of the impression it made upon me than to say it inspired me with an ardent love of the man and a profound veneration of his character. It was so massive and noble, so grand in its proportions, that all men must admire its heroism and gallantry, yet so gentle and tender that a woman might adopt and claim it as her own."[291]
— General John Cabell Breckinridge, C.S.A.

☛ ". . . it may be worth while to correct some popular errors in regard to him. First as to his size and personal appearance. He was strikingly handsome, but not a very large man. I have read accounts of him which described him as being over six feet high and weighing over two hundred pounds. He stood five feet and eleven inches in his cavalry boots. His maximum weight was one hundred and seventy pounds. He carried himself very erect; had broad shoulders and narrow hips. His neck was short and very thick, forming a fit support for a massive head. His arms were long, his hands large and his feet small. These features gave him the appearance when on horseback or seated at a table of being a very large man. The same impression is made by half-length photographs of him; whereas, among men of the Scotch-Irish race in the Valley of Virginia where I knew him, he was constantly overtopped by men taller and heavier than himself. His clothes were always well fitting and extremely neat. He did not use tobacco in any form, nor partake of intoxicating liquors, except an occasional glass of wine. He never used slang nor told a joke which his wife and daughters might not have listened to with perfect propriety.

"It is also supposed by many that General Lee was a man of an easy temper, naturally calm, mild and gentle, with no special propensity to violent expression. This was not the case. He had unquestionably great delicacy and tenderness of feeling, constantly manifested in his regard for animals, his love for children, his consideration for the distressed. But these characteristics were combined with what I may call a fierce and violent temper, prone to intense expression.

"When I knew him he had almost perfect control of this temper; but in the Confederate Army it was an open secret that, when he was organizing Virginia's forces at the beginning of the war, he was regarded by the militia and other colonels who brought their regiments to Richmond as a sort of 'bear,' that when aroused should be avoided by wise people.

"It is also certain that he was fond of war. He deliberately chose the career of a soldier. In this respect he was a true son of his race. He plunged with ardor into the Mexican war. When the Federal hosts were driven back from the heights of Fredricksburg, an officer said to him: 'Isn't it splendid?' He replied: 'Yes; but it is well war is so terrible, or we would become too fond of it.'"[292] — Edward Clifford Gordon

On Lee's love of animals:

☛ "At one time he picks up a dog lost and swimming wildly in 'the Narrows,' and cared for it through life; at another he takes a long, roundabout journey by steamer for the sake of his horse; at another he writes: 'Cannot you cure poor "Spec"?' (his dog). 'Cheer him up! take him to walk with you—tell the children to cheer him up.' In fact, his love for animals, like his love for children, was a marked characteristic throughout his life, and long after the war he took the trouble to write a description of his horse 'Traveller,' which none but a true lover of horses could have written.

"On his return from Mexico, after an absence so long that he failed to recognize his own child whom he had left a babe in arms, he was, like Ulysses, first recognized by his faithful dog."[293] — Thomas Nelson Page

☛ "Lee was always, and especially in every great crisis, a leader among men. During the four years of his education at West Point he did not receive a single reprimand. As a cavalry-officer, wherever he went he was a marked man; and when General Scott made his wonderful march to the capital of Mexico, Captain Lee was his right arm. At the commencement of the late [Mexican-American] war, though only a lieutenant-colonel of cavalry, he was offered the command of the armies of the United States. What a prize for ambition! Fortune, fame, and honors, awaited him. Where would he have been to-day? Probably in the presidential chair of this great nation. But he rejected all to take his chance with his own people, and to unite with them in their resistance to the vast numbers and resources which he knew the North was able to bring against them.

"There is nothing more remarkable in the annals of warfare than the success with which General Lee defeated for years the armies of the United States. Consider the six-days' battles around Richmond; the second battle of Manassas; the battles at Antietam, Fredericksburg, and Gettysburg; the wonderful contest at Chancellorsville; then again the remarkable battle of the Wilderness, in which it has been said by Federal authority that General Lee actually killed as many men as he had under his command; the defence at Cold Harbor, the prolonged defence of Richmond and Petersburg, and the admirably-conducted retreat with but a handful before an immense army. Well has he been spoken of as 'the incomparable strategist.' Did any man ever fight against more desperate odds or resources?

"But not merely as a great general is General Lee to be admired. He claims our admiration as a great man—great in adversity. I think there is nothing more admirable in all his life than his conduct in assuming the sole responsibility at Gettysburg. In the midst of defeat Lee was calm, unmoved, showing no fear where despair would have been in the heart of any other general, and saying to his officers and men, 'The fault is all mine.'

"Let the monument be raised, not merely by soldiers of General Lee, but by all men, no matter of what political feelings, who appreciate and honor that which is manly, great, and patriotic. The monument [dedicated to the General] at Richmond will be the resort of pilgrims from the North as well as from the South, and the grave of Lee will be second only in the hearts of the people to the grave of [George] Washington."[294] — George William Brown

Blair Lee, born in 1857 at Silver Spring, Maryland, is the only child of Samuel Philip Lee and Elizabeth Blair. A lawyer and a Maryland senator, Blair is General Lee's third cousin.

☛ "Calm, dignified and commanding in his bearing, a countenance strikingly benevolent and self-possessed, a clear honest eye, that could look friend or enemy in the face; clean-shaven, except a closely trimmed moustache which gave a touch of firmness to the well-shaped mouth; simply and neatly dressed in the uniform of his rank; felt hat, and top-boots reaching to the knee; sitting his horse as if his home was in the saddle: such was Robert E. Lee as he appeared when he assumed command of the Army of Northern Virginia."[295] — an unnamed eye-witness during Lincoln's War

☛ "[My father] entertained very simply, made every one feel at home, and was always considerate and careful of the amusement and welfare of his guests."[296] — Captain Robert E. Lee, Jr., C.S.A.

☛ "As I recall the past, and the four years of the war come back and move in silent procession before me, I can easily forget that more than twenty years have passed away since I selected for General Lee the spot at Appomattox where his tent was pitched for the last time. His image stands out clearly before me, but it is unnecessary to describe his personal appearance. The majesty of his form will endure in marble and bronze, while his memory will pass down the ages as representing all that is greatest in military art, as well as what is truest, bravest, and noblest in human life—a soldier who never failed in duty, a man who feared and trusted God and served his generation."[297] — General Armistead L. Long, C.S.A.

☞ "[His] keen sense of honesty and honor, this abiding consciousness of perfect rectitude of intention, were, I believe, one source of that calm courage which was so characteristic of General Lee. He was no stoic, no haughty patrician, looking down upon and disregarding the sentiments of others. He loved his fellow men. He desired their esteem; but, as it seemed to me, he had never done anything of which he was ashamed and which it was necessary for him to conceal; and so he never feared to face any man or set of men: not even General Grant and his imposing staff, flushed with victory, at Appomattox.

"When cross-examined at President Davis's preliminary trial for treason, counsel for the United States' Government tried to get him to exculpate himself by seeking to make the Confederate President responsible for the war and General Lee's conduct of it. He at once perceived the counsel's design. He admitted that President Davis was the commander-in-chief of the Confederate army; and, of course, was often consulted by him and other officers. He then added: 'I am responsible for what I did; and I cannot now recall any important movement I made which I would not have made had I acted entirely on my own responsibility.'"[298] — Edward Clifford Gordon

☞ "Possibly Lee's chief, if not his one, fault as a soldier was that he was not always rigorous enough with his subordinates; that is, if such a thing be possible, he was too magnanimous. He took blame on himself where it should rightly have been adjudged to others. Yet, this weakness as a soldier but added to his nobility as a man, and it is as a man that we would now consider him.

"While many competent critics in his army were charging [Confederate General James] Longstreet with having been the cause of the disaster at Gettysburg, Lee gave no hint of dissatisfaction with him. His reports contain no suggestion that he had failed to secure his approval. He wrote him a letter such as only a man of noble nature could have written to an old comrade who had failed him. He showed him a magnanimity which was ill requited when Longstreet wrote his own story of the war."[299] — Thomas Nelson Page

☛ "General [Armistead L.] Long, of Lee's staff, has said that his chief never used any bitter or violent language in speaking of the Federal officers and their men. Indeed, he often alluded to some of the Northern officers, whom he had known in other days, in terms of great friendliness."[300] — Bradley Gilman

☛ "General Lee's cheeks were ruddy, and his eye had that clear light which indicates the presence of the calm, self-poised will. But his hair had grown grey, like his beard and mustache, which were worn short and well trimmed. His dress, as always, was a plain and serviceable grey uniform, with no indications of rank save the stars on the collar. Cavalry boots reached nearly to his knees, and he seldom wore any weapon. A broad-brimmed, grey-felt hat rested low upon the forehead; and the movements of this soldierly figure were as firm, measured, and imposing as ever. It was impossible to discern in General Lee any evidences of impaired strength, or any trace of the wearing hardships through which he had passed. He seemed made of iron, and would remain in his saddle all day, and then at his desk half the night, without apparently feeling any fatigue."[301] — an unnamed eyewitness (from the battlefield, November 1864)

When asked whom he regarded as the greatest living soldier:
☛ "Robert E. Lee is not only the greatest soldier of America, but the greatest soldier now living in the world. This is my deliberate conviction, from a full knowledge of his extraordinary abilities, and, if the occasion ever arises, Lee will win this place in the estimation of the whole world."[302] — General Winfield Scott, U.S.A.

☛ "Robert E. Lee was my associate and friend in the [West Point] Military Academy, and we were friends until the hour of his death. We were associates and friends when he was a soldier and I a Congressman, and associates and friends when he led the armies of the Confederacy and

I held a civil office, and therefore I may claim to speak as one who knew him.

"In the many sad scenes and perilous circumstances through which we passed together our conferences were frequent and full, yet never was there an occasion on which there was not entire harmony of purpose and accordance as to means. If ever there was difference of opinion, it was dissipated by discussion, and harmony was the result.

"I repeat, we never disagreed, and I may add that I never in my life saw in him the slightest tendency to self-seeking. It was not his to make a record, it was not his to shift blame to other shoulders; but it was his, with an eye fixed upon the welfare of his country, never faltering, to follow the line of duty to the end. His was the heart that braved every difficulty: his was the mind that wrought victory out of defeat."[303] — President Jefferson Davis, C.S.A. (at the meeting of the Memorial Association, at Richmond, Virginia, November 3, 1870)

☛ "I have taught my sons—I have no daughters—my friends and my neighbors to love General Lee and honor his memory. I have never seen his equal upon this earth and never expect to. What he was, I ardently wish all men could be."[304] — W. W. Estill

Anne Clymer Brooke, born in 1870, is the wife of Blair Lee, the General's third cousin. Anne and Blair had three sons together. She died in 1903 and is buried at Rock Creek Cemetery, Washington, D.C.

☛ "The day will come when the evil passions of the great [American] civil war will sleep in oblivion, and the North and South do justice to each other's motives, and forget each other's wrongs. Then history will speak with clear voice of the deeds done on either side, and the citizens of the whole Union do justice to the memories of the dead, and place above all others the name of the great chief of whom we have written. In strategy, mighty; in battle, terrible; in adversity, as in prosperity, a hero indeed; with the simple devotion to duty and the rare purity of the ideal Christian knight,—he joined all the kingly qualities of a leader of men. It is a wondrous future indeed that lies before America; but in her annals of the years to come, as in those of the past, there will be found few names that can rival in unsullied lustre that of the heroic defender of his native Virginia, Robert Edward Lee."[305] — Colonel Charles Cornwallis Chesney, English army

☛ "Lee is a phenomenon. He is the only man whom I would follow blindfolded."[306] — General Stonewall Jackson, C.S.A.

☛ "He was always fond of farming, and took great interest in the improvements he immediately began at Arlington [House] relating to the cultivation of the farm, to the buildings, roads, fences, fields, and stock, so that in a very short time the appearance of everything on the estate was improved. He often said that he longed for the time when he could have a farm of his own, where he could end his days in quiet and peace, interested in the care and improvement of his own land. This idea was always with him."[307] — Captain Robert E. Lee, Jr., C.S.A.

☛ "The inside of his tent, which he would never leave for the shelter of a house, although often entreated to do so, afforded no object of luxury. The covering of the commander-in-chief was the same as that of the soldier, and his food often inferior to that of the majority of his officers and men.

"Everywhere he was presented with dainties, cases packed with turkeys, hams, wines, spirits, and other things very tempting in the rough life of a soldier: he sent them nearly always to the sick and wounded. His guiding principle was that of setting his officers an example of not faring better than their soldiers.

"For the rest, to lie hard, to eat little, and that little of poor quality, to drink only water, were not to him privations. It was the life he had led for years on the frontiers of Texas and Mexico. He liked neither wine nor spirits, and made no use of tobacco under any form; very rarely did he allow himself a moment's relaxation. When not traversing his camp to note that the soldiers were not in want of anything, or when not inspecting the outposts, his time was spent in his tent at work, going through reports, corresponding with the authorities at Richmond, and occupying himself about all that touched the well-being of the army under his orders.

"Sometimes, also, if in the neighbourhood of country houses, he would pay a visit to the ladies there, and caress the children, thus revealing an unexpected side of his character. His goodness, sweetness, and affectionate smile, singularly attracted children, and inspired them with a touching confidence.

"One day a little girl, in the neighbourhood of Fredericksburg, confided to him as to her best friend, trembling all the while, that she would like to kiss General Jackson. The brave Stonewall blushed like a young girl, when Lee, with a mischievous smile, told him of the child's wish. In such moments Lee was charming. The pleasure he felt was true and unalloyed; he forgot himself, and one found it difficult to believe that this officer, in a simple grey uniform, so affectionate and childlike, was the commander-in-chief of the Confederate army."[308] — Edward Lee Childe

☛ "[After Lincoln's War] General Lee was investigated by high commissions; his every act was examined by hostile prosecutors. His conduct was inquired into by those who had every incentive of hostility to secure his downfall and his degradation. Yet, amid these fierce assaults, he remained as unmoved as he had stood when he had held the heights of Fredericksburg against the furious attacks of Burnside's intrepid infantry. From this inquisition he came forth as unsoiled as the mystic White Knight of the Round Table. In that vivid glare he stood revealed in the full measure of nobility—the closest scrutiny but brought forth new virtues and disclosed a more rounded character: 'Like Launcelot brave, like Galahad clean.'"[309] — Thomas Nelson Page

☛ "No commander was ever more careful, and never had care for the comfort of an army given rise to greater devotion. He was constantly calling the attention of the authorities to the wants of his soldiers, making every effort to provide them with food and clothing. The feeling for him was one of love, not of awe or dread. They could approach him with the assurance that they would be received with kindness and consideration, and that any just complaint would receive proper attention. There was no condescension in his manner, but he was ever simple, kind, and sympathetic, and his men, while having unbounded faith in him as a leader, almost worshipped him as a man. These relations of affection and mutual confidence between the army and its commander had much to do with the undaunted bravery displayed by the men, and bore a due share in the many victories they gained."[310] — General Armistead L. Long, C.S.A. (Autumn 1864)

Confederate General Ambrose P. Hill fought bravely in Lee's Army of Northern Virginia throughout the entire War. Sadly, he was killed on April 2, 1865, by a Yankee soldier just days before the South's "surrender" at Appomattox on April 9. Though some view Hill's service as "inconsistent," General Lee thought that his fellow Virginian was the South's best major general.

☛ "General Lee is known to the world only as a military man, but it is easy to divine from his history how mindful of all just authority, how observant of all constitutional restrictions, would have been his career as a civilian. When, near the conclusion of the war, darkness was thickening about the falling fortunes of the Confederacy, when its very life was in the sword of Lee, it was my proud privilege to note with special admiration the modest demeanor, the manly decorum, and the respectful homage which marked all his intercourse with the constituted authorities of his country. Clothed with all power, he hid its every symbol behind a genial modesty, and refused to exert it save in obedience to law. And even in his triumphant entry into the territory of the enemy, so regardful was he of civilized warfare that the observance of his general orders as to private property and private rights left the line of his march marked and marred by no devastated fields, charred ruins, or desolated homes."[311] — General John Brown Gordon, C.S.A.

On why Lee was loved by his soldiers:

☛ "And why was this the predominant sentiment of his soldiery ? . . . The answer is obvious: Because he loved his men. His military achievements may have been rivalled, possibly surpassed, by other great commanders. Alexander, Marlborough, Wellington, Napoleon, each and all excited the admiration, enjoyed the confidence, and aroused the enthusiasm of their soldiers; but none of these were loved as Lee was loved. They considered their soldiers as mere machines prepared to perform a certain part in the great drama of the battlefield. They regarded not the question of human life as a controlling element in their calculations: with unmoved eye and unquickened pulse they hurled their solid columns against the very face of destruction without reck or care for the destruction of life involved.

"But General Lee never forgot that his men were fellow-beings as well as soldiers. He cared for them with parental solicitude, nor ever relaxed in his efforts to promote their comfort and protect their lives. A striking exemplification of this trait can be found in the fact that it was his constant habit to turn over to the sick and wounded soldiers in the hospital such delicate viands as the partiality of friends furnished for his personal consumption, preferring for himself the plain fare of the camp that his sick soldiers might enjoy the unwonted luxuries. These facts were well known throughout the army, and hence his soldiery, though often ragged and emaciated, though suffering from privations and cold and nakedness, never faltered in their devotion nor abated one tittle of their love for him. They knew it was not his fault."[312] — Colonel Robert E. Withers, C.S.A.

☛ "Perhaps the highest illustration of [General Lee's ability to induce loyalty from other men] . . . is presented in the fact that his surrender at Appomattox brought speedily the Confederate War to its close. For a brief period after that surrender the Confederate counsels were divided. In North Carolina, as President Davis and his cabinet were moving south from Richmond, I heard him say in a public address that he expected soon to be at the head of sixty thousand troops. Imagination staggers when we calmly consider what would have been the result of a continued prosecution of the war. The North went wild over the assassination of President Lincoln. Had the war continued, the South would have been swept with fire and sword without mercy, and to the North's everlasting dishonor. Mr. Charles Francis Adams [Jr.], in his Lee's Centennial Address, has testified that 'from that crown of sorrows Lee saved the country. He was the one man in the Confederacy who could exercise decisive influence.'"[313] — Edward Clifford Gordon

☛ "The parting of Lee with his devoted followers was a sad one. Of the proud army, which, dating its victories from Bull Run, had driven McClellan from before Richmond, and withstood his best efforts at Antietam, and shattered Burnside's hosts at Fredericksburg, and worsted Hooker at Chancellorsville, and fought Meade so stoutly, though unsuccessfully, before Gettysburg, and baffled Grant's bountiful resources and desperate efforts in the Wilderness, at Spottsylvania, on the North Anna, at Cold Harbor, and before Petersburg and Richmond—a mere wreck remained. It is said that 27,000 men were included in Lee's capitulation; but of these not more than 10,000 had been able to carry their arms thus far in their hopeless and almost foodless flight."[314] — Horace Greeley, Northern editor

☛ "It was generally believed in [Washington] college that General Lee was acquainted with the standing of each student in all of his classes. Certain it is that his knowledge of the students and of their work was wonderful. He kept up with the absences and was quick to mark a change in a student's grades, whether by way of improvement or the reverse. His signature was on all the monthly reports sent to parents; and he frequently wrote them personal letters concerning their sons, sometimes of praise, and sometimes of censure. The catalogue of those days declared: 'The President attends all examinations.'"[315] — Professor C. A. Graves

From a Northern newspaper on the day of Lee's death:

☛ "Never had mother a nobler son. In Robert E. Lee the military genius of America was developed to a greater extent than ever before. In him all that was pure and lofty in mind and purpose found lodgment. Dignified without presumption, affable without familiarity, he united all those charms of manners which made him the idol of his friends and of his soldiers, and won for him the respect and admiration of the world.

Even as, in the days of his triumph, glory did not intoxicate, so, when the dark clouds swept over him, adversity did not depress.

"From the hour that he surrendered his sword at Appomattox to the fatal autumn morning, he passed among men, noble in his quiet, simple dignity, displaying neither bitterness nor regret over the irrevocable past. He conquered us in misfortune by the grand manner in which he sustained himself, even as he dazzled us by his genius when the tramp of his soldiers resounded through the valleys of Virginia. And for such a man we are all tears and sorrow to-day.

"Standing beside his grave, men of the South and men of the North can mourn with all the bitterness of four years of warfare erased by this common bereavement. May this unity of grief—this unselfish manifestation over the loss of the Bayard of America—in the season of dead leaves and withered branches which this death ushers in, bloom and blossom like the distant coming spring into the flowers of a heartier accord!"[316] — The New York *Herald*

From the same Northern newspaper:

☛ "On a quiet autumn morning, in the land which he loved so well, and, as he held, served so faithfully, the spirit of Robert Edward Lee left the clay which it had so much ennobled, and traveled out of this world into the great and mysterious land. The expressions of regret which sprang from the few who surrounded the bedside of the dying soldier and Christian, on yesterday, will be swelled to-day into one mighty voice of sorrow, resounding throughout our country, and extending over all parts of the world where his great genius and his many virtues are known. For not to the Southern people alone shall be limited the tribute of a tear over the dead Virginian.

"Here in the North, forgetting that the time was when the sword of Robert Edward Lee was drawn against us—forgetting and forgiving all the years of bloodshed and agony—we have long since ceased to look upon him as the Confederate leader, but have claimed him as one of ourselves; have cherished and felt proud of his military genius as belonging to us; have recounted and recorded his triumphs as our own; have extolled his virtue as reflecting upon us—for Robert Edward Lee was an American, and the great nation which gave him birth would be to-day unworthy of such a son if she regarded him lightly."[317] — The

New York *Herald*

☛ "Among Lee's characteristics his humanity stands forth to distinguish him forever from possibly nearly all his noted contemporaries. Colonel Charles Marshall, of his staff, who knew him best among men, declares that he never put a spy to death, and the story is well known of his clemency in the case of a deserter who had been found guilty by a court-martial and condemned to death.

"It was during the terrible campaign of 1864, when the women at home wrote such heart-rending accounts of their want to their husbands in the field, that Lee was compelled to forbid the mails to be delivered. A soldier who had disappeared from his regiment and gone home was arrested and tried as a deserter. His defence was a letter which he had received from his wife, which showed that she and her children were starving. It was held insufficient, and he was sentenced to be shot. The case, however, was so pitiful that it was finally presented to General Lee. Lee's views on the mistaken mercy of reversing courts-martial in cases of desertion . . . [have been widely noted]. In this case, however, he wrote beneath the finding his approval, and then below this an order that the man should immediately rejoin his regiment."[318] — Thomas Nelson Page

☛ "If there was anything which unfitted Lee for the leadership of a great revolution it was that he lacked or suppressed that intense ardor, that persistent and overpowering energy and determination, which comes from great personal ambition, and which prompts men to use any means needed to secure success. He would not use his influence over the army to coerce the civil government of the Confederate States and compel it to do what he thought ought to be done in order to secure its independent existence. He would not make a dictator of himself. He would not violate the modern usages of war in laying waste his enemy's country with fire and sword. All this may detract from his merits as a soldier and a revolutionist. It immensely exalts his character as a Christian. He would not do what his enlightened conscience told him was wrong to save either himself or his country."[319] — Edward Clifford Gordon

☛ ". . . there is a chapter in [General Lee's] . . . life which the world does not know so well, which ought to be told, to the greater honor of the illustrious dead. The war was over. The Northern armies had returned victorious, while the veterans of the South, defeated, but not dishonored, took their way back to their desolate homes. The army disbanded and dispersed, what should its leader do? His old ancestral home, standing on the noble height which looks down on the Potomac and across to the dome of the Capital, was in the hands of those against whom he had been fighting for four years, and had even been turned into a national cemetery, in which slept thousands of the Union dead, whose very ghosts might rise up against his return. But if he was an exile from his own home, there were thousands of others open to him all over the South, and across the sea where his fame had gone before him, and would have made him a welcome guest in princely halls. But such a flight from his country (for so he would have regarded it) was impossible to one of his chivalrous spirit. He had cast in his lot with his people; they had believed in him and had followed him, as they thought, to certain triumph; he would not desert them in the day of their adversity.

Another image of Fitzhugh Lee. Born in 1835 at Clermont, Fairfax County, Virginia, he is the son of Sydney Smith Lee and Anna Maria Mason. The Confederate general and Virginia governor is a nephew of General Lee.

"Of course, had he been willing to listen to them, he could have received any number of 'business' proposals. Rich, moneyed corporations would have been glad to 'retain' him at any price as President or Director, so that they could have the benefit of his great name. One, it is said, offered him $50,000 [about $700,000 in today's currency] a year. But he was not to be allured by such temptations.

"The very fact that they were coupled with offers of money was reason enough why he should reject them all, as he did, without a moments hesitation. Nor could he be allured by any military proposals. [Emperor] Maximilian offered to place him at the head of his army if he would go to Mexico, thinking that his genius might save the fortunes of the falling empire. But Lee would not accept any exile, however splendid. His answer was, 'I love the mountains of Virginia still.' His work must be at home, for work he must have. After his active life, he would not sink down into ildeness. With his military career ended, he must find a new career in civil life. Besides, he had a proud spirit of independence, which would not permit him to live on the bounty of the rich at home or the titled abroad. 'He would work for a living,' like the poorest of his soldiers.

"At length came a proposal that seemed most alien to his former pursuits; that the Commander of the Southern Armies should become the President of a college. And yet this change from a military to an academic career was not so violent as it might seem. He had been for three years Superintendent of the Military Academy at West Point, where he was associated with young men. He had been himself a student there, and had been through all the stages of scholarly discipline. Besides, the position of the college to which he was invited, in Lexington, Virginia, was attractive to him. It was remote from cities, among the mountains, and yet within the limits of that 'Old Dominion,' which he looked upon as his mother.

"When it was known that he had accepted the position, his coming was looked for with great eagerness by the people of Lexington; but he did not fix the time, as he wished to avoid any public demonstration. But it had been arranged that when he came he should spend a few days in the hospitable dwelling in which I was so fortunate as to be a guest. While thus in expectancy, the Professor was one day taking a walk, when he saw riding up the street, a figure that he instantly recognized as the same he had so often seen at the head of the army; and to make the picture perfect, he was mounted on his old war horse—a magnificent iron gray, called 'Traveler'—that had so often borne his master through the smoke of battle. He wore no military uniform, nor sign of rank, but a light summer dress, while a broad Panama hat shaded a face that no one could mistake. Advancing toward him, the professor told of the arrangements for his entertainment till he could be established in a house for himself, and led the way to his home.

"Naturally my friend's family were at first somewhat awed by the presence of their illustrious guest. But this was soon dissipated by his simple and unaffected manner. What 'broke the ice' most completely was his manner with the children. He was always very fond of little people, and as soon as they appeared, 'Uncle Robert' as he was affectionately called in the army, had them in his arms and on his knees, till they soon felt perfectly at home with him. They 'captured' him at once, and he 'captured' them, and in this captured their parents also. From that moment all constraint disappeared, though nothing could ever take from the profound respect and veneration with which they looked up to 'General Lee.'

"This was in September, 1865, and on the 2d of October, after solemn prayer by the venerable Dr. White, he took the oath of office, as required by the laws of the college, and thus became its President. Naturally his name drew great numbers of students, not only from Virginia, but from all parts of the South, who were eager to 'serve' under such a leader, and the number of undergraduates rose from one hundred and fifty to over four hundred.

"In one respect his influence was immeasurable. Every man in the South looked up to General Lee as the highest type of manhood, and his very presence was an inspiration. This is the influence which young men feel more than any other—that inspired by intense admiration—an influence that would have been very potent if the object of their admiration had been merely a great soldier, dazzling them by his genius, but destitute of high principals. Had that been the case, his influence would have been demoralizing as now it was elevating, since his superiority in other respects was united with a character that was so gentle and so good.

"That he might reach the young, he sought their acquaintance, not standing apart in icy dignity. Professor White tells me that, if they were walking together in the college grounds, and a student was seen approaching, he would ask who he was, and when he came up, instead of passing him with a stately bow, would stop and call him by name, and ask him about his family and his studies, and speak a few words of encouragement, which the young man would not forget to his dying day. To be under the authority and influence of such a man was an education in manliness. There was not a student who did not feel it, and to whom it was not the highest ambition to be guided by such a leader, to be infused with his spirit, and to follow his example. . . .

"He knew that whatever fell from his lips would be repeated, and not always as he had said it, but with a change of words, or in a different tone of voice, that might give it another meaning. Indeed, with all his caution, he was often quoted in saying what he did not say. As an illustration, Professor White told me that a story had gone the rounds of the papers to the effect that in a conversation, General Lee had brought his clenched hands down on the table, to give emphasis to his utterance, as he said, 'If I had had Stonewall Jackson with me, I should have won the battle of Gettysburg and established the Southern Confederacy.' Now said the professor, without ever asking him, I know that such an occurrence never took place, for in the first place General Lee 'never brought his hand down on the table'—he was not that sort of a man—it is impossible to conceive of him as using any violence of gesture or of language.

Another image of Confederate General William Henry Fitzhugh Lee, born in 1837 at Arlington House. William, known as "Fitzhugh" by his family, is the son of General Lee and Mary Anne Randolph Custis.

"And as to Stonewall Jackson, while he did feel keenly the absence of that great corps commander, he was not the man to indulge in sweeping and positive statements; he never spoke with such absolute assurance of anything, but always with a degree of reserve, as once, when we were riding together, he said in his usual guarded and cautious manner; 'If I had had Stonewall Jackson with me—so far as man can see—I should have won the battle of Gettysburg.' So careful was he to put in this qualification: for he always recognized an overruling Power that may disappoint the wisest calculations, and defeat the most careful combinations of courage and skill."[320] — Reverend Henry M. Field, Northern editor

☛ "Robert Edward Lee was a scion of an ancient family. Launcelot Lee, who fought at Hastings under the banner of William the Conqueror, in 1066, and Lionel Lee, who won fame at the Siege of Acre with Richard Coeur de Lion, in 1192, were his ancestors; and on his maternal side the blood of Robert Bruce flowed in his veins. In American history the Lees of Virginia had been distinguished for character and achievement since the middle of the seventeenth century; but Gen. Robert E. Lee, though he was proud of his name, and resolved never to tarnish it, was yet so far from wishing to exploit his ancestry, that when the project of publishing a Lee genealogy was submitted to him he said: 'I think the money had better be appropriated to relieve the poor.'"[321] — Major General Randolph H. McKim, C.S.A.

☛ "As a mere military man, Washington himself cannot rank with the wonderful war chief who, for four years, led the Army of Northern Virginia. Lee will rank with the greatest of all English-speaking military leaders; and this holds true, even when the last and chief of his antagonists, Ulysses S. Grant, may claim to stand as the full equal of Marlborough and Wellington."[322] — U.S. President Theodore Roosevelt

☛ "Uttering no complaints, entering into no disputes, he was as one in suffering all, that suffers nothing. He accepted fortune's buffets and rewards with equal thanks. His record and appearance during those final years are pleasant to dwell upon, for they reflect honor on our American manhood."[323] — Colonel Charles Francis Adams, Jr., U.S.A.

☛ "During and after the war General Lee manifested in the highest degree the Christian spirit of forgiveness. He hated all wrong and wrongdoing with all the ardor of his intense and passionate nature. He regarded the attempt of the [U.S.] federal government to force Virginia into a war against her southern neighbors as an enormous political wickedness, to be resisted at whatever cost of blood and treasure. Yet he cherished no sentiments of personal hate against the authors and promoters of this wickedness.

". . . After the war General Lee was indicted for treason though never tried. He would have been punished but for the respect General Grant had for his own word pledged at Appomattox. [Lee] . . . asked for amnesty. It was refused. He died a prisoner of war, disfranchised, in a country which gave the right of suffrage to the negro who could neither read nor understand its laws, and to aliens who could not speak its language. Yet he did not depart from his sage plan of action."[324] — Edward Clifford Gordon

☛ "What I had seen General Lee to be at first—child-like in simplicity and unselfish in his character—he remained, unspoiled by praise and by success. While he was always the dignified Virginia gentleman, and never free or familiar with any one, he won the hearts of his men as entirely as ever did Napoleon or Washington."[325] — Vice President Alexander H. Stephens, C.S.A.

☛ "[He had a] wonderful influence over the troops under his command. I can best describe that influence by saying that such was the love and veneration of the men for him that they came to look upon the cause as General Lee's cause, and they fought for it because they loved him. To them he represented cause, country, and all."[326] — Colonel Charles Marshall, C.S.A.

☛ "I think we may conclude that the cardinal fact of Lee's life was God. [German philosopher Friedrich] Schleiermacher said that [Portuguese philosopher Baruch] Spinoza was God-intoxicated. It would be indecorous to speak of Lee as intoxicated with anything. But everywhere and always he had God in his heart, not so much the God of power, or the God of justice, or even the God of beauty, but the God of love, tempering the austerity of virtue, sweetening the bitterness of failure, above all, breathing loving kindness into the intolerable hell of war. There have been fierce saints who were fighters. There have been gentle saints who were martyrs. It is rare to find a soldier making war—stern war—with the pity, the tenderness, the sympathy of a true follower of Christ."[327] — Gamaliel Bradford

☛ "[My father] was the same in victory or defeat, always calm and contained."[328] — Captain Robert E. Lee, Jr., C.S.A.

☛ "In his own home, he was the embodiment of hospitality, his manner always charming and affable, his conversation often quietly humorous, and at all times interesting and unaffected. No one would have recognized in the man as he appeared under his own roof, the cold and austere leader who had so recently directed the movements in great battles."[329] — Philip Alexander Bruce

☛ "The highest head, the noblest and grandest character of our continent, the most conscientious, humane, and faithful soldier, the most chivalrous gentleman in this world, the best, the most superb sample of the American warrior, has fallen like a mighty tree in the forest; and men wonder, after the first shock of the news, to find that there is such a gap, such a blank in the world. What is wanting to the fame of this illustrious American?"[330] — John Mitchell (in the New York *Citizen*)

☛ "[There can be no] doubt that to the soul of Robert E. Lee the cause of the Confederacy was [not slavery, it was] the cause of Liberty and Self-government, and that history must recognize in him an illustrious champion of Freedom and Democracy."[331] — Major General Randolph H. McKim, C.S.A.

☛ "It was characteristic of General Lee that ordinarily, wherever he might be, he slept in a tent, for fear of incommoding the occupants of the houses he might have taken for his head-quarters, and at times when he was inspecting the long lines from Richmond to Petersburg, he even hesitated to seek shelter at night in the camp of an acquaintance lest he might inconvenience him. On his return from Appomattox he, even at his brother's home, slept in a tent in his yard."[332] — Thomas Nelson Page

☛ "[General Lee's] delicate sense of honor gave him a horror of debt. This is all the more noticeable because he was fond of elegance of every sort: fine houses, furniture, plate, clothing, ornaments, horses, equipage. But he could and did deny himself and his family the enjoyment of such things when he did not have the money to buy them.

I have seen him in garments which many men of smaller income and far less reputation would have been unwilling to wear. He was not ashamed to eat a plain dinner plainly served with his friends. He impressed these ideas and habits on his family. Mrs. Lee's usual occupation in the dining room . . . during the evenings was mending her husband's and son's underclothing."[333] — Edward Clifford Gordon

☛ "[My father's] disappointment in the Gettysburg campaign . . . was not shown in anything he said or did. He was calm and dignified with all, at times bright and cheerful, and always had a playful smile and a pleasant word for those about him."[334] — Captain Robert E. Lee, Jr., C.S.A.

Just days before Lee's "surrender" at Appomattox:
☛ "So denuded was the country of all that would sustain life, that [Lee's] men thought themselves well off when a corn-house was found with grain yet left in it and corn was distributed to them to be parched. Even this was not always to be had, and as corn was necessary for the artillery horses, guards were posted where they fed to prevent the men from taking it from the horses. They were reduced to the necessity of raking up the scattered grains from the ground where the horses had been fed and even to picking the grains from the droppings of the horses. Many of the men became too weak to carry their muskets. Small wonder that they dropped out of the ranks by hundreds! Yet still the remainder kept on, with unwavering courage, unwavering devotion, and unwavering faith in their commander.

"In their rags and tatters, ill-clad, ill-shod, ill-fed, ill-armed, and, whenever armed, armed for the most part with the weapons they had captured from brave foes on hard-fought battle-fields, they were the abiding expression of Southern valor and fortitude; the flower of Southern manhood; the pick of every class; the crystallized residue of the Army of Northern Virginia, with which Lee had achieved his fame and on which to future ages shall rest the fame of the South."[335] — Thomas Nelson Page

☛ "The great-hearted Lee must receive praise for setting before his countrymen a personal demeanour that remains unsurpassed in quiet dignity and forbearance. He suffered with his people and taught them how to suffer and be strong. Not a murmur escaped his lips. Not a word of recrimination against the North did he utter. By reason of the example which he set before them, his countrymen likewise laboured in silence to restore prosperity to their beloved land."[336] — Henry Alexander White (on Lee during so-called "Reconstruction")

Cassius Francis Lee I, born in 1808 at Alexandria County, Virginia, is the son of Edmund Jennings Lee I and Sarah Lee. A lawyer, U.S. court clerk, and a devout Episcopalian, Cassius is the first cousin of General Lee.

☛ ". . . The retreat from the lines of Richmond and Petersburg began in the early days of April [1865], and the remnant of the Army of Northern Virginia fell back, more than one hundred miles, before its overpowering antagonist, repeatedly presenting front to the latter and giving battle so as to check his progress.

"Finally, from mere exhaustion, less than eight thousand men with arms in their hands, of the noblest army that ever fought 'in the tide of time,' were surrendered at Appomattox to an army of 150,000 men; the sword of Robert E. Lee, without a blemish on it, was sheathed forever; and the flag, to which he had added such luster, was furled, to be, henceforth, embalmed in the affectionate remembrance of those who remained faithful during all our trials, and will do so to the end."[337] — General Jubal A. Early C.S.A. (1872)

☛ "Robert E. Lee believed in the Union and loved the stars and stripes. He hoped against hope that the Southern states would not secede, and did everything in his power to prevent it. He believed slavery to be a moral and political evil. He freed his own [wive's] slaves long before the war, saying that if all the slaves in the South were his, he would give them up to save the Union. But when it came to choosing between the Union and Virginia, he said: 'I can not draw my sword against my native state.' The decision cost him a terrible struggle.

"[U.S.] General [Winfield] Scott, his old commander, who believed in him so much that he said Lee's service would be worth that of fifty thousand common men, begged of him to remain true to the Union, and President Lincoln informally offered him the command of the entire army of the United States. He gave up his commission as Colonel and declined the President's offer, saying that, though he opposed secession and deprecated war, he could take no part in an invasion of the Southern states. He was still hoping for peace, and had then not the most distant thought of taking part on either side of the conflict if there should be one. Two days afterwards the State of Virginia seceded from the Union and offered Colonel Lee a commission as commander of its forces. He accepted the trust, and I believe there is no one living, South or North, who doubts that he acted with clear conscience and the most perfect sincerity."[338] — Evelyn Harriet Walker

☛ "[As president of Washington College, General Lee] seemed to avoid contact with men, and the impression which he made on me, seeing him every day, and which has since clung to me, strengthening the impression then made, was, that he was bowed down with a broken heart. I never saw a sadder expression than General Lee carried during the entire time I was there. It looked as if the sorrow of a whole nation had been collected in his countenance, and as if he was bearing the grief of his whole people. It never left his face, but was ever there to keep company with the kindly smile.

"He impressed me as being the most modest man I ever saw in his contact with men. History records how modestly he wore his honors, but I refer to the characteristic in another sense. I dare say no man ever offered to relate a story of questionable delicacy in his presence. His very bearing and presence produced an atmosphere of purity that would have repelled the attempt. As for any thing like publicity, notoriety or display, it was absolutely painful to him."[339] — John B. Collyar

☛ "The war had scarcely ceased and General Lee's condition of narrow circumstances become known, when offers of places of honor and profit began to come to him: offers of the presidency of insurance companies and of other industrial enterprises—proposals that he should allow his name to be used for the highest office in the gift of the State; even offers from admirers in the old country [England] of an asylum on that side of the water, where a handsome estate was tendered him, as a tribute of admiration, so that he could spend the residue of his life in peace and comfort. His reply to all these allurements was that which we now know was the only one he could make: a gracious but irrevocable refusal.

Edwin Gray Lee, born in 1835 at Leeland, Jefferson County, West Virginia, he is the son of Edmund Jennings Lee II and Henrietta Bedinger. A colonel in the Confederate army who served as an aide to Stonewall Jackson, Edwin is General Lee's first cousin.

"During the war, when a friend had suggested to him the probability that the people of the South would demand that he should be their president, he had promptly and decisively declared that he would never accept such a position. So now, when the governorship of Virginia was proposed to him, he firmly refused to consider it. With the same firmness he rejected all proposals to provide him with honorable commercial positions at a high salary."[340] — Thomas Nelson Page

To Robert E. Lee, Jr., son of General Lee:

☛ "I never heard your father discuss public matters at all, nor did he express his opinion of public men. On one occasion, I did hear him condemn with great severity the [U.S.] Secretary of War, [Edwin M.] Stanton. This was at the time Mrs. [Mary] Surratt was condemned and executed [for allegedly participating in the murder of Lincoln]. At another time I heard him speak harshly of [Union] General [and war criminal David] Hunter, who had written to him to get his approval of his movements, during the Valley Campaign, against [Confederate] General [Jubal A.] Early. With these exceptions, I never heard him speak of public men or measures."[341] — Captain Edmund R. Cocke, C.S.A.

☛ "When offered the presidency of an insurance company at a princely salary he excused himself on the ground that he knew nothing of insurance business; and when he was told in reply that no duties would be required of him—nothing was asked but the use of his name, his answer was that his good name was about all he had saved from the wreck of the war, and that was not for sale."[342] — Major General Randolph H. McKim, C.S.A.

☛ "In common with the great body of the youths of the South my reverence for General Lee was a matter of inheritance. We revered his name little short of worship, and three years of association with him increased rather than diminished this feeling. He was one of a very few men I have known who impressed me as being *great*. I know of no other word that expresses the idea I wish to convey."[343] — J. W. Ewing

☛ "In the case of Lee we admire much that was Napoleonic in the conception of his plans."[344] — Count Yorck von Wartenburg

☛ "[General Lee's] last official act was to request that all his private soldiers, who owned the horses they used, might be allowed to carry them home, 'for the spring plowing;' so, to the last, [he] was the commander thoughtful of the welfare of his men."[345] — Frederick Warren Alexander

☛ "The conduct of Lee's soldiers, after the close of the war, has excited the attention and elicited the admiration of the world. There was much in the state of things, just after the surrender, to excite the serious apprehension of thinking men that these disbanded soldiers would render the condition of the South far worse by entering upon a career of lawlessness.

"After long exposure to the demoralizing influences of the camp, and a long cessation from any industrial pursuit, these young men returned to find their fondly-cherished hopes blighted, their fortunes ruined, their fields laid waste, and, in not a few instances, blackened ruins marking the spot of their once-happy homes. It would not have been surprising if they had yielded to despair, and had sought redress by taking the law into their own hands.

"I claim to have thoroughly known the veterans of Lee's army, and to have had some peculiar opportunities of seeing them after the close of the war. In traveling very extensively through the South, I made it a point always to inquire after them, and the invariable response was, 'They have gone to work, and are quiet, orderly members of society.' Many of them, who had been raised in luxury and ease, took off their coats and went into the corn, tobacco, or cotton fields of the South, or entered upon other pursuits, with a zeal and earnestness truly marvelous to those who did not know the stuff of which these heroic men were made.

"They 'accepted the situation,' and, amid provocations and insults not a few, have proved themselves 'loyal' to their every pledge—law-abiding citizens of whom any community might be proud.

"If asked the explanation of this, the simplest answer would be, 'The soldiers have continued to follow their commander-in-chief.' General Lee was most scrupulous in observing the terms of his parole. He refused to attend political gatherings, avoided discussing the war, or its issues (except with intimate friends, and in the freedom of private intercourse), and gave the young men of the South a striking example of quiet submission to the United States authorities.

"He was accustomed to say: 'I am now unfortunately so situated that I can do no good; and, as I am anxious to do as little harm as possible, I deem it wisest for me to remain silent.' And yet, as has been intimated, the good order and law-abiding spirit of the soldiers and people of the South were due, in no small measure, to the quiet example and influence of this noble man."[346] — Reverend John W. Jones, chaplain, Army of Northern Virginia, C.S.A.

☛ "The greatest general of the day."[347] — Colonel Thomas L. Livermore, U.S.A.

☛ "The highest tribute to Lee's army is the simple fact that with its surrender the war was over. The fortunes of the Confederacy had been nailed to its tattered standards and with them went down."[348] — Thomas

Nelson Page

☛ "If ever man made his life a true poem it was Lee."[349] — Gamaliel Bradford

☛ "Turning to the political bearing of the important question at issue, the great Southern general [Lee] gave me, at some length, his feelings with regard to the abstract right of secession. This right, he told me, was held as a constitutional maxim at the South. As to its exercise at the time on the part of the South, he was distinctly opposed, and it was not until Lincoln issued a proclamation for 75,000 men to invade the South, which was deemed clearly unconstitutional, that Virginia withdrew from the United States."[350] — Herbert C. Saunders, of London, England, 1866

☛ "Lee had one intimate friend—God."[351] — Gamaliel Bradford

☛ "In every particular he possessed the requisites of a true soldier. He was brave; his whole military record and his lifelong scorn of danger alike bear testimony to his bravery. He was wise; his great successes against great odds and his almost constant anticipation of the enemy's movements were proofs of his wisdom. He was skillful; his forced marches and unexpected victories assert his skill. He was patient and unyielding; his weary struggle against the mighty armies of the North and his stern defence of Richmond will for ever preserve the memory of his patience and resolution. He was gentle and just; the soldiers who fought under him and who came alive out of the great fight, remembering and cherishing the memory of the man, can one and all testify to his gentleness and his justice. Above all, he was faithful; when he gave up his sword there was no man in his own ranks or in those of the enemy that doubted his faith or believed that he had not done all that mortal could do for the cause for which he had made such a noble struggle."[352] — The Halifax *Morning Chronicle*

☛ "[Lee was] the most manly man and entire gentleman I ever saw."[353] — Vice President Alexander H. Stephens, C.S.A.

☛ "As Hannibal, notwithstanding Zama, towers over the very inferior Scipio, the figure of Lee eclipses Grant."[354] — Colonel Charles Cornwallis Chesney, English army

☛ "Lee's religious feeling seemed only to be intensified by the Confederacy's declining fortunes. The profound impression made upon him by the Gettysburg campaign, and his less hopeful outlook on the future thereafter, are clearly revealed in the deeper and more fervent religious tone of his correspondence from that date to the end of the contest.

Sydney Smith Lee, born in 1802 at Stratford Hall, is the son of Henry "Light Horse Harry" Lee and Ann Hill Carter. Sydney, who unlike his cousin Samuel Phillips Lee, remained loyal to the South at the start of Lincoln's War, is the brother of General Lee.

"He seemed to lean more on Providence the more Providence appeared to be deserting his cause. When the Confederacy finally sank in ruins, it was this unshaken trust in God, this confidence in Divine wisdom, that inspired him with calm resignation to the inevitable as well as with a sanguine expectation of a happier day for the Southern people. So deep was this trust and so firm this confidence that not even the relentless Acts of Reconstruction aroused in him bitterness or animosity toward the North. That era of submersion was to him but a passing wave of darkness; the light from Heaven would be obscured only for a time."[355] — Philip Alexander Bruce

☛ "[After the ratification of the Thirteenth Amendment in December 1865] Lee declared, what every one now knows to have been the fact, that every one with whom he associated expressed the kindest feelings toward the freedmen [that is, the freed slaves], and wished to see them get on in the world, and particularly to take up some occupation for a living and to turn their hands to some work, and that efforts were being made among the farmers near his home to induce them to engage for the year at regular and fair living wages. He did not know, he stated, of any combination to keep down wages or establish any rate which the people did not think fair.

"Lee further stated that where he had been the [Southern] people were not only willing that the blacks should be educated, but were of the opinion that this would be for the advantage of both the blacks and the whites."[356] — Thomas Nelson Page

☛ "The fatherlands of Sidney and Bayard never produced a nobler soldier, gentleman and Christian than Gen. Robert E. Lee."[357] — The London *Standard*

☛ "Every incident in that visit is indelibly stamped on my memory. All he said to me then and during subsequent conversations is still fresh in my recollection. It is natural it should be so, for he was the ablest general and to me seemed the greatest man I ever conversed with, and yet I have had the privilege of meeting Von Moltke and Prince Bismarck.

"General Lee was one of the few men who ever seriously impressed and awed me with their inherent greatness. Forty years have come and gone since our meeting and yet the majesty of his manly bearing, the genial, winning grace, the sweetness of his smile, and the impressive dignity of his old-fashioned style of dress come back to me among my most cherished recollections. His greatness made me humble, and I never felt my own insignificance more keenly than I did in his presence. . . . He was, indeed, a beautiful character, and of him it might truthfully be written, 'In righteousness did he judge and make war!'"[358] — British General Garnet J. Wolseley (after a brief meeting with Lee in the Summer of 1862)

☛ "It is an advantage to have a subject like Lee that one cannot help loving. . . . I have loved him, and I may say that his influence upon my own life, though I came to him late, has been as deep and as inspiring as any I have ever known."[359] — Gamaliel Bradford

☛ "General Lee was no original secessionist; he was no politician; he was personally a man of great moderation and wisdom. In the months immediately following the war, he had struggled very hard to reconcile himself and his fellow-citizens to their defeat. He was also an eminent Christian: and in August, 1870, he well knew that he was a dying man, for his intimate friends were aware that he understood the symptoms of his decaying health, and knew that death was not far off.

"But now, after five years' experience of subjugation and reconstruction, this great martyr, this wise, grand old man, looking eternity in the face, forms this deliberate estimate of the illegality, the perjury and cruelty, the mischievousness of the reconstruction measures; that had he foreknown clearly that the results of submission would be such, he would have preferred to die with his face to the foe.

"Impartial history will surely form the same estimate concerning this conclusion of the unconstitutional war of coercion and of the subjugation of the Southern States by other States, pretending to be their equals."[360] — Robert Lewis Dabney, 1870 (after having Lee tell him that he regretted surrendering to the Yanks and would have preferred dying on the battlefield, "with my brave men, my sword in this right hand")[361]

☛ "No one, certainly, since the time of Napoleon, has conquered as much against such immense odds."[362] — The London *Times*

☛ "[Here is a prime example of] Lee's self renunciation. The impossible had happened; Lee had surrendered; his glorious battle flag was furled forever. The war was over.

"What now should be the course of this man who had given all his genius, and all his marvellous energy to establish the Confederacy—and given it in vain? Doors of ease and comfort and honor opened to him across the sea. Should he accept them? Why not? Had he not done all that mortal man could do for the Southern people? Had he not sacrificed all he was, and all he possessed, on their behalf? Then why not leave the scene of his defeat and his losses, and rest in peace and quietness in Old England, where he was admired and revered almost as much as in the South itself?

"No,—a thousand times no! Lee would not for sake his people in their dire calamity. If he could do no more for them, at least he could do this—he could suffer with them. And so again a great renunciation is made. This hero of faith turned away from a life of ease and chose a life of toil. He refused honor and accepted reproach. He turned his back on the luxurious homes offered him beyond the seas, and chose rather to suffer affliction with his people—in their poverty, in their disfranchisements, in all their dire calamities! He would share their sorrows. He would bear their burdens with them. They were his people still, and he would put his neck under the yoke imposed upon them—however grievous it might be.

"But if he was to remain in the South, might he not accept some easy, lucrative post, with only nominal duties—and thus far at least consult his ease? You know that offers of such places were freely made him. Let him allow himself, for example, to be chosen a president of a great business enterprise with a princely salary and practically nothing to do. But again No! This royal soul turned resolutely away from all such offers. Once more the spirit of self renunciation triumphed, and Lee chose a life of toil, and care, and self-denial. He accepted the presidency of Washington College in its day of small things when it was wrecked and almost ruined by the cruel hoof of war, at a salary which was, in fact, a mere pittance, and gave himself to the task of educating the young men of the South in a little mountain town, far from the haunts of men and the stir and clamor of the busy world.

"Why? Because he loved his people. Because he saw that the education of their young men was the first and most pressing task of those trying times. Because he believed in the gospel of work, and would set an example to the Southern people to go to work with all their might to rebuild their shattered fortunes."[363] — Major General Randolph H. McKim, C.S.A.

When, on April 9, 1865, Lee returned to his troops after signing Grant's letter of surrender, the men let out a great cheer:

☛ "It was reported in some of the Northern papers that it was the sound of jubilation at the surrender. But it was not. It was the voice of jubilation, yet not for surrender: but for the captain who had surrendered their muskets but was still the commander of their hearts."[364] — Thomas Nelson Page

☛ "Like Napoleon, Lee's troops soon learned to believe him equal to every emergency that war could bring. . . . Like Caesar he mixed with the crowd of soldiers freely, and never feared that his position would be forgotten."[365] — Colonel Charles Cornwallis Chesney, English army

☛ "Who that once looked on it can ever forget it?—that array of tattered uniforms and bright muskets—that body of incomparable infantry, the Army of Northern Virginia, which, for four years, carried the revolt on its bayonets, opposing a constant front to the mighty concentration of power brought against it; which, receiving terrible blows, did not fail to give the like, and which, vital in all its parts, died only with its annihilation."[366] — William Swinton (historian of the Army of the Potomac), U.S.A.

☛ "Lee and the Army of Northern Virginia never sustained defeat."[367] — Colonel Charles Francis Adams, Jr., U.S.A.

☛ "From the bottom of my heart I thank Heaven for the comfort of having a character like Lee's to look at, standing in burnished glory above the smoke of Mammon's altars."[368] — Morris Schaff

☛ "Lee made five campaigns in a single year; no other man and no other army ever did as much."[369] — Colonel Eben Swift, U.S.A.

☛ "Speaking advisedly and on full reflection, I say that of all the great characters of the Civil War, and it was productive of many whose names and deeds posterity will long bear in recollection, there was not one who passed away in the serene atmosphere and with the gracious bearing of Lee. From beginning to end those parting years of his will bear closest scrutiny. There was about them nothing venal, nothing querulous, nothing in any way sordid or disappointing. In his case there was no anti-climax: for those closing years were dignified, patient, useful; sweet in domesticity, they in all things commanded respect."[370] — Colonel Charles Francis Adams, Jr., U.S.A.

☛ "[Stratford Hall] has a unique distinction among historical houses in this country; for in one of its chambers were born two signers of the

Another view of the Lee home at 707 East Franklin St., Richmond, VA.

Declaration of Independence: Richard Henry Lee, who, in obedience to the mandate of the Virginia Convention, moved the resolution in Congress to declare the Colonies free and independent States, and Francis Lightfoot Lee, his brother.[371]

"But it has a yet greater distinction. In one of its chambers was born, on the 19th of January, 1807, Robert E. Lee, whom many students of military history believe to have been not only the greatest soldier of his time, and, taking all things together, the greatest captain of the English-speaking race, but the loftiest character of his generation; one rarely equalled, and possibly never excelled, in all the annals of the human race."[372] — Thomas Nelson Page

☛ "Partisans and leaders, aiming at the overthrow of our [Southern] institutions, may, while temporarily in high places, by fraud and usurpation, keep up the false cry of rebel and traitor; but these irrepressible outburstings of popular sentiment, regarding no restraints on great occasions which cause Nature to speak, show clearly how this cry and charge are regarded and looked upon by the masses of the people everywhere.

"Everywhere Lee is honored; not only as a hero, but as a patriot. This is but the foreshadowing of the general judgment of the people of the whole United States, and of the world, not only upon Lee, but upon all of his associates who fought, bled, and died in that glorious cause in which he won his immortality. That cause was the sovereign right of local self-government by the people of the several States of this continent. That cause is not dead! Let it never be abandoned; but let its friends rally to its standard in the forum of reason and justice, with the renewed hope and energy from this soul-inspiriting sign that it lies deeply impressed upon the hearts of the great majority of the people in all sections of this country.

"In these popular manifestations of respect and veneration for the man who won all his glory in maintaining this cause, present usurpers should read their doom, and all friends of constitutional liberty should take fresh courage in all political conflicts, never to lower their standard of principles."[373] — Vice President Alexander H. Stephens, C.S.A.

☛ ". . . if today the South is strong and prosperous and rich, holding her place in the Union by as firm a tenure as the North, it is due, more than to any other one influence, to the compelling power of the life and example of Robert E. Lee from 1865 to 1870, informed as they were, always and everywhere, by the Christ-like spirit of self-sacrifice."[374] — Major General Randolph H. McKim, C.S.A.

☛ "How well they [Generals Lee and Stonewall Jackson] fought is a matter of history. They fought as they could not have fought, had they not been led by a great Commander. From the very beginning of his military career, all around him recognized his extraordinary capacity. General Scott, with whom he served in Mexico, pronounced him 'the very best soldier that he ever saw in the field.' But the greatest proof of his ability was when he did not serve under anybody, but planned his own campaigns. Some military critics I know assume to criticize him even here. To such I have only to say that it is a very poor compliment to our leaders and our armies, to question the ability of one who, with less than half the numbers, kept back for two years the tremendous forces of the North that were pressing in on every side. Whatever others may say of General Lee, the great soldiers who fought against him, fully concede his splendid military genius."[375] — Reverend Henry M. Field, Northern editor

☛ "The mighty campaign of 1864 before Richmond was as much a masterpiece of defensive warfare as Napoleon's campaign of 1814."[376] — Captain Cecil Battine, British officer

☛ "There is, seemingly, no character in all history that combines power and virtue and charm as Lee does. He is with the great captains, the supreme leaders of all time. He is with the good, pure men and chivalrous gentlemen of all time . . ."[377] — William Peterfield Trent

☛ "He was the head and front, the very life and soul of the Army."[378] — General Jubal A. Early, C.S.A.

☛ "[General Lee was] tested in war and in peace, in adversity and in prosperity, under the exaltation of victory, and amid the commonplace duties of a daily routine. And everywhere and always he met the experiences that came to him with so poised and perfect a spirit that all who beheld him marveled at him. When Socrates said that 'No harm could come to a good man,' it was of a man like Robert E. Lee that he spoke. Lee met discouragement and defeat with patience and fortitude; he met success and victory with self-restraint and dignity; he passed through sunshine and through shadow as one whose soul was lighted by an inner glory which paled the flickering lights of earth."[379] — Bradley Gilman

On the secret of Lee's greatness:
☛ ". . . this good citizen, this gallant soldier, this great general, this true patriot, had yet a higher praise than this, or these,—*he was a true*

Christian."[380] — President Jefferson Davis, C.S.A.

☛ "In strategy mighty, in battle terrible, in adversity as in prosperity a hero indeed, with the simple devotion to duty and the rare purity of the ideal Christian knight, he joined all the kingly qualities of a leader of men."[381] — Colonel Charles Cornwallis Chesney, English army

☛ "Great in victory, greater still in defeat; great as descried through the red haze of war, greater still as contemplated through the clear air of peace; great as a general, but greatest as a man—behold in him a character which, if not perfect, conceals its faults with the effulgence of its virtues, even as the sun conceals the spots on its dazzling disk. I need not call his name; nor need History, when she carves for the highest niche in her Pantheon a statue to represent manhood apotheosized by its own glory, inscribe beneath it a name which the very design of the statue speaks aloud—the immortal name of Lee."[382] — Reverend R. A. Holland

SEA RAVEN PRESS
SRP
SEARAVENPRESS.COM

APPENDIX A

General Lee's Military Staff

ALEXANDER, E. PORTER: Lieutenant-colonel, Chief of Ordnance Nov. 1862, from June 1, 1862.

BALDWIN, BRISCOE G.: Lieutenant-colonel, Chief of Ordnance Nov. 1862, Sept., 1863, April 9, 1865.

BROOKE, JOHN M.: Lieutenant Virginia Navy, Acting A. D. C. May 4-8, 1861.

CHILTON, R. H.: Colonel, A. A. General June 1862, July 31, Aug. 31, 1863; Brigadier-general, A. and I. General, Dec. 1863.

COLE, ROBERT G.: Lieutenant-colonel, Chief Commissary of Subsistence June 1862-April 9, 1865.

COOKE, GILES B.: Major, A. A. General Nov. 4, 1864.

CORLEY, JAMES L.: Lieutenant-colonel, Chief Quartermaster June 1862-April 1865.

CRENSHAW, JOSEPH R.: Major, Acting Commissary-general April 29, 1861.

DEAS, GEORGE: Major, A. A. General, Chief of Staff June 15, 1861; Lieutenant-colonel, A. A. General July 4, 1861 (Virginia State Forces).

GARNETT, R. S.: Colonel, A. A. General April 26, 1861; Colonel, A. A. General May 7, 1861 (Virginia State Forces).

GILL, WILLIAM G.: Lieutenant-colonel, P. A. C. S., Ordnance Officer Nov. 1, 1861.

GUILD, LAFAYETTE: Surgeon, Medical Director Nov. 26, 1862, March 6, Aug. 31, 1863, April 9, 1865.

HARVIE, EDWIN J.: Lieutenant-colonel, Inspector-general June 1862.

HETH, HENRY: Lieutenant-colonel, Acting Q. M. General Virginia State Forces April 29, 1861; promoted Brigadier-general Jan. 6, 1862; Major-general May 24,1863.

IVES, JOSEPH C.: Captain C. S. A., Chief Engineer Nov. 6,1861.
JOHNSON, S. K.: Captain, Engineer Officer Nov. 1862-Sept. 1863.
LAY, GEORGE W.: Colonel, A. I. General March 6, 1863.
LONG, ARMISTEAD L.: Major, Chief of Artillery Department S.C., Ga., and Fla. Nov. 1861; Colonel, Military Secretary April 21, 1862-Sept. 1863; promoted Brigadier-general of Artillery Sept. 21, 1863.
MANIGAULT, JOSEPH (a cousin of the author): Vol. A. D. C. Nov., 1861.
MARSHALL, CHARLES: Major, A. D. C. Aug. 1862; Major, A. D. C. March, Aug. 1863; Lieutenant-colonel, A. A. General Nov. 4, 1864-April 1865.
MASON, A. P.: Captain, A. A. General Aug. 1862, March 6,1863.
MURRAY, E.: Lieutenant-colonel, A. A. General July 31-Sept. 1863, Nov. 4, 1864.
PAGE, THOMAS J.: Lieutenant Virginia Navy, Acting A. D. C. May 3, 1861.
PENDLETON, W. N.: Brigadier-general, Chief of Artillery Mar. 6-Aug. 31, 1863-1865.
PEYTON, HENRY E.: Major, A. A. General Nov. 1862; Lieutenant-colonel July 31-Nov. 4, 1864.
RICHARDSON, W. H.: Captain, A. A. General May 11, 1861.
SMITH, F. W.: Captain, Military Secretary May 27, 1861.
SMITH, WILLIAM PRESTON: Lieutenant-colonel, Chief of Engineers July 31-Sept. 1863.
TALCOTT, T. M. R.: Major, A. D. C. Nov. 1862, July 31-Aug. 1863.
TAYLOR, WALTER H.: Captain C. S. A., A. D. C. Nov. 8, 1861-March 27, 1862; Major, A. D. C. Aug. 1862, July 31, Aug. 31, 1863; Lieutenant-colonel, A. A. General Nov. 4, 1864-1865.
VENABLE, CHARLES SCOTT (a cousin of the author): Major, A. D. C. July 31-Aug. 31,1863; Lieutenant-colonel, A. A. General Nov. 4, 1864-April 1865.
WASHINGTON, JOHN A. (a cousin of the author): Captain, A. D. C. May 6, 1861.
WASHINGTON, THORNTON A. (a cousin of the author): Captain, A. A. General Nov. 6, 1861.
YOUNG, H. E.: Captain, A. A. General July-Sept. 1863; Major, A. A. General Nov. 4, 1864.

APPENDIX B

General Lee's Civil War Engagements

Campaign in Western Virginia: August-October 1861
The Battle of Cheat Mountain: September 12-15, 1861
The Battle of Oak Grove: June 25, 1862
The Seven Days' Battle: June 26-July 2, 1862
- The Battle of Beaver Dam Creek: June 26, 1862
- The Battle of Gaines' Mill (Battle of Cold Harbor I): June 27, 1862
- The Battle of Glendale: June 30, 1862
- The Battle of Malvern Hill: July 1, 1862

The Battle of Second Manassas: August 30, 1862
The Battle of South Mountain: September 14, 1862
The Battle of Sharpsburg (Antietam): September 16-18, 1862
The Battle of Fredericksburg I: December 11-15, 1862
The Battle of Chancellorsville: April 30-May 6, 1863
The Battle of Salem Church: May 3-4, 1863
The Battle of Gettysburg: July 1-3, 1863
The Battle of Williamsport: July 6-16, 1863
The Battle of Rappahannock Station: November 7, 1863
The Battle of Mine Run: November 27-December 2, 1863
The Battle of the Wilderness: May 5-7, 1864
The Battle of Spotsylvania Court House: May 8-21, 1864
The Battle of North Anna: May 23-26, 1864
The Battle of Totopotomoy Creek: May 28-30, 1864
The Battle of Cold Harbor II: May 31-June 12, 1864
The Battle (Siege) of Petersburg II: June 15-18, 1864
The Battle of Jerusalem Plank Road: June 21-24, 1864
The Battle of the Crater: July 30, 1864
The Battle of Deep Bottom II: August 13-20, 1864
The Battle of Globe Tavern: August 18-21, 1864
The Battle of Chaffin's Farm: September 29-30, 1864
The Battle of Darbytown and New Market Roads: October 7, 1864
The Battle of Fort Stedman: March 25, 1865
The Battle of White Oak Road: March 31, 1865
The Battle of Petersburg III: April 2, 1865
The Battle of Cumberland Church: April 7, 1865
The Battle of Appomattox Court House: April 9, 1865

APPENDIX C

Lees Who Were Born at Stratford Hall

1. Phillip Ludwell Lee, 4th generation, Feb. 24, 1727
2. Hannah Lee, 4th generation, Feb. 6, 1728
3. John Lee, 4th generation, Mar. 28,1729
4. Lucy Lee, 4th generation, 1730
5. Thomas Ludwell Lee, 4th generation, Dec. 13, 1730
6. Richard Henry Lee, 4th generation, Jan 20, 1732
7. Francis Lightfoot Lee, 4th generation, Oct. 14, 1734
8. Alice Lee, 4th generation, June 4, 1736
9. William Lee, 4th generation, Aug. 31, 1739
10. Arthur Lee, 4th generation, Dec. 21, 1740
11. Matilda Lee, 5th generation
12. Flora Lee, 5th generation
13. Phillip Lee, 5th generation, Feb. 24, 1775
14. Nathaniel Greene Lee, 6th generation, 1784
15. Phillip Ludwell Lee, 6th generation, 1785
16. Lucy Grymes Lee, 6th generation, 1786
17. Henry Lee, 6th generation, May 28, 1787
18. Algernon Sydney Lee, 6th generation, April 2, 1795
19. Charles Carter Lee, 6th generation, Nov. 9, 1798
20. Anne Kinloch Lee, 6th generation, June 19, 1800
21. ROBERT EDWARD LEE, 6th generation, January 19, 1807
22. Margaret Lee, 7th generation

Lees who lived at Stratford but were not born there:

- Thomas Lee, 3rd generation, born at Mt. Pleasant, VA, 1690
- Richard Lee, 4th generation, born at Mt. Pleasant, VA, June 17, 1723.
- Henry Lee, 5th generation, born at Leesylvania, VA, Jan. 29, 1756.[383]

APPENDIX D

Robert E. Lee's Paternal Family Tree

Twenty-Six Generations - From Launcelot De Le to General Lee's Grandchildren

From the Author's Personal Family Tree

NOTES

- The names of those in the direct Lee line are bolded, with the first number indicating the generation.
- Spouses are listed below their husband or wife and are marked with a cross (+).
- Children are listed below their parents.
- The General and his descendants descend from European royalty, through both his father and his mother.
- I have limited the tree to twenty-six generations to protect the privacy of living relations.
- Warning: while I believe most of this information is accurate, not all of it has been genealogically validated. Generations one through eighteen, for example, are not yet known with complete certainty.
- Currently the General's earliest known ancestor is Launcelot De Le, born at Loudon, France, in the 11th Century. In 1066 Launcelot crossed the English Channel with William the Conqueror and fought valiantly at the Battle of Hastings. For his service, William, now king of England, gave Launcelot an estate in Essex County, England, from whence the English Lees originated and spread across Europe and into America. The surname Lee (or De Le or Lega) is extremely old, even appearing numerous times in the *Doomsday Book* of 1086.[384] One of Launcelot's descendants married a descendant of King William (see Hugo and Beatrice below); thus like the author, General Robert E. Lee descends from William the Conqueror.
- The surname Lee is an ancient place-name that derives from the French word *léaz*, meaning a "plain" or "untilled land."[385] (To this day there is a village in France named Léaz.) In Medieval England *léaz* was spelled *leie*, giving rise to the Old English word *leah*, meaning "woodland" or a "clearing in the woods," and later "meadow."[386] Thus someone living near or in a forest or pasture had the word *leah* appended to their first name. There are many Old and Middle English spelling variations of the Old English surname Leah: Lega, Lege, Leage, Leie, Le, Legh, Legha, Leghe, Leigh, Ley, Lea, Lee, Ley, Leys, Lay, Laye, Leye, Leygh, Lie, Lye, and Lyes.[387] A number of these surnames derive from the actual names of old villages and towns in England named Lee or Leigh, many which still exist.[388] The early Lee surnames contained the preposition *de* ("of"), or its variations: *de la*, *del*, *a la*, and *atte*. All have the rough meaning of "at the" or "of the." Thus the full name of General Lee's twenty-first great-grandfather, Launcelot De Le, literally means, "Launcelot who lives at the clearing in the woods."

1 **Launcelot De Le** (French progenitor of the English Lees), b: bet. 1020 and 1040 at Loudon, France; d: probably in Essex Co., England; Number of children: ? Gender: Male
..+_____ _____?, b: abt. 1050 in England? Number of children: ? Gender: female

..2_____ **De La Leigh**, b. abt. 1070 in Essex Co., England; Number of children: ? Gender: Male
....+_____ _____?, b: abt. 1072 in England; Number of children: ? Gender: female

...3_____ **De La Leigh**, b. abt. 1100 in Essex Co., England; Number of children: ? Gender: Male
.....+_____ _____?, b: abt. 1110 in England; Number of children: ? Gender: female

....4 **Hugo De La Leigh**, b: 1135 at Lea Hall, Shropshire, England; d: 1180; Number of children: ? Gender: Male
......+Beatrice De Glanville, b: abt. 1135 at Thurleigh, Bedfordshire, England; m: abt. 1151 at Bedfordshire, England; Number of children: ? Father: William De Glanville; Mother: Countess Gundred De Warren of Warwick, England; (Note: Gundred, of royal European lineage, was the second great-granddaughter of William the Conqueror, twenty-second King of England); Gender: Female

.....5 **Reginald De La Lee**, b: 1160 at Lea Hall, Shropshire, England; d: 1203; Number of children: ? Gender: Male
.......+_____ _____?, b: abt. 1162; Number of children: ? Gender: Female

......6 **John De La Lee**, b: 1201 at Lea Hall, Shropshire, England; d: 1301; Number of children: ? Gender: Male
.......+_____ _____?, b: abt. 1203; Number of children: ? Gender: Female

.......7 **Thomas De Lee**, b: 1230 at Moreton Corbet, Shropshire, England; Number of children: ? Gender: Male
.........+Petronella De Corbet, b: abt. 1238; m: abt. 1155; Number of children: ? Father: Richard De Corbet; Mother: Petronella De Booley, Lady; Gender: Female

........8 **Thomas De Lee**, b: 1260 at Shropshire, England; d: 1319; Number of children: ? Gender: Male
..........+Petronella De Stanton, b: abt. 1262 at England; m: 1286; Number of children: ? Gender: Female

.........9 **John De Lee**, b: 1290 at Pimhill, Shropshire, England; d: 1350; Number of children: ? Gender: Male
..........+Matilda De Erdington, b: abt. 1292 at Erdington, Shropshire, England; Father: Henry De Erdington; Mother: Joan De Wolvey; Number of children: ? Gender: Female

..........10 **Thomas De Lee**, Sir/Sheriff, b: abt. 1320 at Stanton, Shropshire, England; Number of children: ? Gender: Male
............+Sibella ______?, b: abt. 1320 in England; Number of children: ? Gender: Female

...........11 **Rodger De Lee**, b: abt. 1356 at Coton Hall, Nordley Regis, Alveley Parish, Shropshire, England; d: 1419; Number of children: ? Gender: Male
.............+Margaret Astley, b: abt. 1358 at Coton Hall, Nordley Regis, Alveley Parish, Shropshire, England; d: 1423; Father: Thomas De Astley; Number of children: ? Gender: Female

............12 **Robert Lee**, b: 1396 at Langley, Shropshire, England; Number of children: ? Gender: Male
..............+Petronella Lee, b: abt. 1385 at Langley, Shropshire, England; m: abt. 1405; Number of children: ? Father: Roger Lee; Mother: Joanna Burnell; Gender: Female

.............13 **Ralph Lee**, b: abt. 1406 at Langley, Shropshire, England; d: 14 Dec 1479; Number of children: ? Gender: Male
...............+Isabella Ridley, b: 1410 at Alkington, Shropshire, England; m: in Shropshire, England; Father: Jacob Ridley; Number of children: ? Gender: Female

..............14 **Richard Lee**, b: 1432 at Langley, Shropshire, England; d: 1496; Number of children: ? Gender: Male
................+Margery Sprencheaux, b: abt. 1450 at Langley, Shropshire, England; Father: Fulco Sprencheaux; Number of children: ? Gender: Female

...............15 **Fulke Lee**, b: abt. 1478 at Langley, Shropshire, England; Number of children: ? Gender: Male
.................+Alice Cornwall, b: abt. 1482 at Berington, Hereford, England; Number of children: ? Father: Henry Cornwall; Mother: Jane Milbourne; Gender: Female

................16 **Thomas Lee**, b: abt. 1509 at Langley, Shropshire, England; d: bef. 1619 in England; Number of children: ? Gender: Male
..................+______ Hoke, b: abt. 1513 at Langley, Shropshire, England; m: abt. 1531 at Langley, Shropshire, England; d: bef. 1623; Number of children: ? Gender: Female

.................17 **Johannes Lee**, b: 1530 at Colton, Shropshire, England; d: 14 May 1605 in Shropshire, England; Number of children: ? Gender: Male
...................+Joyce Romney, b: 1529 in England; m: 1553 in England; d: 1609 in England; Number of children: ? Gender: Female

.................18 **John Lee**, b: 12 July 1590 at Worcestershire, England; Number of

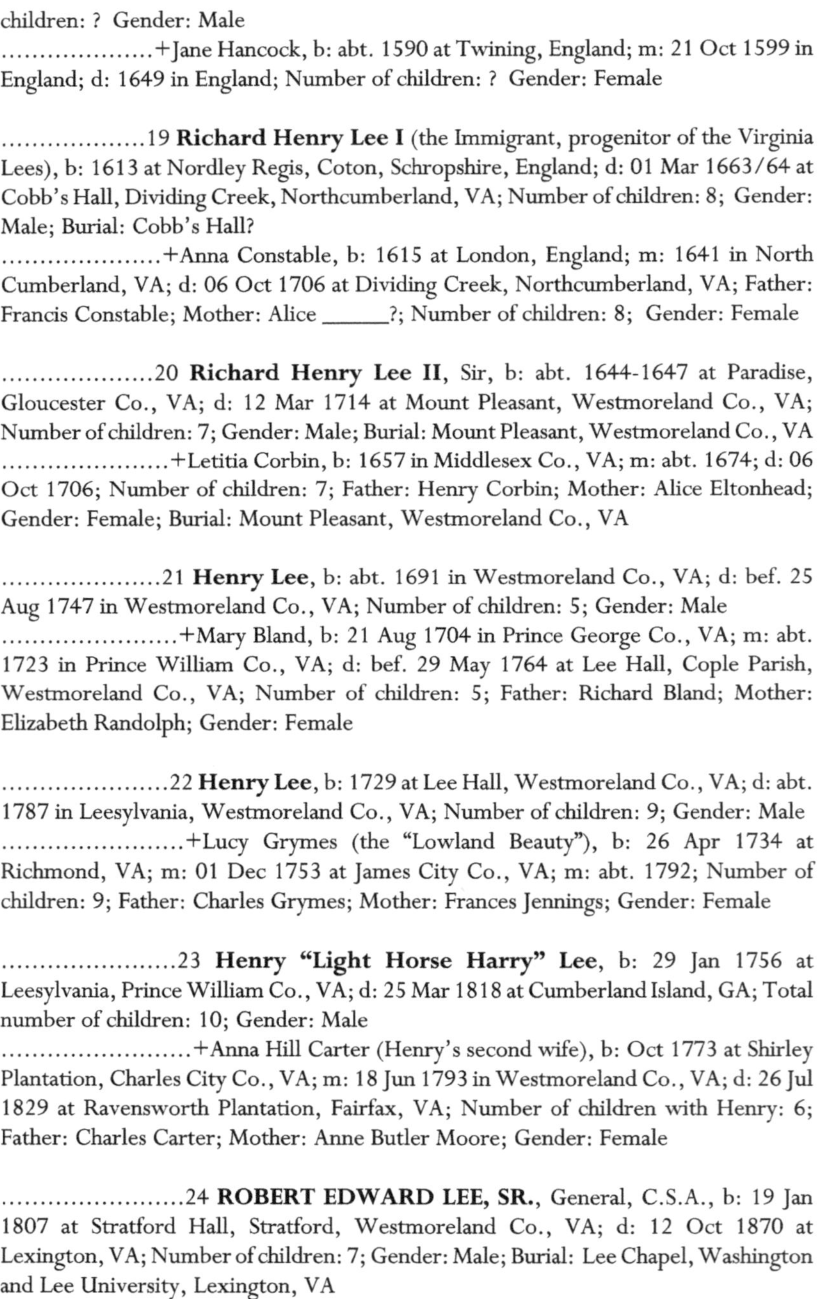

children: ? Gender: Male
....................+Jane Hancock, b: abt. 1590 at Twining, England; m: 21 Oct 1599 in England; d: 1649 in England; Number of children: ? Gender: Female

...................19 **Richard Henry Lee I** (the Immigrant, progenitor of the Virginia Lees), b: 1613 at Nordley Regis, Coton, Schropshire, England; d: 01 Mar 1663/64 at Cobb's Hall, Dividing Creek, Northcumberland, VA; Number of children: 8; Gender: Male; Burial: Cobb's Hall?
.....................+Anna Constable, b: 1615 at London, England; m: 1641 in North Cumberland, VA; d: 06 Oct 1706 at Dividing Creek, Northcumberland, VA; Father: Francis Constable; Mother: Alice ______?; Number of children: 8; Gender: Female

....................20 **Richard Henry Lee II**, Sir, b: abt. 1644-1647 at Paradise, Gloucester Co., VA; d: 12 Mar 1714 at Mount Pleasant, Westmoreland Co., VA; Number of children: 7; Gender: Male; Burial: Mount Pleasant, Westmoreland Co., VA
......................+Letitia Corbin, b: 1657 in Middlesex Co., VA; m: abt. 1674; d: 06 Oct 1706; Number of children: 7; Father: Henry Corbin; Mother: Alice Eltonhead; Gender: Female; Burial: Mount Pleasant, Westmoreland Co., VA

.....................21 **Henry Lee**, b: abt. 1691 in Westmoreland Co., VA; d: bef. 25 Aug 1747 in Westmoreland Co., VA; Number of children: 5; Gender: Male
.......................+Mary Bland, b: 21 Aug 1704 in Prince George Co., VA; m: abt. 1723 in Prince William Co., VA; d: bef. 29 May 1764 at Lee Hall, Cople Parish, Westmoreland Co., VA; Number of children: 5; Father: Richard Bland; Mother: Elizabeth Randolph; Gender: Female

......................22 **Henry Lee**, b: 1729 at Lee Hall, Westmoreland Co., VA; d: abt. 1787 in Leesylvania, Westmoreland Co., VA; Number of children: 9; Gender: Male
........................+Lucy Grymes (the "Lowland Beauty"), b: 26 Apr 1734 at Richmond, VA; m: 01 Dec 1753 at James City Co., VA; m: abt. 1792; Number of children: 9; Father: Charles Grymes; Mother: Frances Jennings; Gender: Female

.......................23 **Henry "Light Horse Harry" Lee**, b: 29 Jan 1756 at Leesylvania, Prince William Co., VA; d: 25 Mar 1818 at Cumberland Island, GA; Total number of children: 10; Gender: Male
.........................+Anna Hill Carter (Henry's second wife), b: Oct 1773 at Shirley Plantation, Charles City Co., VA; m: 18 Jun 1793 in Westmoreland Co., VA; d: 26 Jul 1829 at Ravensworth Plantation, Fairfax, VA; Number of children with Henry: 6; Father: Charles Carter; Mother: Anne Butler Moore; Gender: Female

........................24 **ROBERT EDWARD LEE, SR.**, General, C.S.A., b: 19 Jan 1807 at Stratford Hall, Stratford, Westmoreland Co., VA; d: 12 Oct 1870 at Lexington, VA; Number of children: 7; Gender: Male; Burial: Lee Chapel, Washington and Lee University, Lexington, VA

..........................+Mary Anne Randolph Custis (the great-granddaughter of Martha Dandridge, the wife of U.S. President George Washington), b: 01 Oct 1808 at Arlington, VA; m: 30 June 1831 at Arlington House; d: 05 Nov 1873 at Stratford Hall, Westmoreland Co., VA; Number of children: 7; Father: George Washington Parke Custis; Mother: Mary Anne Randolph Fitzhugh; Gender: female

........................25 **George Washington Custis "Boo" Lee**, b: 16 Sep 1832 at Arlington House, Arlington, VA; d: 18 Feb 1913 at Ravensworth, Fairfax, VA; Gender: Male; Burial: Lee Chapel, Lexington, VA (he never married)
........................25 **Mary Custis Lee**, b: 12 Jul 1835 at Arlington House, Arlington, VA; d: 22 Nov 1918 in VA; Gender: Female; Burial: Lee Chapel, Lexington, VA (she never married)
........................25 **William Henry "Rooney" Fitzhugh Lee**, b: 31 May 1837 at Arlington House, Arlington , VA; d: 15 Oct 1891 in VA; Total number of children: 7; Gender: Male; Burial: Lee Chapel, Lexington, VA
..........................+Charlotte Georgiana Wickham (first wife of William Henry Fitzhugh Lee), b: 1841 in Fairfax Co., VA; m: 23 Mar 1859 at Shirley Plantation, Richmond, VA; d: 26 Dec 1863; Number of children: 2; Father: George Wickham; Mother: Charlotte Carter; Gender: Female; Burial: Shockoe Hill Cemetery, Richmond, VA

..........................26 **Robert Edward Lee III** (a), b: 09 Mar 1860 in New Kent Co., VA; d: 30 June 1862 at Richmond, VA; Burial: Shockoe Hill Cemetery, Richmond, VA
..........................26 **Charlotte Carter Lee**, b: 19 Oct 1862 in VA; d: 06 Dec 1862, VA; Burial: Shockoe Hill Cemetery, Richmond, VA

............................+Mary Tabb Bolling (second wife of William Henry Fitzhugh Lee), b: 27 Aug 1846 at Petersburg, VA; m: 28 Nov 1867, VA; d: 05 May 1924; Number of children: 5; Father: George Washington Bolling; Mother: Martha Smith Nichols; Gender: Female; Burial: Lee Chapel, Lexington, VA

..........................26 **Anne Agnes Lee**, b: unknown; d: 1874; Gender: Female; Burial: Lee Chapel, Lexington, VA (died young)
..........................26 **William Henry Fitzhugh Lee, Jr.**, b: unknown; d: 1875; Gender: Male; Burial: Lee Chapel, Lexington, VA (died young)
..........................26 **Mary Tabb Lee**, b: unknown at Petersburg, VA; d: 1871; Gender: Female; Burial: Lee Chapel, Lexington, VA (died young)
..........................26 **Robert Edward Lee III** (b), b: 11 Feb 1869 at Petersburg, VA; d: 07 Sep 1922 at Petersburg, VA; Gender: Male; Burial: Magnolia Cemetery, Charleston, SC
............................+Mary Wilkerson Middleton, b: 14 Aug 1874 at Charleston, SC; d: 19 May 1959 at Asheville, NC; Father: Ralph Izard Middleton; Mother: Sarah Virginia Memminger; Gender: Female; Burial: Magnolia Cemetery, Charleston, SC

............................26 **George Bolling Lee**, b: 31 Aug 1872 at Fairfax Co., VA; d: 13 Jul 1948 at New York, NY; Gender: Male; Burial: Lee Chapel, Lexington, VA
..............................+Helen Keeney, b: 26 Sep 1895 at San Francisco, CA; d: 08 Jul 1968; Father: Charles C. Keeney; Mother: Adele Maria Jones; Gender: Female; Burial: Lee Chapel, Lexington, VA

.........................25 **Anne Carter "Annie" Lee**, b: 18 Jun 1839 at Arlington House, Arlington, VA; d: 20 Oct 1862 at Warrenton, NC; Gender: Female; Burial: Lee Chapel, Lexington, VA (she never married)
.........................25 **Eleanor Agnes "Wigs" Lee**, b: 27 Feb 1841 at Arlington House, Arlington, VA; d: 1873 at Lexington, VA; Gender: Female; Burial: Lee Chapel, Lexington, VA (she never married)
.........................25 **Robert Edward Lee, Jr.**, b: 27 Oct 1843 at Arlington House, Arlington, VA; d: 19 Oct 1914 at Richmond, VA; Number of children: 2; Gender: Male; Burial: Lee Chapel, Lexington, VA
............................+Charlotte Taylor Haxall (first wife of Robert E. Lee, Jr.), b: 23 Oct 1848 at Orange Co., VA; m: 16 Nov 1871; d: 22 Sep 1872 at West Point, King William Co., VA; Father: Richard Barton Haxall; Mother: Octavia Robinson; Number of children: none known; Gender: Female; Burial: Hollywood Cemetery, Richmond, VA
............................+Juliet Carter (second wife of Robert E. Lee, Jr.), b: 06 Apr 1860; m: abt. 1896; d: 17 Nov 1915; Number of children: 2; Father: Thomas Hill Carter; Mother: Susan Elizabeth Roy; Gender: Female; Burial: Lee Chapel, Lexington, VA

............................26 **Anne Carter Lee**, b: 21 Jul 1897; d: 08 Nov 1978 at Upperville, Fauquier Co., VA; Number of children: 2; Gender: Female; Burial: Ivy Hill Cemetery, Upperville, Fauquier Co., VA
..............................+Hanson Edward Ely, Jr., b: 31 Mar 1896 in MT; d: 29 Sep 1938 in NJ; Number of children: 2; Father: Hanson Edward Ely, Sr.; Mother: Mary Barber; Gender: Male: Burial: Arlington National Cemetery, Arlington, VA
............................26 **Mary Custis Lee**, b: 23 Dec 1900 at Richmond, VA; d: 26 Dec 1994 in VA; Number of children: 3; Gender: Female
..............................+William Hunter De Butts, b: 23 Oct 1899 in VA; m: 01 Oct 1925; d: 23 Nov 1987; Number of children: 3; Father: Dulaney Forrest De Butts; Mother: Emma Ashby; Gender: Male; Burial: Ivy Hill Cemetery, Upperville, Fauquier Co., VA

.........................25 **Mildred Childe "Precious Life" Lee**, b: 10 Feb 1846 at Arlington House, Arlington, VA; d: March 27, 1905 at New Orleans, LA; Gender: Female; Burial: Lee Chapel, Lexington, VA (she never married)

APPENDIX E

Lee Family Real Estate

A partial alphabetized list of the names of the American homes, estates, farms, and plantations built, owned, or lived in by the Lees and/or their collateral relations

Note: Only a handful of the Lees' original homes survive into the present day. Some were intentionally burned by Yankee troops during Lincoln's War, some were demolished in the 20th Century to make way for new roads and housing developments, many were simply abandoned and fell into disrepair. A number, known only by a reference in a 200-year old letter or an obscure court document, completely disappeared, were recently rediscovered, and are now archaeological sites. Of those residences still standing, at least one has been turned into a modern organic farm. A few have been beautifully restored and are now popular tourist sites. Sadly, we can be sure that a number of Lee family dwellings have vanished without leaving a trace, and whose beauty and history will thus never be known.

All Hallows
Allstadt House
Anchorage
Annefield
Arch Hall
Arlington House
Belleview/Bellevue
Belmont
Blair-Lee House
Bland House
Blenheim
Brookfield
Buckland Hall
Cabin Point
Carter Hall
Cedar Grove
Chantilly
Charles Lee House
Chatham
Clarens
Clermont
Clifts Plantation
Cobb's Hall
Coton
Derwent
Ditchly/Ditchley
Dungeness
Duvall House
Eagle's Nest
Eckington
Edmund Jennings Lee House
Effingham
Fairfield
Farmwell

Glebe House
Gordansdale
Greenspring
Henry Lee House
Hickory Hill
Highland Home
Horn Quarter
Lansdowne
Law-Lee House
Lee Cabin
Lee-Fendall House
Lee Hall
Lee-Hopkins House
Leeland
Leeland Orchards
Lee-Longsworth House
Lee's Greenbrier Cottage
Lee's Quarters at Fortress Monroe
Lee's Richmond Home
Leesylvania
Leeton
Leeton Forest
Lloyd House
Ludwell House
Mansfield
Meadow Farm
Menokin
Mount Airy
Mount Pleasant
Norwood
Pagebrook
Pampatike
Paradiose
Park Gate
President's House
Ravensworth
Richland
Richard Bland Lee House
Robert E. Lee's Boyhood Home
Rockland
Sabine Hall
Salona
Selma
Shirley Plantation
Shooter's (or Shuter's) Hill
Stratford Hall
Strawberry Vale Manor
Sully Plantation
Thomas Law House
Wakefield
Walnut Farm
White House
White Marsh
Windsor Forest

NOTES

1. See Seabrook, L, p. 635.
2. To learn the truth about the Emancipation Proclamation, see Seabrook, EYWTACWW, pp. 136-145.
3. Riley, p. 200.
4. Howe, pp. 510-511.
5. Jones, LL, pp. 13-14.
6. F. Lee, p. 2.
7. Williamson, p. 10.
8. Cooke, p. 13.
9. Speer, p. 47.
10. Cooke, p. 17.
11. Williamson, pp. 14-16.
12. Alexander, p. 205.
13. R. E. Lee, Jr., pp. 325-326.
14. Walker, p. 304.
15. Alexander, pp. 204-205.
16. Alexander, pp. 206-207.
17. Walker, p. 304.
18. McKim, p. 9.
19. McGuire, p. 39.
20. R. E. Lee, Jr., p. 17.
21. Jones, PR, pp. 133-134.
22. R. E. Lee, Jr., p. 14.
23. Speer, p. 55.
24. Long and Wright, p. 44.
25. Walker, pp. 306-307.
26. Gilman, pp. 22-23.
27. Munford, p. 156.
28. Trent, pp. 9-11.
29. Walker, pp. 305-306.
30. McKim, p. 10.
31. Long and Wright, p. 463.
32. Long and Wright, p. 463.
33. R. E. Lee, Jr., pp. 9-10.
34. R. E. Lee, Jr., p. 324.
35. R. E. Lee, Jr., p. 12.
36. R. E. Lee, Jr., p. 271.
37. R. E. Lee, Jr., p. 13.
38. R. E. Lee, Jr., p. 245.
39. R. E. Lee, Jr., pp. 249-250.
40. Foote, p. 171.
41. Cooke, p. 28.
42. Alexander, pp. 212-216.
43. Pollard, LHL, pp. 54-55.
44. In 1913 Henry Lee's remains were removed to Lee's Chapel, Lexington, Virginia.
45. Bruce, p. 23.
46. Jones, PR, p. 484.
47. Long and Wright, pp. 241-242.
48. Hopkins, pp. 49-50.
49. White, pp. 230-231.
50. Long and Wright, pp. 259-260.
51. White, p. 300.
52. White, pp. 318-319.

53. Long and Wright, p. 302.
54. White, p. 325.
55. Stiles, p. 189.
56. White, p. 334.
57. Jones, PR, p. 162.
58. White, p. 349.
59. R. E. Lee, Jr., pp. 118-119.
60. Jones, LL, p. 449.
61. Long and Wright, p. 301.
62. Jones, PR, pp. 162-163.
63. R. E. Lee, Jr., pp. 76-77.
64. Long and Wright, p. 306.
65. White, p. 413.
66. White, pp. 334-335.
67. Hopkins, pp. 115-116.
68. White, pp. 349-350.
69. Hopkins, pp. 91-92.
70. Long and Wright, p. 338.
71. R. E. Lee, Jr., p. 200.
72. Hopkins, pp. 128-129.
73. Stiles, p. 239.
74. Long and Wright, pp. 386-387.
75. White, pp. 361-362.
76. Gilman, pp. 123-124.
77. Long and Wright, pp. 387-388.
78. Hopkins, pp. 217-218.
79. Jones, PR, p. 410.
80. R. E. Lee, Jr., pp. 77-78.
81. Long and Wright, p. 388.
82. Jones, LL, p. 401.
83. R. E. Lee, Jr., pp. 106-107.
84. Long and Wright, p. 387.
85. Long and Wright, pp. 388-389.
86. R. E. Lee, Jr., pp. 73-74.
87. Jones, LL, pp. 454-455.
88. Long and Wright, pp. 240-241.
89. R. E. Lee, Jr., p. 74.
90. Hopkins, pp. 182-184.
91. Longstreet, pp. 620-621.
92. Jones, PR, p. 411.
93. Childe, p. 190.
94. White, p. 363.
95. R. E. Lee, Jr., p. 87.
96. Speer, p. 72.
97. Stiles, pp. 259-260.
98. Hopkins, pp. 193-194.
99. Hopkins, pp. 155-156.
100. Jones, PR, p. 169.
101. Jones, PR, p. 148.
102. Riley, p. 103.
103. White, p. 235.
104. White, p. 335.
105. White, pp. 375-376.
106. Jones, PR, pp. 409-410.

107. White, p. 421.
108. White, p. 421.
109. Long and Wright, pp. 421-422.
110. McCabe, p. 634.
111. Long and Wright, p. 426.
112. Long and Wright, p. 426.
113. White, pp. 426-427.
114. Long and Wright, pp. 240-241.
115. White, p. 424.
116. W. H. Taylor, p. 153.
117. Swinton, p. 621.
118. R. E. Lee, Jr., p. 155.
119. R. E. Lee, Jr., p. 265.
120. Riley, p. 136.
121. Riley, p. 68.
122. R. E. Lee, Jr., p. 279.
123. Riley, p. 68.
124. Riley, pp. 73-74.
125. McGuire, pp. 179-182.
126. Riley, p. 127.
127. Riley, pp. 137-138.
128. Riley, p. 107.
129. R. E. Lee, Jr., pp. 314-315.
130. R. E. Lee, Jr., pp. 315-316.
131. Riley, pp. 142-143.
132. Riley, pp. 50-51.
133. R. E. Lee, Jr., p. 346.
134. Riley, p. 107.
135. Riley, pp. 108-109.
136. R. E. Lee, Jr., p. 132.
137. R. E. Lee, Jr., p. 332.
138. Riley, p. 50.
139. General Lee's U.S. citizenship was restored to him by an act of the U.S. Congress in 1975. Seabrook, TQREL, p. 231; Phillips, FWNE, s.v. "Robert Edward Lee."
140. R. E. Lee, Jr., pp. 347-348.
141. R. E. Lee, Jr., p. 410.
142. R. E. Lee, Jr., p. 410.
143. R. E. Lee, Jr., pp. 408-409.
144. Riley, p. 32.
145. Walker, p. 312.
146. Riley, p. 60.
147. Jones, PR, pp. 410-411.
148. Page, p. 670.
149. Page, p. 671.
150. Riley, p. 47.
151. R. E. Lee, Jr., p. 325.
152. Riley, pp. 135-136.
153. Riley, pp. 65-66.
154. Riley, p. 49.
155. R. E. Lee, Jr., p. 275.
156. Seabrook, ARB, p. 8; Riley, pp. 71-72.
157. Riley, pp. 80-81.
158. Riley, p. 110.
159. R. E. Lee, Jr., p. 351.

160. Riley, p. 111.
161. Riley, p. 109.
162. Riley, p. 114.
163. Riley, p. 51.
164. Riley, pp. 49-50.
165. Gilman, p. 196.
166. Jones, LL, p. 402.
167. R. E. Lee, Jr., p. 267.
168. Riley, pp. 153-154.
169. Jones, CITC, pp. 59-60.
170. Riley, pp. 128-129.
171. Riley, p. 154.
172. Riley, pp. 36-37.
173. Long and Wright, pp. 437-438.
174. R. E. Lee, Jr., p. 405.
175. R. E. Lee, Jr., p. 316.
176. Long and Wright, p. 461.
177. Jones, PR, p. 433.
178. R. E. Lee, Jr., p. 160.
179. Riley, pp. 52-53.
180. Jones, LL, p. 453.
181. Long and Wright, p. 461.
182. Bond, pp. 24-26.
183. Riley, p. 39.
184. Riley, p. 17.
185. R. E. Lee, Jr., p. 317.
186. R. E. Lee, Jr., p. 165.
187. R. E. Lee, Jr., pp. 357-358.
188. Long and Wright, p. 462.
189. Long and Wright, pp. 462-463.
190. Riley, p. 55.
191. Riley, p. 125.
192. Riley, p. 62.
193. Riley, p. 43.
194. Iles, pp. 76-79.
195. R. E. Lee, Jr., pp. 371-372.
196. R. E. Lee, Jr., p. 388.
197. R. E. Lee, Jr., pp. 392-393.
198. R. E. Lee, Jr., pp. 289-290.
199. Riley, pp. 63-64.
200. Riley, p. 19.
201. Page, pp. 664-665.
202. Riley, p. 21.
203. Long and Wright, p. 474.
204. Childe, p. 334.
205. R. E. Lee, Jr., pp. 434-439.
206. Riley, p. 31.
207. McGuire, pp. 197-198.
208. Walker, p. 312.
209. Riley, p. 128.
210. Riley, p. 130.
211. Jones, LL, p. 479.
212. Long and Wright, pp. 474-475.
213. Jones, PR, p. 61.

214. Williamson, p. 148.
215. Riley, p. 66.
216. Jones, PR, p. 71.
217. Long and Wright, p. 61.
218. Long and Wright, p. 35. This quote was constructed from the words of Long and Wright.
219. R. E. Lee, Jr., p. 407.
220. Long and Wright, p. 37. This quote was constructed from the words of Long and Wright.
221. R. E. Lee, Jr., p. 141.
222. Page, p. 597.
223. Hopkins, pp. 76-77.
224. Jones, PR, p. 58.
225. R. E. Lee, Jr., p. 6.
226. Page, p. 114.
227. Long and Wright, pp. 66-67, 70.
228. Riley, p. 62.
229. See Munford, p. 156.
230. Long and Wright, pp. 489-490.
231. Jones, LL, pp. 36-37.
232. McGuire, p. 39.
233. Jones, PR, pp. 134-135.
234. White, p. 37.
235. Long and Wright, pp. 79-80.
236. R. E. Lee, Jr., p. 137.
237. Jones, PR, p. 60.
238. Williamson, pp. 149-150.
239. Jones, LL, pp. 397-399.
240. Childe, p. 185.
241. Pollard, LC, pp. 654-655.
242. Pollard, EL, p. 44.
243. Page, p. 609.
244. Jones, PR, pp. 60-61.
245. Cooke, pp. 518-519.
246. G. Bradford, p. 232.
247. Long and Wright, pp. 228-229.
248. Cooke, pp. 31-32.
249. Page, p. 666.
250. Riley, p. 204.
251. Jones, LL, p. 450.
252. Jones, PR, p. 59.
253. McGuire, pp. 184-185.
254. Long and Wright, p. 423.
255. Page, pp. 120-121.
256. Jones, LL, p. 470.
257. Riley, p. 185.
258. White, p. 170.
259. Long and Wright, p. 451.
260. Page, pp. 666-667.
261. Lee, of course, did not try to "destroy" the U.S. government. It was Lincoln who demolished the "voluntary union of friendly states," ingeniously envisioned and carefully crafted by the Founding Fathers. Lee and the rest of his Confederate brothers and sisters tried to preserve it. This bold fact has been suppressed by pro-North historians and writers for the past 150 years in an effort to justify Lincoln's unjustifiable War. In its place, out of Lincoln's great anti-South propaganda machine, arose one of the North's most cherished myths, that "it was the South's aim to destroy the Union." For detailed discussions on the Confederate Republic intended by the Founding Generation—which the Southern Confederacy fought

to maintain—see Seabrook EYWTACWW, pp. 40-53; Seabrook, AL, pp. 31-102; Seabrook, L, pp. 202-214; Seabrook, TMCP, pp. 278-369.
262. In my opinion, and in the opinion of many other Southerners as well as Northerners, the U.S. today is still a divided nation South from North. This cultural divide has existed since the days of the original Thirteen Colonies, and was only widened and deepened by Lincoln's War. I personally believe it will always exist, despite the best efforts of so many Yankees to Northernize Dixie; a futile and egotistical attempt to make the spiritual, leisurely-paced, conservative, agriculturally oriented South an exact duplicate of the atheistic, fast-paced, liberal, industrially oriented North. As a traditional Southern agrarian, I will continue to personally resist this trend, and it is hoped that my fellow traditionalists, and those who come after me—whether Southern or Northern—will fight it as well. The South is unique, and always has been. We would like it to remain that way.
263. Alexander, pp. 224-233.
264. Childe, pp. 188-190.
265. F. Lee, pp. 398-399.
266. Riley, pp. 197-198.
267. Stiles, p. 165.
268. Long and Wright, p. 433.
269. Riley, p. 116.
270. Cooke, p. 541.
271. Hopkins, p. 87.
272. Jones, PR, p. 147.
273. White, p. 41.
274. Hopkins, pp. 139-140.
275. Cooke, p. 488.
276. Riley, p. 117.
277. Jones, PR, p. 411.
278. R. E. Lee, Jr., pp. 231-232.
279. Garrison began calling slavery a "crime" and slave owners "criminals," despite the fact that slavery was legal all across the U.S. While Garrison's feelings are understandable to us today, referring to Southern owners of black servants as felons could only anger the inhabitants of Dixie and postpone the inevitable destruction of Southern slavery—which is precisely what occurred. For delaying emancipation by many decades *and* contributing so heavily to the sectional bitterness that fueled Lincoln's War, traditional Southerners continue to deplore the name of William Lloyd Garrison. For more on this topic see Seabrook, EYWTACWW, pp. 105-108.
280. White, p. 28.
281. Fremantle, pp. 253-254.
282. Walker, p. 305.
283. Childe, pp. 35-36.
284. R. E. Lee, Jr., p. 19.
285. Page, p. 616.
286. Riley, p. 120.
287. Jones, PR, pp. 168-169.
288. Long and Wright, p. 435.
289. Riley, p. 120.
290. Riley, p. 77.
291. Cooke, p. 509.
292. Riley, pp. 77-79.
293. Page, pp. 32-33.
294. Cooke, pp. 555-556.
295. White, p. 142.
296. R. E. Lee, Jr., p. 244.
297. Long and Wright, p. 436.
298. Riley, pp. 96-97.
299. Page, p. 617.

300. Gilman, p. 130.
301. White, p. 414.
302. Jones, PR, p. 482.
303. Long and Wright, pp. 478-479.
304. Riley, p. 53.
305. Alexander, p. 217.
306. R. E. Lee, Jr., p. 95.
307. R. E. Lee, Jr., p. 20.
308. Childe, pp. 190-191.
309. Page, pp. 685-686.
310. R. E. Lee, Jr., p. 137.
311. Long and Wright, p. 479.
312. Long and Wright, pp. 479-480.
313. Riley, p. 98.
314. Alexander, pp. 262-263.
315. Riley, p. 26.
316. Jones, PR, pp. 62-63.
317. Jones, PR, pp. 61-62.
318. Page, pp. 617-618.
319. Riley, pp. 100-101.
320. Alexander, pp. 219-224.
321. McKim, p. 3.
322. Gilman, p. 172.
323. Williamson, p. 150.
324. Riley, p. 101.
325. Long and Wright, p. 495.
326. R. E. Lee, Jr., p. 138.
327. G. Bradford, p. 246.
328. R. E. Lee, Jr., p. 75.
329. Bruce, p. 364.
330. Jones, PR, p. 56.
331. Mckim, p. 29.
332. Page, p. 619.
333. Riley, pp. 95-96.
334. R. E. Lee, Jr., p. 103.
335. Page, pp. 563-564.
336. White, pp. 441-442.
337. R. E. Lee, Jr., p. 148.
338. Walker, pp. 307-308.
339. Riley, p. 67.
340. Page, p. 647.
341. R. E. Lee, Jr., p. 172.
342. McKim, p. 180.
343. Riley, p. 72.
344. McKim, p. 80.
345. Alexander, p. 263.
346. Jones, PR, pp. 198-199.
347. McKim, p. 80.
348. Page, p. 579.
349. McKim, p. iii.
350. R. E. Lee, Jr., p. 233.
351. McKim, p. 194.
352. Long and Wright, p. 491.
353. Long and Wright, p. 492.

354. McKim, p. 80.
355. Bruce, pp. 356-357.
356. Page, p. 651.
357. McKim, p. 3.
358. Page, pp. 682-683.
359. McKim, p. 194.
360. T. C. Johnson, p. 500.
361. Seabrook, TQREL, p. 213; Seabrook, EYWTACWW, p. 206.
362. McKim, p. 154.
363. McKim, pp. 198-200.
364. Page, p. 639.
365. McKim, p. 116.
366. Johnston, p. 308.
367. McKim, p. 116.
368. McKim, p. 194.
369. McKim, p. 40.
370. "Lee's Centennial," *Washington and Lee University, October 1916 Bulletin*, Vol. 15, No. 5, Address of Charles Francis Adams, Jr., January 19, 1907, p. 19.
371. Both Richard and Francis were first cousins twice removed of General Robert E. Lee. From the author's personal family tree.
372. Page, pp. 4-5.
373. Cooke, p. 577.
374. McKim, p. 202.
375. Field, pp. 295-296.
376. McKim, p. 68.
377. Trent, pp. 130-131.
378. McKim, p. 116.
379. Gilman, p. 205.
380. McKim, p. 208.
381. McKim, p. 94.
382. Jones, PR, p. 473.
383. This information is from Alexander's *Stratford Hall and the Lees Connected With Its History*.
384. Mead, pp. 9, 12.
385. Mead, pp. 11-12.
386. Mills, p. 405.
387. Reaney and Wilson, s.v. "Lea."
388. Mills, s.v. "Lee"; "Leigh."

BIBLIOGRAPHY

Alexander, Frederick Warren. *Stratford Hall and the Lees Connected With its History: Biographical, Genealogical and Historical.* Oak Grove, VA: Historical Society of Virginia, 1912.

Bond, Christiana. *Memories of General Robert E. Lee.* Baltimore, MD: Norman, Remington Co., 1926.

Bowden, Scott, and Bill Ward. *Last Chance For Victory: Robert E. Lee and the Gettysburg Campaign.* 2001. Cambridge, MA: Da Capo Press, 2003 ed.

Bradford, Gamaliel, Jr. *Lee the American.* Boston, MA: Houghton Mifflin Co., 1912.

Bradford, James C. (ed.). *Atlas of American Military History.* New York, NY: Oxford University Press, 2003.

Brock, Robert Alonzo, and Virgil Anson Lewis. *Virginia and Virginians* (Vol. 1). Richmond, VA: H. H. Hardesty, 1888.

Bruce, Philip Alexander. *Robert E. Lee.* Philadelphia, PA: George W. Jacobs and Co., 1907.

Burke, John. *Burke's Peerage: Genealogical and Heraldic History of the Baronetage and Knightage* (104th ed.) 1826. London, UK: Waterlow and Sons, 1967 ed.

Childe, Edward Lee. *The Life and Campaigns of General Lee.* London, UK: Chatto and Windus, 1875.

Cooke, John Esten. *A Life of Gen. Robert E. Lee.* New York, NY: D. Appleton & Co., 1883.

Encyclopedia Britannica: A New Survey of Universal Knowledge. 1768. Chicago, IL/London, UK: Encyclopedia Britannica, 1955 ed.

Field, Henry Martyn. *Bright Skies and Dark Shadows.* New York, NY: Charles Scribner's Sons, 1890.

Figgis, John Neville, and Reginald Vere Laurence (eds.). *Selections From the Correspondence of the First Lord Acton* (Vol. 1). London, UK: Longmans, Green and Co., 1917.

Foote, Henry Stuart. *Casket of Reminiscences.* Washington, D.C.: Chronicle Publishing Co., 1874.

Fremantle, Arthur James Lyon. *Three Months in the Southern States: April-June, 1863.* Edinburgh, UK: William Blackwood and Sons, 1863.

Gilman, Bradley. *Robert E. Lee.* New York, NY: The Macmillan Co., 1915.

Iles, George (ed.). *Little Masterpieces of Autobiography.* 1885. New York, NY: Doubleday, Page and Co., 1908 ed.

Hill, Frederick Trevor. *On the Trail of Grant and Lee.* New York, NY: D. Appleton and Co., 1911.

Hopkins, Luther W. *From Bull Run to Appomattox: A Boy's View.* Baltimore, MD: Fleet-McGinley Co., 1914.

Howe, Henry. *Historical Collections of Virginia.* Charleston, SC: Babcock and Co., 1845.

Johnson, Thomas Carey. *The Life and Letters of Robert Lewis Dabney* (Vol. 3). Richmond, VA: The Presbyterian Committee of Publication, 1903.

Johnston, Robert Matteson. *Leading American Soldiers.* New York, NY: Henry Holt and Co., 1907.

Jones, John William. *Personal Reminiscences, Anecdotes, and Letters of Gen. Robert E. Lee.* New York, NY: D. Appleton & Co., 1874.

——. *Christ in the Camp, or Religion in the Confederate Army.* 1887. Atlanta, GA: The Martin and Hoyt Co., 1904 ed.

——. *Life and Letters of Robert Edward Lee: Soldier and Man.* New York, NY: Neale Publishing Co., 1906.

Lee, Fitzhugh. *General Lee*. New York, NY: The University Society, 1905.

Lee, Henry. *Memoirs of the War in the Southern Department of the United States*. New York, NY: University Publishing Co., 1869.

Lee, Robert E. Lee, Jr. *Recollections and Letters of General Robert E. Lee*. New York, NY: Doubleday, Page, & Co., 1904.

Long, Armistead Lindsay, and Marcus J. Wright. *Memoirs of Robert E. Lee: His Military and Personal History*. New York, NY: J. M. Stoddart & Co., 1887.

Longstreet, James. *From Manassas to Appomattox: Memoirs of the Civil War in America*. Philadelphia, PA: J. B. Lippincott Co., 1908.

McAllister, John Meriwether, and Lura Boulton Tandy. *Genealogies of the Lewis and Kindred Families*. Columbia, MO: E. W. Stephens, 1906.

McCabe, James Dabney. *Life and Campaigns of General Robert E. Lee*. Atlanta, GA: National Publishing Co., 1866.

McGuire, Judith White. *General Robert E. Lee, the Christian Soldier*. Philadelphia, PA: Claxton, Remsen and Haffelfinger, 1873.

McKim, Randolph Harrison. *The Soul of Lee*. New York, NY: Longmans, Green and Co., 1918.

Mead, Edward Campbell. *Genealogical History of the Lee Family of Virginia and Maryland From A.D. 1300 to A.D. 1866*. New York, NY: University Publishing Co., 1871.

Mills, A. D. *A Dictionary of English Place-Names*. 1991. Oxford, UK: Oxford University Press, 1998 ed.

Munford, Beverly Bland. *Virginia's Attitude Toward Slavery and Secession*. New York, NY: Longmans, Green, and Co., 1909.

ORA (full title: *The War of the Rebellion: A Compilation of the Official Records of the Union and Confederate Armies*. (Multiple volumes.) Washington, D.C.: Government Printing Office, 1880.

Page, Thomas Nelson. *Robert E. Lee: Man and Soldier*. New York, NY: Charles Scribner's Sons, 1911.

Phillips, Robert S. (ed.). *Funk and Wagnalls New Encyclopedia*. 1971. New York, NY: Funk and Wagnalls, Inc., 1979 ed.

Pollard, Edward Alfred. *Lee and His Lieutenants: Comprising the Early Life, Public Services, and Campaigns of General Robert E. Lee and His Companions in Arms*. New York, NY: E. B. Treat, 1867.

——. *The Lost Cause*. 1867. Chicago, IL: E. B. Treat, 1890 ed.

——. *The Early Life, Campaigns, and Public Services of Robert E. Lee*. New York, NY: E. B. Treat, 1871.

Reaney, P. H., and R. M. Wilson. *A Dictionary of English Surnames*. 1958. Oxford, UK: Oxford University Press, 1997 ed.

Riley, Franklin Lafayette (ed.). *General Robert E. Lee After Appomattox*. New York, NY: The Macmillan Co., 1922.

Seabrook, Lochlainn. *Nathan Bedford Forrest: Southern Hero, American Patriot: Honoring a Confederate Hero and the Old South*. 2007. Franklin, TN: Sea Raven Press, 2010 ed.

——. *Abraham Lincoln: The Southern View - Demythologizing America's Sixteenth President*. 2007. Franklin, TN: Sea Raven Press, 2013 ed.

——. *The McGavocks of Carnton Plantation: A Southern History - Celebrating One of Dixie's Most Noble Confederate Families and Their Tennessee Home*. 2008. Franklin, TN: Sea Raven Press, 2011 ed.

——. *Everything You Were Taught About the Civil War is Wrong, Ask a Southerner! - Correcting the Errors of Yankee "History."* Franklin, TN: Sea Raven Press, 2010.

——. *The Quotable Jefferson Davis: Selections From the Writings and Speeches of the Confederacy's First President*. Franklin, TN: Sea Raven Press, 2011.

——. *Lincolnology: The Real Abraham Lincoln Revealed in His Own Words - A Study of Lincoln's Suppressed,*

Misinterpreted, and Forgotten Writings and Speeches. Franklin, TN: Sea Raven Press, 2011.
——. *The Unquotable Abraham Lincoln: The President's Quotes They Don't Want You to Know!* Franklin, TN: Sea Raven Press, 2011.
——. *The Quotable Robert E. Lee: Selections From the Writings and Speeches of the South's Most Beloved Civil War General*. Franklin, TN: Sea Raven Press, 2011.
——. *Give 'Em Hell Boys! The Complete Military Correspondence of Nathan Bedford Forrest*. Franklin, TN: Sea Raven Press, 2012.
——. *The Quotable Stonewall Jackson: Selections From the Writings and Speeches of the South's Most Famous General*. Franklin, TN: Sea Raven Press, 2012.
——. *Encyclopedia of the Battle of Franklin: A Comprehensive Guide to the Conflict That Changed the Civil War*. Franklin, TN: Sea Raven Press, 2012.
——. *Honest Jeff and Dishonest Abe: A Southern Children's Guide to the Civil War*. Franklin, TN: Sea Raven Press, 2012.
——. *Forrest! 99 Reasons to Love Nathan Bedford Forrest*. Franklin, TN: Sea Raven Press, 2012.
——. *The Quotable Nathan Bedford Forrest: Selections From the Writings and Speeches of the Confederacy's Most Brilliant Cavalryman*. Franklin, TN: Sea Raven Press, 2012.
——. *The Constitution of the Confederate States of America Explained: A Clause-by-Clause Study of the South's Magna Carta*. Franklin, TN: Sea Raven Press, 2012.
——. *The Great Impersonator: 99 Reasons to Dislike Abraham Lincoln*. Franklin, TN: Sea Raven Press, 2012.
——. *Saddle, Sword, and Gun: A Biography of Nathan Bedford Forrest For Teens*. Franklin, TN: Sea Raven Press, 2012.
——. *The Alexander H. Stephens Reader: Excerpts From the Works of a Confederate Founding Father*. Franklin, TN: Sea Raven Press, 2013.
——. *The Quotable Alexander H. Stephens: Selections From the Writings and Speeches of the Confederacy's First Vice President*. Franklin, TN: Sea Raven Press, 2013.
Speer, Emory. *Lincoln, Lee, Grant, and Other Biographical Addresses*. New York, NY: Neale Publishing Co., 1909.
Stiles, Robert. *Four Years Under Marse Robert*. New York, NY: Neal Publishing Co., 1910.
Swinton, William. *Campaigns of the Army of the Potomac*. New York, NY: Charles B. Richardson, 1866.
Taylor, Walter Herron. *Four Years With General Lee*. 1877. New York, NY: D. Appleton and Co., 1878 ed.
Tilley, John S. *Facts the Historians Leave Out: A Confederate Primer*. 1951. Nashville, TN: Bill Coats Ltd., 1999 ed.
Tomes, Robert. *Battles of America By Land and Sea*. 2 vols. New York, NY: James S. Virtue, 1878.
Trent, William Peterfield. *Robert E. Lee*. London, UK: Kegan Paul, Trench, Trübner and Co., 1899.
Tyler, Lyon Gardiner (ed). *Encyclopedia of Virginia Biography*. 5 vols. New York, NY: Lewis Historical Publishing Co., 1915.
Walker, Evelyn Harriet (ed.). *Leaders of the 19th Century With Some Noted Characters of Earlier Times*. Chicago, IL: A. B. Kuhlman Co., 1900.
Warner, Ezra J. *Generals in Gray: Lives of the Confederate Commanders*. 1959. Baton Rouge, LA: Louisiana State University Press, 1989 ed.
——. *Generals in Blue: Lives of the Union Commanders*. 1964. Baton Rouge, LA: Louisiana State University Press, 2006 ed.
White, Henry Alexander. *Robert E. Lee and the Southern Confederacy, 1807-1870*. 1897. New York, NY: G. P. Putnam's Sons, 1900 ed.
Williamson, Mary Lynn. *Life of Robert E. Lee*. 1895. Richmond, VA: Johnson Publishing Co., 1918 ed.

MEET THE AUTHOR

LOCHLAINN SEABROOK, winner of the Jefferson Davis Historical Gold Medal for his "masterpiece," *A Rebel Born: A Defense of Nathan Bedford Forrest,* is an unreconstructed Southern historian, award-winning author, Forrest scholar, and traditional Southern Agrarian of Scottish, English, Irish, Welsh, German, and Italian extraction. An encyclopedist, lexicographer, musician, artist, graphic designer, genealogist, and photographer, as well as an award-winning poet, songwriter, and screenwriter, he has a thirty year background in historical nonfiction writing and is a member of the Sons of Confederate Veterans, the Civil War Trust, and the Grange.

Due to similarities in their writing styles, ideas, and literary works, Seabrook is referred to as the "American ROBERT GRAVES," after his cousin, the prolific English writer, historian, mythographer, poet, and author of the classic tomes *The White Goddess* and *The Greek Myths*.

(Illustration © Sea Raven Press)

The grandson of an Appalachian coal-mining family, Seabrook is a seventh-generation Kentuckian, co-chair of the Jent/Gent Family Committee (Kentucky), founder and director of the Blakeney Family Tree Project, and a board member of the Friends of Colonel Benjamin E. Caudill. Seabrook's literary works have been endorsed by leading authorities, museum curators, award-winning historians, bestselling authors, celebrities, noted scientists, well respected educators, renown military artists, esteemed Southern organizations, and distinguished academicians from around the world.

As a professional writer Seabrook has authored some thirty popular adult books specializing in the following topics: the American Civil War, pro-South studies, Confederate biography and history, the anthropology of religion, genealogical monographs, Goddess-worship (thealogy), ghost stories, the paranormal, family histories, military encyclopedias, etymological dictionaries, ufology, social issues, comparative analysis of the origins of Christmas, and cross-cultural studies of the family and marriage.

Seabrook's eight children's books include a Southern children's guide to the Civil War, a dictionary of religion and myth, a rewriting of the King Arthur legend (which reinstates the original pre-Christian motifs), two bedtime stories for preschoolers, a naturalist's guidebook to owls, a worldwide look at the family, and an examination of the Near-Death Experience.

Of blue-blooded Southern stock through his Kentucky, Tennessee, Virginia, West Virginia, and North Carolina ancestors, he is a direct descendant of European royalty via his 6th great-grandfather, the EARL OF OXFORD, after which London's famous Harley Street is named. Among his celebrated male Celtic ancestors is ROBERT THE BRUCE, King of Scotland, Seabrook's 22nd great-grandfather. The 21st great-grandson of EDWARD I "LONGSHANKS" PLANTAGENET), King of England, Seabrook is a thirteenth-generation Southerner through his descent from the colonists of Jamestown, Virginia (1607).

The 2nd, 3rd, and 4th great-grandson of dozens of Confederate soldiers, one of his closest connections to the War for Southern Independence is through his 3rd great-grandfather, ELIAS JENT, SR., who fought for the Confederacy in the Thirteenth Cavalry Kentucky under Seabrook's 2nd cousin, Colonel BENJAMIN E. CAUDILL. The Thirteenth, also known as "Caudill's Army," fought in numerous conflicts, including the Battles of Saltville, Gladsville, Mill Cliff, Poor Fork, Whitesburg, and Leatherwood.

Seabrook is also related to the following Confederates and other 19th-Century luminaries: ROBERT E. LEE, MARY ANNA RANDOLPH CUSTIS (General Lee's wife), STEPHEN DILL LEE, JOHN SINGLETON MOSBY, STONEWALL JACKSON, NATHAN BEDFORD FORREST, JAMES LONGSTREET, JOHN HUNT MORGAN, JEB STUART, P. G. T. BEAUREGARD (designer of the Confederate Battle Flag), JOHN BELL HOOD, ALEXANDER PETER STEWART, EDMUND W. PETTUS, JOHN B. WOMACK, ALEXANDER H. STEPHENS, THEODRICK "TOD" CARTER, ARTHUR M. MANIGAULT, JOSEPH MANIGAULT, CHARLES SCOTT VENABLE, THORNTON A. WASHINGTON, JOHN A. WASHINGTON, JOHN H. WINDER, GIDEON J. PILLOW, STATES RIGHTS GIST, EDMUND WINCHESTER RUCKER, HENRY R. JACKSON, JOHN C. BRECKINRIDGE, LEONIDAS POLK, ZACHARY TAYLOR, SARAH KNOX TAYLOR (the first wife of JEFFERSON DAVIS), RICHARD TAYLOR, DAVY CROCKETT, DANIEL BOONE, MERIWETHER LEWIS (of the Lewis and Clark Expedition) ANDREW JACKSON, JAMES K. POLK, ABRAM POINDEXTER MAURY (founder of Franklin, TN), WILLIAM GILES HARDING, ZEBULON VANCE, THOMAS JEFFERSON, GEORGE WYTHE RANDOLPH (grandson of Jefferson), FELIX K. ZOLLICOFFER, FITZHUGH LEE, NATHANIEL F. CHEAIRS, JESSE JAMES, FRANK JAMES, ROBERT BRANK VANCE, CHARLES SIDNEY WINDER, JOHN W. MCGAVOCK, CARRIE (WINDER) MCGAVOCK, DAVID

(Photo © Lochlainn Seabrook)

Harding McGavock, Lysander McGavock, James Randal McGavock, Randal William McGavock, Francis McGavock, Emily McGavock, William Henry F. Lee, Lucius E. Polk, Minor Meriwether (husband of noted pro-South author Elizabeth Avery Meriwether), Ellen Bourne Tynes (wife of Forrest's chief of artillery, Captain John W. Morton), South Carolina Senators Preston Smith Brooks and Andrew Pickens Butler, and famed South Carolina diarist Mary Chesnut.

Seabrook's modern day cousins include: Patrick J. Buchanan (conservative author), Rebecca Gayheart (Kentucky-born actress), Shelby Lee Adams (Letcher County, Kentucky, portrait photographer), Bertram Thomas Combs (Kentucky's fiftieth governor), Edith Bolling (wife of President Woodrow Wilson), and actors Robert Duvall, Reese Witherspoon, Lee Marvin, and Tom Cruise.

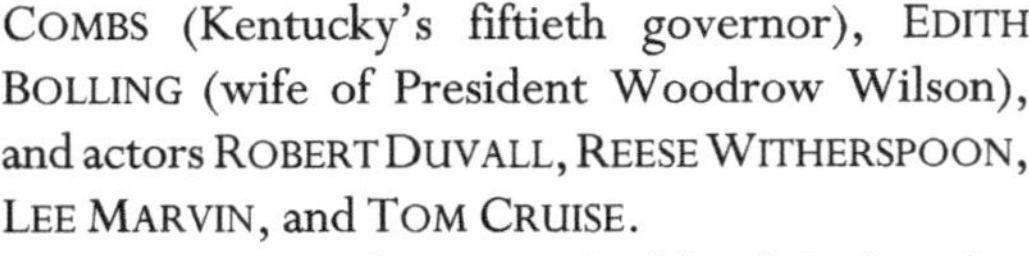

Born with music in his blood, Seabrook is an award-winning, multi-genre, BMI-Nashville songwriter and lyricist who has composed some 3,000 songs (250 albums), and whose original music has been heard on TV and radio worldwide. A musician, producer, multi-instrumentalist, and renown performer—whose keyboard work has been variously compared to pianists from Hargus Robbins and Vince Guaraldi to Elton John and Leonard Bernstein—Seabrook has opened for groups such as the Earl Scruggs Review, Ted Nugent, and Bob Seger, and has performed privately for such public figures as President Ronald Reagan, Burt Reynolds, and Senator Edward W. Brooke.

Seabrook's cousins in the music business include: Johnny Cash, Elvis Presley, Billy Ray and Miley Cyrus, Patty Loveless, Tim McGraw, Lee Ann Womack, Dolly Parton, Pat Boone, Naomi, Wynonna, and Ashley Judd, Ricky Skaggs, the Sunshine Sisters, Martha Carson, and Chet Atkins.

Seabrook lives with his wife and family in historic Middle Tennessee, the heart of Forrest country and the Confederacy, where his conservative Southern ancestors fought valiantly against liberal Lincoln and the progressive North in defense of Jeffersonianism, constitutional government, and personal liberty.

If you enjoyed Mr. Seabrook's *The Old Rebel*
you will be interested in his excellent companion work:

THE QUOTABLE ROBERT E. LEE
SELECTIONS FROM THE WRITINGS & SPEECHES OF THE SOUTH'S MOST BELOVED CIVIL WAR GENERAL

Available from Sea Raven Press and wherever fine books are sold.

SeaRavenPress.com

www.ingramcontent.com/pod-product-compliance
Lightning Source LLC
Chambersburg PA
CBHW032053090426
42744CB00005B/192
9780983818540